Into the Canyon

Into the Canyon

Seven Years in
Navajo Country

Lucy Moore

UNIVERSITY OF NEW MEXICO PRESS ▲ ALBUQUERQUE

10 09 08 07 06 05 04   1 2 3 4 5 6 7

Library of Congress Cataloging-in-Publication Data

Moore, Lucy, 1944–
Into the canyon : seven years in Navajo country / Lucy Moore.
p. cm.
ISBN 0-8263-3416-4 (cloth : alk. paper)
1. Navajo Indians—Arizona—Chinle—Social conditions.
2. Navajo Indians—Legal status, laws, etc.—Arizona—Chinle.
3. Navajo Indian Reservation—Social life and customs. I. Title.

E99.N3M6865 2004
305.897'2607913—dc22

2004010254

This book is typeset in Minion 11/14

The display type is also Minion

Book and cover design and type composition:
Kathleen Sparkes

Cover photograpy:
Richard W. Hughes

All other photographs in book as noted.

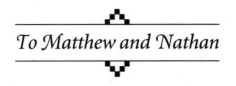

To Matthew and Nathan

Contents

Acknowledgments   IX

Introduction   1

ONE
Tracks In   5

TWO
Legal Crusaders   19

THREE
On the Home Front   35

FOUR
More Learning than Teaching   45

FIVE
Role Models   59

SIX
The Del Muerto Connection   71

SEVEN
Wildlife and Women's Lib   87

EIGHT
A Career Appears   99

PHOTOGRAPHS   119

NINE
The Grassroots Wake Up   137

TEN
Having Faith   161

ELEVEN
Bucking the System   173

TWELVE
Identity Crises   187

THIRTEEN
Tracks Out   199

FOURTEEN
Tracks Back   213

Acknowledgments

This book would not have happened without Emlen Hall who introduced me to Beth Hadas of UNM Press, who dropped a hint that she would be interested in a book about young people in the 1960s who came to the Southwest intending to do good. With Beth I was in the best possible editorial hands, and she spoiled me badly by making the process so enjoyable. I am also grateful to Peter Iverson for his wise reviews and guidance, and Leslie Silko for her enthusiasm.

The book is richer and more accurate, thanks to reviews by Michael Benson and Bob Hilgendorf. It is a clearer and more grammatical book, thanks to my mother, Honora Moore. Thanks also to friends who helped along the way: Richard Barlow, Jon Colvin, Pat D'Andrea, Judy Goldberg, Richard Jones, Ann Lacy, Ella Natonabah, Dana Newmann, Elise Turner, Anne Valley Fox, and Lorain Varela. A special thanks to Tara Travis, who gave me a reassuring perspective from Chinle in the year 2003.

I also appreciate more than ever the lessons and memories from friends in Chinle, Ben and Irene Teller, Eunice Lee and her family, Peterson and Roz Zah, Robert and Verna Salabye, Sybil Baldwin and her Headstart crew, Headstart classes of 1969 and 1970, the staff at DNA Legal Services, and Lillie Charley and her family. Their generosity has given me a standard for the rest of my life.

Finally, I owe so much to my partner, Roberto, for his firm and loving pressure in this direction.

Before the driver gave me the keys to the Headstart van,
he told me the facts of muddy roads on the Chinle route.
The road could be slick with a chocolate pudding glaze.
Or, it could be covered by a huge puddle masking a foot or
more of ooze. He made sure that I understood the importance
of stopping before driving into one of these small lakes.
"Look at that puddle. If you see fresh tire tracks going
in and you see them coming out the other side, it's
probably ok to go through." He added, smiling,
"If you see them going in and *not* coming out . . .
maybe it's quicksand!"

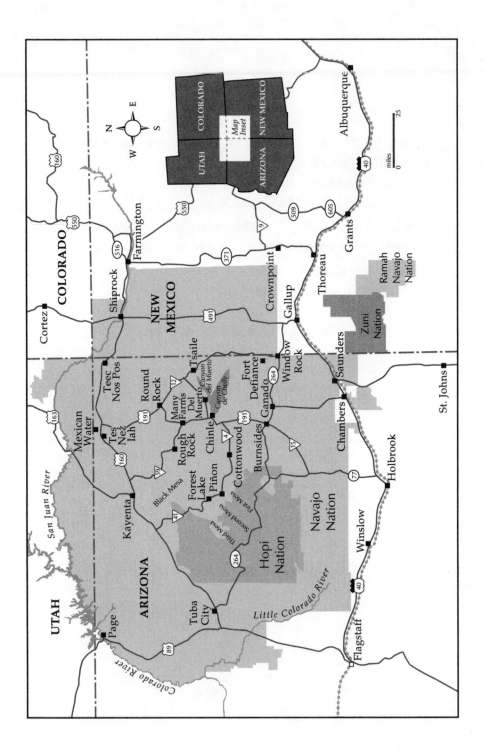

Introduction

Over the years, I have wondered, as I think most people do, what I would do if my family were taken from me through some disaster and I were the sole survivor. In that moment of hypothetical hopelessness and despair, I always seize on Chinle. I see in my mind the silhouette of Black Mesa with Fish Point at the south end, the giant cottonwoods along the Chinle Wash, and the gentle mouth of Canyon de Chelly. I tell myself I would go back to Chinle, for comfort, for an identity, for a meaning to life. That is the depth of my roots in this place, so foreign in the beginning, so beloved now.

This book is a collection of memories, some accurate, some probably enhanced, of seven and a half years spent on the Navajo Indian Reservation (now the Navajo Nation) from 1968 through 1975. As newlyweds, Bob and I moved from Cambridge, Massachusetts, to Chinle, Arizona, a leap in geography, culture, and perspective. We made friends, we had two children, we entered into the culture—from cake walks to puberty ceremonies. We learned lessons about what it means to be an outsider, and about ourselves in that role. We arrived, hoping that we could be useful, Bob as a legal services attorney, and I as . . . well, that was harder to predict. The depth of our experience in Chinle was reflected in our painful departure, and our connections to Navajoland since then.

I had some surprises in the writing of this book. There were moments of revelation about myself and others that I had forgotten. One of them involved the incident when Ted Mitchell, founder and director of DNA Legal Services, was thrown out of the Navajo Tribal Council Chambers for rude behavior. What I had forgotten, and was reminded of by my ex-husband, was that I had planned on wearing cut-off jean shorts to the meeting that afternoon. Fortunately, I was saved from this embarrassment, and showed up in a modest skirt, modest at least by 1968 standards. Looking back, I am horrified that I could have been so ignorant and insensitive, just like the many outsiders, Anglos, whom I scorned later—rather quickly, in fact—for *their* insensitivities. I had never realized that I *was* one of them, at twenty-four, fresh from Cambridge, Massachusetts, hotbed of radicalism and freedom of expression.

It is easy to fool oneself into thinking that the enlightened, experienced, maybe wiser person that one becomes in later life is the same person one was back then. We think the significant difference between then and now is that the one back then was younger and wrinkle-free. The kernel of this older, wiser me was present, of course, in that younger me. But my experience to that point in 1968 had not prepared me to be an aware, enlightened newcomer, the kind of outsider who left in 1975. In reminiscing about those days, I tend to assume that I had the more mature sensibilities that I now have. But I didn't. This is a little painful to realize, and I apologize for the many offenses this younger me undoubtedly committed.

Another surprise was that my memory of events was so clear, and could be so wrong. I *knew* that Bob and I had been sitting in the Council Chambers when Ted Mitchell insulted a Navajo leader and that we had seen him evicted from the Chambers. Peter Iverson's *Dine: A History of the Navajo People* told me this was not possible. The insult happened one day; the eviction happened the next. We were only there the first day. This means that the version of the story I originally wrote, where Annie Wauneka pummels Ted with her large hand bag, is not true. In fact, she beat him on the head with her fist. How is it that I can see her charging down the aisle toward us, swinging back that pitching arm, purse flying?

Peter's response to my confession that I had made up a memory and called it history, is very comforting:

"What is important about memory, I think, is not that it is always accurate (it isn't, of course), but that it is so powerful . . . the heart of history is the power of memory, the creation of tradition, the significance of place, the importance of stories, the richness of language, the meanings of silence, and the employment of imagination."

My sources for the book were my own letters and random writings from those years, newspaper clippings, and a variety of correspondence, flyers and newsletters. I have done my best to be as accurate as I can. Where I miss the mark, I hope that I succeed in meeting Peter's criteria described above.

ONE

Tracks In

Two days after our wedding in late June 1968, Bob and I piled the essentials into our brand new blue-and-white Ford Bronco and set out for Chinle, Arizona. We had searched the Boston car lots for a vehicle appropriate for our southwestern adventure and were thrilled with our find. It would be perfect for the trip west, and for whatever terrain might challenge us in our new homeland. Our years in Cambridge had been a luxury, we had degrees to be envied—mine from Radcliffe, Bob's from Harvard Law School—and now it was time to make a difference, as well as make an escape.

The times were increasingly stressful. Just when we seemed to be on the brink of major social change, the country was coming apart at the seams. There were daily reports from Viet Nam and footage on television that drove some to violence, others to depression. As the civil rights movement blossomed, Martin Luther King, Jr., was shot in April 1968, and Bobby Kennedy in early June, just three weeks before we were married. The country seemed doomed to self-destruction at home and abroad. John F. Kennedy, assassinated just five years earlier, was still an inspiration to many of us, and we wanted to live up to his expectations, to do something for our country. We were determined to use our valuable education, our fortunate background, our youth and energy to improve the lives of others.

We were not alone. In the late 1960s thousands of young people left the security, or at least the familiarity, of college and graduate school life and headed into the unknown. Like pioneers or missionaries of any era and any place, they set out for a variety of reasons including exploration, adventure, fame—if not fortune—and perhaps above all, doing good. Some went abroad via the Peace Corps. Others joined domestic equivalents, like Legal Services, Headstart and VISTA, that would take them to equally foreign places in the inner city, in rural America, or on Indian reservations. President Johnson's Poverty Program was young and full of promise, and so were we.

Hoping to do some good while escaping the insanity of the times, we chose the newly formed legal services program on the Navajo Indian Reservation. We expected a Peace Corps–like experience, helping people in need, experiencing exotic customs, making friends across cultural boundaries. Our families were excited for us, our friends admiring and perhaps a little envious (or at least that is what we imagined) as we set out for Chinle.

The previous fall Bob had been browsing the bulletin board at Harvard Law School looking for work. It was the season when law firms set up appointments with law schools and came recruiting, looking for good prospects in the crop graduating that year. The firms were from the eastern urban centers of power, and had very fancy names, many awesome and seductive to law students. The law school bulletin board was dense with opportunity, in the form of index cards with the names of the firms, and the date, time, and room number where each would be interviewing. Bob's glance stumbled over one card. Diné Bee'iiná' Náhiilnah Bee Agha'diit'aahe, Inc,* would be interviewing the next day in room 115. Who on earth was that and what were they doing on that bulletin board among that prestigious company?

---

*Literal translation: Lawyers who contribute to the economic revitalization of the Navajo people.

He went to find out, and met Ted Mitchell, the founder and director of the legal services program on the Navajo Reservation, and his Navajo associate Peterson Zah. The two were interviewing at Harvard, Yale, Princeton, Columbia, NYU, and Stanford, unabashedly looking for the best and brightest young attorneys. They were a charismatic pair. Mitchell, a young Anglo attorney, was an aggressive, almost messianic promoter of his cause. Zah, later to become president of the Navajo Nation, was quiet, handsome, and able to flash a magnetic smile at just the right moment. Although the two were competing with high-powered and high-paying law firms in Boston, New York, Philadelphia, and Washington, D.C., they were confident they could fill the positions. They were offering an alternative that was very appealing to those who wanted to take a chance and who hoped to make a difference.

We wanted to be in that category, but wrestled with the decision. Would we regret it? Would Bob lose out on some other career opportunity? What would *I* do on an Indian reservation? On the other hand, what would I do anywhere? My year as a caseworker with the Boston Welfare Department was certainly challenging, and surely I was helping people at least monetarily. But this was not how I wanted to spend my life, or even another year. Bob flew out to visit the Navajo legal services program and to get a look at this new world that might be home for us. He was intrigued and brought back tales of mutton stew and fry bread, beautiful rugs and jewelry, incredibly appealing children, warm people who needed a good lawyer, and a landscape that was, well, indescribable—not necessarily inviting, he admitted, but incredible. There would be plenty of things for me to do, too, with one of the many government agencies or with the tribe. We gave ourselves a push and said yes to Diné Bee'iiná' Náhiilnah Bee Agha'diit'aahe, Inc. After all, if we hated it, we could leave after the mandatory two years.

Besides, there were deeper connections that drew us to Chinle. In the 1950s Bob's father had rejected a job offer in Window Rock, Arizona, the capital of the Navajo Nation. The children were little, and he feared the wilds of Indian country, the poor schools, and the uncertainty of a career as an attorney in the Tribal Justice Department. The family stayed in Whitefish Bay, Wisconsin, and now his lawyer son, raised in the safety and familiarity of that Milwaukee suburb, and with the best possible education, chose to make this trip into the unknown. It was pleasing to us, that revisiting of an old decision and re-deciding in a new direction. We felt bold and superior, as is appropriate for a younger generation reflecting on itself.

For me, there was the feeling that I was going somewhere that I belonged—at least a little more than the ordinary Anglo. I was raised with the knowledge that I was part Indian, a very few drops, but to me it had always seemed a very special part of me. In the amusing way that we all do, I chose *that* part to hold significantly more importance than the other parts of me. My grandfather's mother was part Chippewa. She died when her four children were very young. Her husband, a lumberjack in northern Minnesota, did his best, but my grandfather grew up hungry, poor, and without any connection to his mother's people.

Although I had never been to Chippewa country, and was raised in a middle-class suburb of Seattle, I felt some kind of kinship to things Indian. My ideas, my imaginings were embarrassingly romantic and unrealistic. All I had to cling to in terms of Indian culture was a copy of Longfellow's *Song of Hiawatha*—a strange totem indeed! It was a small, satin-covered edition with gold edges on the pages and a silk ribbon to mark your place, and it had belonged to my grandmother. Married to the mixed-blood, she probably had also romanticized and, in the absence of any real connection to Chippewa culture, had seen a vision in this poem that she liked and decided to adopt. I did the same and carried that little volume with me from Seattle to Cambridge in my college-bound trunk, along with a beloved stuffed rabbit, a large photo of my boyfriend, and a favorite white angora sweater that I thought made me look sexy. The book and the rabbit are still with me.

Laden with our material possessions and with these ulterior motives, we left Cambridge at the end of June 1968. It felt like an ocean voyage rather than a trip across country. With all our goods in the hold, the Bronco was like a little sea-going vessel, bobbing along the highway, headed for a point on the horizon that would not come into view for many days. Along the way, of course, there were stops, visits to islands where family dwelled and where we partook in strange customs. In Whitefish Bay, we were feted at a countryside German restaurant, rented by Bob's father for the occasion. There were acres of green lawn and tons of bratwursts, and dozens of extremely warm, extremely smiley relatives, most of them German or Swedish. They were excited for us, pressed checks into our hands, or at least Bob's hand, come to think of it. They gave us wedding gifts including a silver ice bucket and a heating tray which you plugged in to keep the hors d'oeuvres hot. We cashed the checks before setting sail, but left the rest of the gifts in the basement of my mother-in-law, Eleanor Hilgendorf, keeper extraordinaire of all things related to family. We were to return years later to retrieve them, still in their boxes, still with the gift cards tucked inside.

Our next stop was Warner, South Dakota, near Aberdeen, where Eleanor's uncles had settled. Three of six brothers had left home—seriously left home—setting out from the family farm in Sweden, which could not support all six children, and ending up in various parts of Wisconsin, Minnesota, and South Dakota. Bob's great-uncle had changed his name from Swan Nelson to Nels Swanson. Apparently there were too many Swan Nelsons, and he wanted to distinguish himself. At least one brother, still a Nelson, had found a spot in Warner that must have looked very inviting after the cramped, divided, and exhausted land of rural Sweden. His descendants were still there, and welcomed us so warmly. We rode horses, saw wheat and corn growing, ate heavenly fried chicken, mashed potatoes, real gravy, and berry pies. I took many pictures of farming cousins, baby piglets, and other wonders of agricultural life, and not until I developed the roll in Seattle did I realize that I was not advancing the film on our new 35 mm camera. I had innocently pressed the rewind button, and lo and behold when I opened the camera, the film was rewound. I did not know that it had been nowhere during the film shoot, and I had taken thirty-six photos one on top of the other.

We left the farm folks and felt as if we really had an island of well-wishers there in the wilds of South Dakota. They were very interested in our journey, and sent with us two ceramic pheasants and a classic white ceramic cookie jar, with the word "COOKIES" in ornate raised lettering on the side. With Eleanor's basement out of reach, and wanting to have these mementos of rural America and tokens of dedicated, if distant, relatives with us, we wrapped them very carefully in newspaper and tucked them among the blankets in the back of the Bronco.

Driving through Aberdeen, headed west, I was aware that I was leaving roots as well. This was the town where my grandfather (of the

Chippewa grandmother) fell in love with my grandmother (the Longfellow fan) at the dining table in a boarding house in Aberdeen. I had heard the story many times, and found it sweet. Still a bachelor in his forties, he had come to town to work in the bank and had moved into a boarding house. His first night at dinner, he told me many times, he came into the dining room and saw Emma Warner sitting at the table. Having graduated from the one-room school in nearby Webster and having gone to Valparaiso Teacher's College for a year, she was more than qualified to come home and teach, which is what she was doing. He sat down opposite her and never recovered. They were married a few months later, and headed west for the famous rich, red earth of Oregon's Willamette Valley, where my mother was born. Their love was one of the purest and simplest I have ever known, lasting over fifty years, and here I was, probably within sight of the first encounter. I peered at the bank as we drove down the main street, and at houses on the edge of town, wondering if any of them could be reincarnations of that 1890s historic location. Some people leave home and some people stay put. I could see it both ways.

As we headed across Montana, I thought about my other grandfather, on my father's side. He had left his Philadelphia home at sixteen, not happy with a new stepmother and ready to be on his own. He migrated across the Midwest and landed in South Dakota, where he took a job with a railroad crew building bridges and tunnels to accommodate tracks that snaked through the Rocky Mountains. By the time the tracks reached eastern Washington state where he settled down, he was twenty-two, married, and an accomplished surveyor, engineer, and builder. Sixty-five years later we were covering this same migration route in just a few days, over endless miles of pavement.

The Rockies drew us westward under a dome of cloud-dotted blue sky that was almost frightening in its expanse. When we reached Glacier National Park, we suddenly felt quite eastern in our skills, ironic for two people who had never achieved anything near eastern status during our years in New England. We had planned on camping at Glacier, friends had raved about it, and we knew it would be spectacular. But when we pulled out Bob's old Boy Scout tent, I knew that Bob was concerned about not having a real pillow, and I could not even attempt to hide my anxiety over the events of three months previous. While in her sleeping bag at this very campground, a young woman had been mauled to death by a bear. The bear had heard I was coming, and was waiting. I knew it. I remember a relatively sleepless night, and greeting the sunrise with enormous relief—one of the few times in my life that I was a "morning person."

Seattle was within reach. Here was my home town, from which I had fled six years earlier to go to college. My father still lived in the same house, and it was strange to say the least to find myself and a new husband in my old bedroom. It was all perfectly legitimate. How unusual to do such things in your own house—your own bedroom, even—and for there to be nothing wrong with it! It was a mixed experience of relief on the one hand and a lack of thrill on the other. Somehow it had been more fun and less complicated in Bob's pennant-bedecked and sports trophy-clad bedroom in Whitefish Bay. *That* was a kick. I imagine he felt the reverse.

Seattle, too, was full of eager well-wishers. In Whitefish Bay, I had felt the scrutiny—not unkind, but somewhat pointed—of curious friends and relatives. Who was this person that Bob had married? Would she match up to the prospects he had left behind? This time the curiosity was about Bob, and he was on the receiving end of the overly attentive looks and probing conversations. Here was Lucy, back from the East, with a husband! Let's look him over! My father, who perhaps had the most reason to be scrutinizing, was generous in his welcome and only a little teary (compared to me) in his goodbye.

From Seattle, we sped south to visit my mother in San Francisco. She had not lived there long, and there was no need for a welcoming and send-off party like those we had had in Whitefish Bay and Seattle. It was a relief to have a little leisure to visit with her and stock up on some big-city experiences. She had a special treat for us, tickets for *Hair*. That evening, and an afternoon at a Golden Gate Park love-in, were our last interactions with a counterculture we would only have glimpses of during the next seven years. I remember an awareness that we were making a choice, that this was a kind of political and cultural fork in the road. I hoped it would work out and that I would look back on the choice as a smart one. My fears were that (1) we would not do any good, and (2) I would miss out on a good time.

We looped south through San Diego and across the desert to Phoenix. By now it was late July, and our timing was perfect—if one were interested in experiencing extreme heat inside a metal container. Our Bronco, which had served us so well in the northern and coastal regions, was now our enemy. With no insulation on the roof or the floor, no air conditioning, and wrap-around, untinted windows, it was a kind of solar oven. We learned the physics of water-cooling, and held wet washcloths out the window as we drove through the Mojave. They cooled immediately and we slapped them on our foreheads, receiving at best thirty seconds of relief before they heated up and dried out again. It was a competition between the need to keep the washcloths wet and the need to save water in case the Bronco needed a drink. At the sign an nouncing Plaster City, Population 165, we made a rare stop. It was a photo to send the folks back home—Lucy, leaning with one arm against the sign, face red, wearing tank top, cut-offs, sandals, and an expression of squinting desperation. Another stop was El Centro, for immersion in the public swimming pool. The temperature was 120.

We lived in another swimming pool in a Phoenix motel for a couple of days and then turned northward for the coolness of Flagstaff, in the shadow of the San Francisco Peaks, the westernmost of the four mountains sacred in Navajo belief. Although we had not yet reached the legal boundary of the reservation, this mountain marked our entry into the area believed by Navajos to be traditionally theirs. The other three sacred mountains are, to the north, Hesperus Peak in southwestern Colorado, to the east Blanca Peak in south central Colorado, and to the south Mount Taylor in west central New Mexico. We knew this from our cursory reading about Navajo culture and history. Neither of us was scholarly—in spite of, or perhaps because of, our years in academia— and our inclination was to learn by doing. But we did want to know enough in advance so as not to embarrass ourselves or offend any sooner than was inevitable, so we read Clyde Kluckhohn's *The Navaho*, which taught us the rudiments of Navajo religion and culture.

Years later I heard from a Navajo friend in Ramah that some of the Navajos interviewed by the unsuspecting anthropologist had enormous fun, at his expense, telling him all kinds of invented traditions and cultural practices, which they then delighted in seeing in print. As we passed the [truly] sacred peaks, we were ignorant of the richness of the Navajo relationships that lay ahead. There was no preparation possible for the surprises, the humor, the depth of feeling that would bless us in the next few years.

We had also made an effort to learn some Navajo before we arrived, and as we left Phoenix, I reached for our reel-to-reel tape recorder. We had used it sparingly on the trip because it needed eight C batteries to operate, but it had seen us through some long miles in the Dakotas and Montana, and now it was time to get serious. I put on our tape of Navajo language phrases and vocabulary recorded by Jim Parrish, a Navajo from Monument Valley who spent a semester at M.I.T. speaking Navajo to Kenneth Hale, a linguistics scholar who was studying and teaching the language. Bob had visited with Jim when we were still in Cambridge, and had asked him to record a tape for us to take with us to Chinle. He kindly obliged and chose the topics that he felt were most important for the new immigrant.

The first hour of the tape covered coming and going. "*Háágóó'shá díníyá*—Where are you going?" was followed by an endless string of possibilities, each with a pause for us to repeat. "*Na'nízhoozhígóó déyá*— I am going to Gallup," "*Tótagóó déyá*—I am going to Farmington," "*Chinlegóó déyá*—I am going to Chinle," "*Tségháhoodzánígóó déyá*— I am going to Window Rock," and on and on through every place that a Navajo might want to go. It was monotonous, and in our impatience we wished to get down to business and learn the basics of grammar, key words of greeting and getting things done. But I did take notice of the huge number of different words that related to travel. *Deya* meant *I am going*, and *niya* meant *I arrived*. But the words for *I come back*, or *I went and came back*, or *I went intending to stay*, or *I went on foot*, or *I came back alone*—all those varieties seemed to be entirely different verbs. Moving about seemed to be very important. The second hour dealt with where you and other people are from, another clue into Navajo priorities that passed us by. And so we entered Navajoland, droning "*Háágóó shá díníyá, shimásání?* [Where are you going, my grandmother?]" and "*Na'nízhoozhígóó déyá.* [I am going to Gallup]."

The monumentalness of our move hit me as we went through Flagstaff, circled east of the sacred peaks, and headed for Tuba City, the center of government and commerce for the western Navajo communities. Up until now the trip had been an adventure, a honeymoon, a farewell to family, friends, and comfortable landscapes. There had been shocks, like the drive through the desert, with its extreme, dry heat and lack of vegetation. I had lived through that and had a picture from Plaster City to prove it. But now I was headed to our new home, and homes were supposed to be in comfortable, familiar places, weren't they? Because Bob had flown out to visit the Reservation the winter before we made the decision, he had a little more preparation than I. But that winter of 1967–68 had been the worst in decades, with feet of snow everywhere, painting the entire landscape white. (Ironically the high and arid Colorado Plateau could receive heavy snowfalls, which often evaporated before they had time to melt and soak into the dry soil.)

So the landscape we encountered in July 1968 was a shock to us both. It was, in fact, just like what we had seen in the movie *2001: A Space Odyssey*. I was appalled and mesmerized at the same time. I was a product of the green and mossy Northwest, where large bodies of water are never far away and the sky hangs low like a comforting gray blanket. A few years in the Boston area had not changed my vision of what landscapes should be. The East was colder in the winter and hotter in the summer, but just as green and wet.

But here, as we approached and passed Tuba City, growth was the exception, the rare exception. I had to turn off the tape player and give all my attention to this strangeness. The landscape looked like the backs of hundreds of elephants, with no vegetation whatsoever. The colors were brown, gray, and dull red. There was no green anywhere. Most unsettling was the openness, the uninterrupted line of sight . . . to nowhere! To everywhere? The eye could travel out farther and farther in any direction and not run into anything, save rock formations and mesas. And even then, the eye, or at least my eye, stumbled only for a moment, before leaping over or darting around these features and plunging on and on to the horizon. The sky was even more formidable than it had been in Montana. It was a huge bowl overhead, blue with clouds, distinct clouds, hundreds of them, maybe millions. There was so much room up there! And it felt as if we were closer to it. I couldn't believe it. My heart raced. Surely this was a phenomenon of the *western* Navajo region. Chinle was still several hours away. Surely Chinle would be different.

Three hours later when we turned north for the last thirty-one miles to Chinle, I knew it was not going to be different. But already my eyes and brain were beginning to acclimatize and I had begun to be more thrilled than appalled by what I was seeing. Maybe there was a kind of peacefulness if you gazed out over the ocean of land, if you told your eyes to give up their frantic search for greenery, their pointless racing in all directions. Maybe there was more than brown and red out there. Weren't those patches of ochre and bands of purple over there? And after all, weren't brown and red in all their varieties kind of pleasing? Looking left, the southern edge of Black Mesa grew on the horizon, deep gray and purple, with graceful dips and points against the blue background. To the right, there was a solitary tree in the distance that looked like a rooster from a certain angle. And as we moved north we caught glimpses of the Beautiful Valley below on our right. Maybe beautiful would not be the first descriptor that would come to mind; maybe stark, bleak, or moon-like would come to my newcomer's lips first. But perhaps there was a beauty there, if one got used to it. As a reward for those generous thoughts, we were given a rainbow, a full and glorious one that arched from the west across the road and dropped on Chinle ahead.

And the horses! How wonderful to see horses, wild horses, dappled and wild-eyed, standing by the road, or off in the distance, tails swishing, ears twitching, nostrils flaring. On that day in early August 1968, we stopped and filled an entire roll of film with pictures of the horses on the road approaching Chinle from the south. I was amused to find those pictures years later, long after the amazement had worn off, and the ever-present horses on the road were notable only for the potential damage they could cause your car.

We followed the rainbow, dropping down off the mesa into the Chinle Valley below. My heart was beating faster. We were approaching a place that would be home for awhile, and I was aware that everything I was seeing for the first time would, in time, be so familiar. The curve in the road at the bottom of the mesa, the bridge over Black Wash, the pock-marked metal sign indicating the shooting range off to the right, the water tower up ahead, on stilts, like some mechanical extraterrestrial. All these landmarks I knew would become significant pieces of a landscape that would be mine, that would be the setting for experiences and feelings of all kinds. Right now, it all looked quietly exotic, holding the potential for great importance behind a very mundane façade.

Bob had been on this road before, the previous winter, when Peterson Zah brought him to look at one of the branch offices of the legal services program. He knew to expect Fleming Begaye's Trading Post, gas station, and café at the junction, and he knew that if we didn't make that right-hand turn into Chinle, we would sail on to Many Farms, Round Rock, and points north. We made the turn and proceeded toward our new home. There was no center of Chinle, just scattered housing, services, and a little commerce. I saw the entrance to a housing project on the right, the post office and police station on the left, a red sandstone church on the right, a sign indicating the Chinle Chapter House on the right, an Indian Health Service Clinic on the left, and finally we turned right into the Bureau of Indian Affairs compound.

Although a Navajo couple, both working at the BIA, were willing to rent a house to the new lawyer and his wife, it was not yet ready. In the meantime, we were allowed to rent an efficiency apartment for $26 a month in the "new BIA compound." The "old BIA compound," built in the 1930s and 1940s was actually much nicer. Located behind the clinic and toward the canyon, the area had real houses, yards with grass, paved roads, and a few big trees. The BIA superintendent and other management-level employees lived in classy stone-and-log houses in the old compound, separate from the rest of the community.

Across the road, the new compound consisted of rows of one-story stuccoed apartments, stuck together, with mud front yards and no trees, facing a once poorly paved street, now more potholes than pavement. But none of this mattered to us. We had our Bronco to maneuver the pot holes, we had enough space for the little we had brought with us, and who needed a lawn anyway? Lawns were part of our past, and this was our future. And besides, if we were hungry for green, the apartment was furnished with a BIA-green vinyl-and-chrome sofa and chairs, as well as a kitchen table, lamp, bed, bookcase, and appliances. The cookie jar went on the kitchen table, the two ceramic pheasants on top of the refrigerator, and soon it looked like home, someone's home, but not exactly ours. But just as I recognized that the features of the landscape would soon be mine, I knew that the apartment would soon be ours. I only needed to leave and come back, and each time I opened the door I would be coming home, and it would begin to feel and look like home.

We made a trip to Gallup the first week and bought a few more furnishings, dishes, and cooking things. *"Na'nízhoozhígóó déyá!"*—I am going to Gallup—we proudly declared. *"Chinledéé naashá!"*—I am from Chinle—we shouted when we got there. That Navajo tape was coming in very handy indeed. And when we drove the two-hour trip back to Chinle it did feel as if we were going home. Black Wash, the shooting range, the water tower, they all welcomed us. We piled our new goods into the apartment. It was looking quite cozy, quite homey. We cracked open an illicit bottle of wine from Gallup, put on our Navajo tape, and let Jim Parrish guide us deeper into the mysteries of the Navajo language. He was now into weather conditions, and we were delighted to learn the word for mud, *hashtł'ish*, a lovely sound, squishy to say. The summer rains had arrived, and mud was everywhere, filling the potholes, turning the road to chocolate pudding, building up on the floor of the Bronco like a brown cement frosting. Sitting on the green vinyl chairs, we marveled at the word, *hashtł'ish*, and happily pointed to it, on our shoes, on the linoleum floor, outside where the lawn could have been—*hashtł'ish!* We were in Navajo country. We were having adventures. And we were going to do good!

Legal
Crusaders

Diné Bee'iiná' Náhiilnah Bee Agha'diit'aahe, Inc., colloquially known as DNA, was one of dozens of federally funded legal services programs around the country in 1968. The programs were designed to give legal assistance in civil, not criminal, cases to individuals who could not afford a lawyer. Priorities and policies for each program were set by a local board of directors, which included representatives from both the legal and the client communities. Legal services for the poor, we believed, was a critical piece in the social justice revolution puzzle. If the poor and disenfranchised could receive quality legal services, they would be able to fight discrimination and oppression, and achieve the quality of life they deserved. If that revolution succeeded, we might have a country that truly lived up to the dreams of Martin Luther King, Jr., Robert and John Kennedy, and so many others. This could be a *better* country, and we could be part of the struggle.

Infused with this vision, and fresh from law school, Bob was one of twenty-four lawyers who arrived that year to fill positions with DNA. The program was only in its second year, and the harvest from the previous year's recruiting trip brought the total legal staff to twenty-eight, still an inadequate number. Although there were many other legal services programs, including six others on Indian reservations, none was like DNA. The Navajo Reservation, as it was called then (now the Navajo Nation), is the size of West Virginia and covers parts of three states, Utah, Arizona, and New Mexico. In 1968, the population of roughly 125,000* was spread out over this huge area, living in small family compounds, herding sheep and goats on foot or horseback, raising a few cattle, and growing corn and squash. Some lived near trading posts, which had sprung up at fifteen mile intervals along all the roads, mostly dirt. I realized years later that this placement probably reflected the distance horses could travel before needing a drink of water. Others lived in the small towns that had grown around the Bureau of Indian Affairs offices. In all statistical measures of health, education, and economic well-being, Navajos scored near the bottom. The need for help of all kinds was undeniable.

Each new attorney was assigned to one of five towns on the reservation. Several stayed in Window Rock, the location of both the central office and the Fort Defiance branch office. Three or four went to each of the other four branch offices, except for Chinle, which received only one. Housing was an issue in Chinle, more than elsewhere. It was in the heart of Navajoland, and perhaps more dominated by government agencies than the other places, which were all within a few miles of the reservation border. In Chinle we were two hours from Gallup, almost two and half from Holbrook or Farmington. That made us more isolated in many ways. It also meant that there was less commerce and less private enterprise, and therefore very little non-governmental housing with utilities. The legal services program had contracted with a couple in Chinle to rent us a house that they had built for their retirement. They had several years left with the BIA and had a house that went with that job. It was a good arrangement, but would only accommodate one attorney, and so Chinle came up short until the next year, when additional housing was found.

---

*The median age was 17, resulting in a population climb to 290,000 in the year 2000.

Most of us bonded with our assigned locations almost immediately. Bob and I felt quite special, especially since we had been lucky enough to have a rainbow guide the way. There were geographical and cultural features that distinguished each place and became our touchstones for this new life. Chinle had the Canyon de Chelly, with Spider Rock and over fifty multi-roomed ruins tucked in the canyon walls. Window Rock was the capital of the Navajo Nation, and its arch-like rock with a natural window in it was a symbol of Navajoland. Shiprock, of course, had the huge rock shaped like a ship, and it was within reach of the Colorado peaks. Crownpoint, the eastern outpost of Navajo country, could claim proximity to Chaco Canyon. Tuba City, besides having the best name, had some beautiful hidden oases, and if you didn't have a problem skiing on a sacred mountain, there was a ski area less than an hour away.

In truth, all the towns were much the same, having been founded by government agencies or by churches that needed to centralize their services. They built Bureau of Indian Affairs boarding schools, clinics, and administrative offices for roads maintenance, social security, and a host of other necessities. After the Navajo Tribal government was established in the 1920s, tribal offices piggy-backed on the federal presence. Tribal police stations, courts, and jails appeared, as well as the center of community life and local government, the chapter house, usually a centrally located stone or cinder-block building with a single large meeting room and adjoining kitchen and storage area. Trading posts, churches, and gas stations—in that order—had arrived as the markets grew in these towns. Later waves of development in the 1980s and 1990s brought Allsups, Blockbuster Video, Bashas Supermarkets, Ace Hardware, and, of course, pizza, chicken, and burgers. In Chinle, Colonel Sanders was the first to break the fast food barrier, opening a restaurant in 1978.

In the 1960s each town was blessed with a HUD housing project, usually poorly built cinder-block houses laid out subdivision style, on a grid of unnamed, potholed streets. No matter in which town, these housing areas were called Low Rent, as in "Where do you live?" "Oh, I live over in Low Rent." "Oh, yeah? which house?" "You go over the cattle guard, stay on that street, look for the yard on the corner with that big dog tied to a rope, turn that way. We're on that street. We have blue curtains." If the dog in that corner yard was out for the day, you would never find the right turn. The rent was indeed low, beginning around $12 a month, and Low Rent was a housing solution for many Navajos who came to one of these towns for work.

The towns also shared an abundance of mud in the rainy season. The rest of the time it was dust and sand, which the wind picked up and flung at you no matter where you were. Red dust regularly came through the cinder blocks in Low Rent, depositing little dunes on the floor next to the wall. On a bad day, it sandblasted your face as you scurried from house to car, or car to trading post. On a really bad day, you had fine sand grinding between your teeth every time you swallowed. On a really, *really* bad day the automatic street lights along the main road in Chinle, triggered by darkness, turned on.

But this was all part of the foreignness and adventure. We were fiercely loyal to Chinle and were very pleased to have been assigned to the heart of Navajoland. Not only did we have the beautiful Canyon de Chelly and Canyon del Muerto, places of great significance in Navajo culture and history, but we also had a horizon defined by Black Mesa in the distance, the huge dark mass whose every point, bump, and gap against the skyline eventually became familiar and comforting to me. We had cottonwood trees along the washes that turned to gold in the fall. It was the best of all possible places. As time went by, we even bragged that in Chinle we had the finest mud and the fiercest sand storms. At that first meeting in Window Rock, we were already bonding with our new locations, and we traded friendly insults with others in our group of immigrants: "We wouldn't be caught dead in Tuba City, there's nothing there. It's so bleak," or "How can you stand it in Shiprock, with that power plant right next door?" And they would gape at us, "God, who would want to be in Chinle?! It's so far from everything!"

❖

In the beginning, Bob's life of doing good was easier than mine. He had a role that was very clear, at least to himself. He was the first lawyer ever to practice in Chinle. His office was waiting for him, above Fleming Begaye's Trading Post, with an entrance at the back, up an outside staircase. Fleming, a Navajo entrepreneur with a prime piece of real estate on the

corner where anyone going to Chinle had to turn, had built a very successful business. He snagged the tourists, whether or not they were turning,
with the Shell station and store. And his café was popular with locals. He
was pleased to increase his little empire by adding the lawyer to his complex, and had remodeled a second story to house the legal services offices.

We wanted to meet Bob's landlord that first day, and stopped at the
trading post to say hello. It was a strange encounter for us, new to Navajo
country. With a compact build, pressed blue jeans and a very white shirt,
Fleming shook hands and stared at us, or rather inspected us through his
glasses. His round face did not give way to even a faint smile, although I
am sure that we were full of excitement and beaming blinding Anglo
smiles at him. He said that the office was not ready for Bob, and he
should come back in two days. We wondered for a long time if Fleming
was angry with us, with DNA Legal Services, with his wife, or with the
world. It turned out that none of the above was true, and we valued him
as a very conscientious landlord and as a friend.

Being a Navajo business person, we learned, was not always easy.
Cultural norms pressured someone with money or goods to share
among family members, and sometimes the definition of family became
very broad indeed. Those who had a salary or owned a business were
probably contributing to the support of a host of unseen relatives. It
made it hard to get ahead in the Anglo sense. If you kept your earnings
to yourself and your immediate family, you appeared to other Navajos
hard-nosed and uncaring, and "un-Navajo." If you spread your earnings
among all those who had a claim on them, it must have seemed hardly
worth the effort to try to get ahead.

The DNA Legal Services office space was roomy, with a reception
area and four separate offices. Bob took one with a view toward the
northeast, over the Chinle Wash. The offices were furnished with desks,
chairs, and telephones, and with secretaries Lucille Begay and Alta
Bluehouse, a receptionist, Lucy Zohannie, and interpreters David Barney
and Florence Paisano. When he arrived for work the first day, it seemed
as if the staff had been waiting for the lawyer to complete the cast so the
film could roll. And roll it did.

The first day in his new office, Bob was visited by the already enraged Chinle Public School District Superintendent, Jodie Matthews.

Matthews had a career which included a variety of briefly held school administration positions in his native Arkansas and elsewhere, and like some other reservation refugees, seemed to have found a place where he could operate a fiefdom as he wished. He had hired his wife to manage the school system's federal programs, resulting in a combined salary of over $70,000, an unconscionable amount in 1968. Complaints about their professional and personal habits were rampant. Matthews understood from Bob's comments at a school board meeting the night before that he intended to support the right of parents to organize a recall election. The parents, who spoke at the meeting, wanted to recall two board members who supported the superintendent.

Red-faced and quivering, Matthews slammed his fist on Bob's desk and began ranting about the fancy furniture, the waste of federal money on lawyers, and the fact that he knew Navajo Tribal Chairman Nakai personally and that he could have the program de-funded. He must have been livid that this ridiculously young radical upstart from some effete eastern college was meddling in his affairs. Bob asked if he could tape the conversation, which was becoming more and more threatening and obscene. "Yes," shouted Matthews, "I want it on tape!" Later that tape would be a major piece of evidence in the *Dodge v. Nakai* lawsuit filed by DNA Legal Services to protect the right of the program to operate without intimidation and threats of de-funding.

But on that first day there were others who waited patiently to see the new lawyer in town. People from miles around had heard that there was now a lawyer in Chinle, an *agha'diit'ahe*, or "one who speaks for another," and they came with a great variety of problems that they hoped might fit within this job description. A Navajo woman from Piñon, more than fifty miles away, breast fed her baby while she told her story through the interpreter. She had received a postcard in the mail months earlier and, not understanding it, hoped the *agha'diit'ahe* could help her. Perhaps, she thought, she was in trouble, or was supposed to do something in order to stay out of trouble. She spoke no English, and the card was a mystery to her. Someone had told her it was from Winslow, Arizona, and that made her think of the jail where her brother-in-law was held for several days for no apparent reason. Yes, she needed to get this postcard taken care of before there was more trouble.

Excited to be handling his first client, and a traditional Navajo at that, Bob invited her into the office with David to interpret. David explained that the woman had a piece of mail that she wanted the lawyer to help her with. Bob geared himself up for a "Denial of Benefits" from the Social Security Administration, or a "Summons to Appear" from tribal court, or whatever legal challenge was coming his way. The woman handed him the card, badly dog-eared from its travels with her over the past nine months. Bob read: *Grand Opening, December 1, 1967, White's Sewing Machine Center, Winslow, Arizona—Demonstrations of our newest models, just in time for Christmas—Refreshments—Free Prizes—Bring this card with you to be eligible for the drawing! Don't miss it.*

He explained the message to her, saying that this was not important and that she was not in trouble. As David interpreted, the woman listened with acceptance, with no apparent regret of the long journey she had made to see the lawyer or of the drawing that she missed. She nodded to Bob and said thank you. As he stood up to say good-bye and shake her hand, he moved to drop the card in the wastebasket. She stopped him, asked for the card back, and replaced it in her purse. They shook hands, Bob's first experience with the traditional Navajo handshake, so long, so gentle, so devoid of pumping. She left the office, with its new lawyer, now experienced, now open for business.

It was not all smooth sailing, however, with his staff. There were wardrobe issues for Bob. He arrived for work that first day dressed in slacks, sports jacket, white shirt, and tie. He wanted to look respectable, and he wanted to respect his clients by looking like a serious lawyer. Already we were hearing rumors of hippies coming through the reservation. Whatever they seemed to be seeking—drugs, someone to do drugs with, love, or enlightenment—it felt frightening and predatory to most traditional and many modern Navajos. The hippies seemed to expect an automatic welcome as soul mates or kindred spirits in Indian country, for reasons that escaped their hosts. They also made the mistake of assuming an anti-government, anti–Viet Nam War position in Indian country, among a population that has been always, and was then, among the most patriotic and heroic fighters on behalf of the United States. Bob and I were both acutely aware of our whiteness, our age, and our potential for being cast as hippies, and we were extremely careful not to dress accordingly. It was tougher on me than on Bob. I have never exactly known what image to put forth in my dress, and it was tempting to just forget it and go hippie. But I knew that could be harmful to the image of the legal services program, and I struggled to dress like the lawyer's wife. Of course, no one had seen a lawyer before in Chinle, and so no one had seen his wife before either... but enough about me and my dress.

Bob was in trouble and didn't know it. He assumed he was dressing appropriately, and although he would have preferred jeans and a button-down shirt, he didn't want to be disrespectful. What he didn't know was that the young Mormon missionaries dressed just like him, and Lucille and David were beginning to wonder if the new lawyer was also a Mormon. Finally, Lucille gathered her courage and asked Bob if he was of that faith. He laughed and said no. He had been raised Lutheran in Wisconsin, but he didn't belong to any church anymore. He had never even met a Mormon that he knew of, although he would be happy to do so if one came along, he quickly added. Lucille suggested that he stop wearing the white shirt and the tie. Bob said he would be happy to oblige, and how about if he wore Levis and cowboy boots? He was secretly thinking about getting a horse and riding it to the office, and leaving me with the Bronco during the day. "Oh, no," she said, "not that either. We don't want you looking like a cowboy." It was a delicate dance—how to dress to avoid looking like a hippie, a Mormon, or a cowboy. He settled on slacks and button-down shirts that were either blue, pink, or yellow. He dropped the tie, and the Harris tweed jackets eventually ended up on a variety of Navajo elders of both sexes, providing warmth against the winter wind.

Within two weeks the folders of clients at the Chinle legal services office filled a filing cabinet drawer. Other offices with more attorneys expanded their caseloads even more rapidly. The DNA lawyers were making an immediate impact, in all sorts of ways.

On his first day on the job in Window Rock in the summer of 1968, Richard Barlow saw a client who breathlessly explained that his pickup had just been repossessed. Richard had been practicing tax law in New York City and was completely unprepared for anything that could have walked in the door on that day. The rest of the staff had all gone to a legal services conference in San Francisco, and he had been left behind, the most junior person, to handle the walk-ins. Fortunately, the truck had been picked up in Chinle, according to a frantic call from the owner's wife, and it would be at least forty-five minutes before the tow truck would roll through Window Rock on its way to Gurley Motors in Gallup. Richard had time to do a little research. A quick consultation of Navajo tribal law revealed that the repo man needed a tribal court order in order to take a vehicle off the reservation. The client reported that his wife had been shown no court order.

Richard called the tribal police and ordered them to arrest the tow truck driver before he reached the New Mexico state line. To his delight, and the relief of the client, it worked. The driver was jailed and the tow truck impounded. The next morning Pat Gurley, owner of Gurley Motors, and his attorney, John Schulke, appeared in Richard's office. Gurley was fuming, outraged at the nerve of these legal services upstarts to impede his practice of commerce with the Navajo people. He threatened to take Richard to court, have *him* jailed, seize *his* vehicle. Richard explained the need for a tribal court order for repossessions on the Reservation. Gurley continued to spew invectives. Schulke took Gurley out in the hall for a few minutes, apparently to explain to his client the facts of law, and when they came back into Richard's office, they were ready to make a deal. The driver and tow truck were released, and the repossessed pickup was returned to its owner, paid in full. There would be no further payments and the vehicle title was given to the ecstatic client. This was the kind of case that endeared Diné Bee'iiná' Náhiilnah Bee Agha'diit'aahe, Inc., to the Navajo people and made them the devil incarnate to those doing illegal business on the reservation.

Another attorney from New York, young and single, was enamored of both the women and the horses native to Navajoland. He established himself in Window Rock and quickly set about to find at least one of each. He settled down with a horse first, and gave Navajo humor one of its great stories. It seems that he bought the horse before he really knew how to care for it. He knew it needed hay, and he bought a couple of bales. He also knew that it needed something else to eat, but he wasn't sure what. He asked a Navajo interpreter at the DNA Window Rock office, who was also a rodeo champion, what he should feed his horse. "Oh, sure," said the interpreter. "You need to give him feed, not just hay."

"Oh, yeah?" he asked. "How do I do that?"

"Well, the best thing is to go to that supermarket, across the road, and get one of those big cans of peaches, you know the really big cans, like for a big family, you know that size?" and he described with his hands a can with a diameter of about eight inches.

"Yeah, I know what you mean." The lawyer was following closely.

"Well, you just use that," concluded the interpreter. He said it with finality and walked off, and the lawyer accepted that as the last word. To the delight of everyone in the region, Navajo and Anglo alike, the lawyer went to the store, bought the big can of peaches, opened it, and tried to feed the peaches to his horse. The interpreter had assumed that he knew about oat feed for horses, and was only telling him about how much feed to administer. The answer, of course, was to use one of those big cans as a measure—after it was empty. The next day the lawyer reported to his adviser the interpreter that his horse wouldn't eat the peaches, and the story was born. Lawyers were making legends, as well as impacts on the law.

One of Bob's first big cases involved an action against the trader at Piñon. The trader had recruited fifteen Navajos to work on the railroad in Utah, and had hired his son to drive them to the job site. The son packed all fifteen into the back of a pickup and took off. At one point he was going much too fast and paid no attention to the men pounding on the window to get him to slow down. The truck rolled, killing two men and seriously injuring several others. Suit was filed against the uninsured trader, as an agent for the railroad, under the Federal Tort Claims Act. Bob had to refer the case to private attorneys in California because of the potential for winning large fees, but those attorneys let a Motion to Dismiss go unanswered and lost the case. Bob was so incensed that he sued the California attorneys for malpractice and eventually won in the 10th Circuit Court of Appeals. When the money came in, Bob set up trusts for the victims' families, giving them a steady income to replace the money that their husbands would have earned.

DNA attorneys saw as part of their mission the nurturing and support of the tribal court system, and part of that nurturing included staying away. The attorneys did not practice in tribal court, leaving that to tribal court advocates (many employed by DNA), who represented defendants, with advice from attorneys as needed. Many of the advocates moved on to private practice, and even to positions as tribal judges. A Navajo Department of Justice was created in the early 1970s, followed in 1978 by the Navajo Nation Bar Association (NNBA). The NNBA now has over 400 members, Navajo and non-Navajo, some attorneys, some tribal court advocates. The enormous increase in Navajo attorneys, from zero in 1968, may be a result of DNA's influence, or the litigious nature of American society, or glamorous lawyer shows on television. Or it may be due to the actions of mothers, like the woman who buried her baby's umbilical cord under the outside staircase of the Chinle DNA office in 1969. She chose that spot, hoping that her son would grow up to be a lawyer. Who knows?

Bob represented clients who had problems with the non-Indian world, which seemed to be on a collision course with traditional ways. The cases multiplied, and we wondered whether they had always been there, waiting for an attorney to come along and pick them up, or whether the legal collisions were really increasing so rapidly. In time, as he became more efficient, Bob was able to step back and try to address some of the systemic problems—the Social Security application process, the handling of pawn transactions, contracts for new and used cars and trucks, students' rights, and more. Some of these efforts resulted in class action lawsuits, enhancing the reputation of the legal services program among many Navajos, and putting the attorneys in the bull's eye of many of those whose boats were being rocked—government agencies, traders, car dealers, school authorities, to name only a few.

Navajo citizens needed legal help in so many ways, and sometimes their own government was the abuser. Until now, there had been no effective way for a Navajo on the reservation to receive legal representation in cases against his/her own government. The tribe had its own staff of attorneys, in the General Counsel's Office, hired from off-reservation, but to us, they often seemed as much the bad guy as the pawn brokers and car dealers. The new legal services attorneys brought cases against tribal police for brutality, against tribal court officials for lack of due process, against tribal administrators for employment discrimination. It was not only the non-Indian world that was threatened by the new legal services program on the Navajo Reservation. Tribal Chairman Raymond Nakai and many members of the Navajo Tribal Council had concerns about this band of outsiders and their potential to disrupt a delicate balance of power between the Navajo people and their elected officials. These new lawyers were talking about civil rights of individual Navajos, not just in the state and federal context, but in the tribal context. Where would this stop? Was this just another chapter in the long and painful tale of colonization? Was it a good thing for the Navajo Nation or a destructive thing? Who were these young, energetic, crusading Anglos, sent by the federal government?

With these questions hanging in the air, a spokesperson from the U.S. Department of Justice came one day in August 1968 to address the Navajo Tribal Council on the new Indian Civil Rights Act of 1968 and its applicability on Indian land. Bob and I were in Window Rock that day. He had a staff meeting in the morning, I was going to shop for food, and then we would go together to the Council Chambers in the afternoon to hear what the man from Waashindoon (Washington in Navajo) had to say. I went into the DNA office with Bob and ran into Ted Mitchell, founder and director of the legal services program, and the one who had recruited and hired Bob the year before.

Ted glared at me. "I certainly hope you're not going to wear that to the Council Chambers!" I was wearing cut-off jeans.

I was suddenly and profoundly embarrassed. "No, I won't."

"It's really important to be respectful of Navajo people, especially in the Council—that's their place of government. It's a very serious place. We can't be running around upsetting people."

"OK. I understand. I'm sorry." I left, adding to my shopping list a skirt of some kind for the afternoon.

Later in the day, and appropriately dressed, Bob and I stopped by the Council Chambers. It was a spectacular building, a giant log hogan, and I was awed by the atmosphere, physical and otherwise. Clearly, serious business of government took place here, much of it interpreted from Navajo to English and back again. But there was also the feeling that other powers resided here. I was very glad that I wasn't wearing shorts. We sat near the back, next to Ted.

Ted was charismatic and a committed troublemaker. Raised Mormon in Arizona, he went east to law school, and his years at Harvard convinced him that Mormonism was not in his future. Rather than simply retire quietly from the faith, as many do, he insisted on being expunged from the church on the grounds that he no longer believed. The long and tortuous process of convincing high officials in the Church is rarely invoked, and even more rarely succeeds. He told of endless sessions with the elders in Boston, where they attempted to re-indoctrinate him with beliefs they felt had been eroded by an ultra-liberal education. Eventually he prevailed and was officially released from the church.

Now, as leader of this band of do-gooders, he had found a new faith. He believed passionately in the cause of Navajo rights and threw himself into creating a legal services program that would be a force to be reckoned with, inside and outside the reservation. After one year of operation, it was clear to those in power that he was messianic in his vision and in his ability to attract followers. It was also clear that the Navajo Tribal government itself was not exempt from his attacks, if he saw abuses or corruption which threatened the safety and well-being of Navajo people. Some would say that he set his sights on the BIA and the tribal government for the pure joy of taking on the power structure, whether or not there were abuses.

A young, energetic Anglo himself, the Department of Justice attorney sat behind a table in front of the Tribal Council and did his best to field questions that were loaded with suspicion and hostility. Annie Wauneka, the only woman on the Council, took him on. Other councilors and those in the audience smiled. Annie was fierce and fearsome, a big presence in every sense. She was outspoken in both Navajo and in English and could be counted on to get her man. She asked him a series of leading questions about the Indian Civil Rights Act and the Navajo Treaty of 1868 and how the two related to each other. Would, for instance, the Tribal Council have the right to expel a "bad white man" from the reservation, a procedure guaranteed the Navajo Tribe by treaty, she asked? The Department of Justice attorney was in trouble, looking through his files for help that was not there. Eventually, he stammered, "Well, if there were someone . . . It would depend on what . . . I mean, is there someone specific that you are thinking about?"

"No," she snapped back. "I'm not talking about anyone in particular. I just want to know the answer to my question."

Everyone in the Council Chamber knew that Annie was talking about Ted. They had already chosen each other as worthy opponents and had engaged in minor skirmishes. Ted, overcome by naughtiness, snorted a loud, raucous laugh, just in case her reference was lost on anyone in the chamber. Annie wheeled her big, multi-skirted frame to face the source of the laugh.

"Don't you laugh at me, Ted Mitchell!" she yelled and shook her finger at him. Carl Beyal, the official interpreter and sergeant-at-arms for the council, quietly rose and walked down the aisle toward us. He leaned into our row and asked us to please behave in a respectful manner while in the Navajo place of government. I was mortified and, again, grateful not to have shorts on. How ironic that Ted would protect the Navajo sensibilities from my bare thighs, and offend those same sensibilities by mocking a respected leader.

The next day in the Council Chamber saw the escalation of the duel between Ted and Annie. The discussions with the man from Waashindoon were continuing. At some point Annie, still piqued from the day before, turned on the now silent Ted in the back row and shouted, "You dared to laugh at me, Ted Mitchell? You will not get away with that!" She strode down the aisle toward him, drew back her pitching arm and beat him about the head with her not insignificant fist. We were not there that day, but apparently she drove him from the chambers, herding him through the back door like a calf to slaughter.

That was only the beginning. The Tribal Council Advisory Committee voted shortly after her whipping to exclude Ted Mitchell from the reservation for life. Ted set up a trailer office about ten feet across the reservation boundary on the outskirts of Window Rock, from which he continued to run the legal services program and from which he filed suit in federal court. *Dodge v. Nakai*, brought by the Legal Services Board president, was a civil rights action against the Navajo Tribal government, claiming that Ted had been excluded without due process. The case dragged on for many months, and became a distraction for those in the legal services program. Employees, Anglo and Navajo, were unsure about the future. If Ted were excluded from the reservation, that would surely make anyone who crossed the government—and lawyers certainly were fitting themselves into that category—vulnerable to exclusion. Would it be feasible to continue the program, or would the funding be pulled and reallocated to a jurisdiction where a little more security existed for staff? If the court ruled that Mitchell could not be excluded and he returned to the reservation, certainly Nakai, Wauneka, and company could make life miserable for the program. The court ultimately did decide in favor of Ted and the applicability of the Civil Rights Act to non-Indians.

Ted returned to the office in Window Rock. The celebration was subdued. Navajo legal services was still in business, but with a new name, DNA People's Legal Services. The original Diné Bee'iiná Náhiilnah Bee Agha'diit'aahe, Inc., had to go, a concession to the Washington officials at the Office of Economic Opportunity who thought the Navajo phrase meant an obscenity, and to the Arizona Bar Association who claimed the phrase was "self-laudatory" and in violation of lawyer ethics. The name change was a relief to some Anglos who had had trouble mastering the long Navajo name, but in general it seemed an affront to the integrity of the program, and a threat to its tie with the Navajo grassroots.

The case had demonstrated growing support at the hogan level for the program, and this was reassuring. It was nice to have won a civil rights battle, and to have people recognize and appreciate it. The legal issues of the case, however, were perplexing. I admired Ted and believed he had been excluded in an arbitrary way. But there was no doubt he had acted badly in the Council Chamber. He was a mischievous force on the reservation and I could see why those in power detested him. Furthermore, there was the issue of tribal sovereignty, the right of a tribe to make its own laws to protect its people, resources, culture, and way of life. I believed deeply in that principle. Anglo American society and government had been forcing itself on Indian country for generations, always claiming to know what was best. It was a painful history, both for the Navajo people, and for those of us who were on the reservation representing the U.S. government.

For many Navajos the abuses began in 1864, when the U.S. government had rounded up Navajos in their traditional areas, including the bottom of Canyon de Chelly, and marched them, supposedly for their own good, eastward to Fort Sumner in what is now eastern New Mexico. They were kept there in a concentration camp until 1868 when the few remaining leaders signed a treaty with the United States and the remainder of the Navajos were allowed to walk back to their old home, now a reservation. Although those who marched, or were carried in mothers' arms, were probably all gone by 1968, the memory of this humiliation was very strong even after 100 years.

In the 1930s the U.S. War Department, in charge of Indians, had declared that the reservation land was becoming seriously overgrazed by the rapidly increasing sheep population. They attempted to convince the Navajos to cut down their numbers of sheep voluntarily in order to save the land. To the Navajo, sheep have always been a sign of wealth, as well as a necessity, and to reduce a family's herd was unthinkable. The government finally resorted to force and sent teams all over the reservation to confiscate sheep and slaughter them. To take away a Navajo's sheep was bad enough, but to slaughter the sheep, dig pits, and burn them right in front of the Navajo owners was a crime beyond comprehension.

The legacy of those disastrous acts continued to spin itself in strange ways. Not long before we arrived in Chinle, the Indian Health Service attempted to improve sanitary conditions in traditional Navajo homes. They sent sanitary engineers (white, of course) to each community to explain to people why sanitation was important and what they could do to clean up their hogans. They offered free spray to kill lice and bedbugs to anyone who was interested. In Lukachukai, an old man stood up and replied to the sanitation expert, "Many years ago Waashindoon came here to our land and told us it was important for our families and our land to give up some of our sheep. They killed our sheep in front of our eyes, and now Waashindoon is back to take away our bedbugs. I do not want any spray." He spoke for most people, and the program was a failure.

And so, I thought, shouldn't tribes be able to make decisions on how they want to govern themselves, what values they want to uphold, what culture they want to preserve, and how? For me the answer was an absolute "yes." I had a little trouble, however, with the fact that the Navajo governmental system had been forced on the tribe by the U.S. government. They modeled the office of Tribal Chairman after the Presidency, the Council after the Congress, and the Tribal Court after the Supreme Court. This particular way of doing business was established for the convenience of the U.S. government officials who needed to deal with Navajo issues and wanted a system to work with that mirrored their own. Now, decades later, was this the legitimate government of the Navajo people, authorized to protect individual rights and the sovereignty of the Navajo Nation? If it wasn't, if it had been a "mistake," what could be done about it now? And, who should do it?

Certainly not me. I needed to look for work.

THREE

On the Home Front

It was late September, and I sat on the concrete stoop of our apartment, picking dried clumps of *hashtł'ish* from my sandals. It was silly to try to keep the mud off the linoleum, but that was not my purpose anyway. In fact, I was without purpose. I was simply enjoying the act. The pieces came out from between the treads in perfect little geometric shapes, little clay figures, smooth, brown, each an individual. I lined them up on the concrete beside me, like strange cuneiform writing. What were they telling me? What should I be doing? Where was my adventure? Bob had a very clear—and admittedly challenging—path. A lawyer didn't wonder where the path was. He just stepped onto it and proceeded. My path . . . well, there was this mud . . . . and it was hard to pick out just which way to go.

I thought about Mr. Koontz, one of the first to try to tell me the facts of life at Navajo. He stuck with me, Mr. Koontz, not unlike *hashtł'ish*.

I replayed our conversation often, sometimes coming out the victor, sometimes the loser, but always piqued and perplexed. Soon after our arrival in Chinle, I had gone to Window Rock and Fort Defiance to apply for work with the Navajo Tribe. All the agency headquarters were there, and if I wanted work in Chinle this was the place to start. I visited the Office of Navajo Economic Opportunity (ONEO), a stepchild of the federal Office of Economic Opportunity (OEO). ONEO was in charge of several education, health, and welfare programs including Headstart.

It was strange to have a college degree so valuable in some quarters, and so meaningless in the place I had chosen to be. It was not an uncomfortable feeling, however, because I felt that now at last I was in the *real* world. My experience in Cambridge had been unreal in many ways. We had protested the war, marched for civil rights, harassed the university administration, all while receiving an excellent education and doing a certain amount of partying as well. It was a privileged position to be in, and we were surrounded by people like ourselves. There must be something else out there, beyond the boundaries of Harvard Square. There must be other people, with other experiences and other views. And here I was, sitting at a massive oak table, vintage BIA, filling out my third all-purpose application and wondering just how that degree in English and French History and Literature was going to fly.

From behind me, I heard "Well, what do *you* know?" It was a strange question, and clearly my answer should not pertain to English and French History and Lit. I looked around and found peering over my shoulder a smiley little Navajo man wearing a suit and horn-rimmed glasses.

I smiled while I searched for an answer. "I know I want a job."

"Where?"

"In Chinle."

"Oh, in *Chin*le." I noted a little sarcasm. "You people are so fussy."

I leapt to my own defense. "My husband and I are living in Chinle. I *have* to be there." After all, I thought, I am not just somebody wandering through looking for a reason to stay here. We *belong* here. We *live* here.

"I bet he's a lawyer."

"Yes, he is." I was surprised, which obviously gave my interrogator deep pleasure.

"I can always tell," he said, and he walked off, still smiling.

I was irritated and a little hurt by what felt like stereotyping. I was not just anybody. How dare he make assumptions about who I am? How dare he say "you people"? What people is that? White people? Well, there are white people, and then there are white people. How does he know what kind of white person I am? I was silently muttering to myself when I was called into the office of Mr. Flake, the Anglo director of Headstart. It was the world's shortest interview, in which I said that I had education credits, which I didn't, and that I loved little children, which I did, and in which Mr. Flake said he didn't have any funds, which he probably didn't, and that he did need some help in Chinle, which he probably did. He would keep me in mind, he said.

I was about to drive back to Chinle, still muttering about "you people," when I decided to make one last application at the personnel office in Fort Defiance. I got there just as the secretary was leaving for lunch. She said that Mr. Koontz would know what positions were available. I thought "Koontz—another Anglo in an administrative position with the Tribe, what a sad state of affairs." She gave me an application, and I sat down to fill it out.

"Ah, we meet again!" said Mr. Koontz as he came out of his office. I recognized the voice.

"Yes, I am *still* looking for a job," and I laughed, surprised to find my nemesis was named Koontz. For some reason I was not unhappy to cross his path again so soon.

He picked up the half-completed application and sat on the desk in front of me. "And what can you do? Type?"

"Fifty words a minute. And I can drive and . . . ."

"Bah!" he tossed the application back at me. "You know what we Indians need on this Reservation? We need someone like you people [I cringe again] to come out here with a great big bag of money, and leave it right here," and he pounded his hands on the desk, "and then go away." He waved his arms toward the east, still smiling.

"Do you mean that if every Anglo left the reservation. . . ."

Mr. Koontz laughed and interrupted again "No, I did not say that. Let me explain. When did the first one of you people [I give up cringing] start coming in here? In 1868. In 1868 a man came and founded the school right here in Fort Defiance. That was 100 years ago, 100 years ago, and ever since then men and money have poured in here and it has ballooned." He made a big balloon with his hands. "The system has grown bigger and bigger, but the Indian never got any drippings from it, and he still isn't getting any drippings from it. It's like a big rain cloud hanging over the dry field, and getting bigger and blacker and fuller with water. But the rain never falls on the field. That's what it's like."

"But isn't ONEO getting money to Indian people?" I tried feebly to participate.

"You know the sawmill up the road?" I couldn't tell if Mr. Koontz was answering me or not. "The man that runs that mill brings in money from all over the country. He sends men up to the mountain to cut timber. They bring it back, and put it through all those banging metal machines, and then the money comes jingling in. The owner of that operation works, and then he gets his money. He deserves his money. He's hiring people, he's making something, and he's selling it. I work for ONEO. I just sit here and I know the money is going to come in to me every week. I should work for it first and then get it. Do you understand?"

I didn't really, but I nodded.

He scooted closer to me on the desk, and smiled. "What else do you do?"

"I do social work," I almost shouted. I had forgotten that I *did* have something to offer. "I was a social worker for a year in Boston, for families on public welfare."

He was shaking his head and chuckling. "But what kind of social work? What do you do?"

I was intent on convincing Mr. Koontz of my worth. "Well, I visited families in their homes, and I kept written case records, and I had conferences with medical...."

He was laughing out loud now, "No, I mean 'social.' What do you do for social?" There was no mistaking the twinkle in his eye.

I laughed, too, and sat back in my chair, giving up my clutch on the application and on my professional credentials. This was clearly about something else, and I should take it in.

"Where are you from?" he asked.

"I'm from Seattle, and my husband is from Milwaukee."

"Well, I don't understand it. What are you two doing out here? With a background like this"—he pointed to the application—"you should be in a good job in the city somewhere."

"We're tired of cities. We like it here."

"How long are you here for?"

"At least two years."

"That's the trouble. That's not long enough. We need you to come here and stay, and live and die with us." I felt real progress was being made. Minutes earlier, I was supposed to bring a big bag of money and leave immediately.

"We've only been here three weeks," I tried to keep it light. "We can't guarantee how long we'll be here. DNA may not get funded again, and then we'd have to leave, or find something else to do. But we may stay here a long time. I'd like to."

"All right, but you and your husband must be lacking something."

I didn't know whether he had said "liking" or "lacking," and hoping for the best, I repeated "We must be *liking* something?"

"No, *lacking* something."

"What do you mean 'lacking' something?" Now I am down again. A roller coaster ride with Mr. Koontz.

"Well, if I were a lawyer and had gone to good schools and came from good families, I would go to the city and make a lot of money. There must be something wrong if you're out here."

"You can't say that." I was flustered. I wanted to connect with this person. I wanted him to understand. "We have always lived in cities and we want to live a different way. This is the kind of life that is new to us, and we want to be here and not in the city. We chose to come here. And, we want to help."

He nodded. "You are professional people. Do you know there are no professional Navajos? None at all. That school was founded in 1868, and what have we got out of it? Not one professional Indian. If I were a professional I would go to the city."

"Have you been to the city?"

"Yes, I lived there awhile."

"And you came back here?"

He smiled and hesitated. "*I* have reasons to be here. Family." He hopped off the desk. " I must go home for lunch. You got me going!" and he headed for the door.

"We'll be in Chinle, maybe for a long time. I enjoyed talking with you . . . and I'm willing to learn," and I laughed.

He smiled. "Yes, I won't forget that. Leave that application for me."

❖

Now, it was two months later and no word from either Mr. Koontz or Mr. Flake. I also had submitted applications to the BIA boarding school in Chinle to be a substitute teacher, but was held up by civil service exam results. In the meantime, I could pick mud out of my sandals and continue to ponder life on the reservation. My pondering sent me in search of a weaving teacher. The rugs were so stunning, and I had seen women weaving on simple upright looms. I could get Bob to make me a loom out of two-by-fours, and I would give it a try. I went to the Navajo Tribal Arts and Crafts Guild, across the street from Fleming Begaye's, where the finest jewelry and rugs were sold. I loved to look at things there, and had been in several times, but this time I had a mission. I was in search of information on how to learn to weave. I approached the woman behind the counter, and said that my husband and I had just moved to Chinle and that I was interested in learning how to weave. Did she know, I asked, where I might buy some spun wool or some of the weaving tools? She looked very blank and shook her head. "No, I don't know," was all she said.

I was discouraged, but didn't give up. I asked more questions. What kind of carder is best? Is it hard to learn to spin? How can the weavers spin the wool so fine? Are there gray sheep, or is gray wool a mixture of black and white wool? Was it hard to build a loom? Did she know someone who could help me get started? Did she think my husband could build the loom? I employed a technique that I later realized was very Navajo. I simply didn't go away. I stayed and asked and listened, and asked some more. Did she think I could learn how, or was it too hard? There was no reply beyond "yes" and "no." Finally, I gave up, and picked up my car keys off the counter. I was going to thank her for her time, when she smiled and said, "I weave, and my daughter, who is eleven, weaves," and she tossed in another smile. "You can do it." She opened up and told me where to buy everything, and how not to get taken by the trader. She said if my husband would build the loom, she would show me how to get started. She was sure that I could do it. She was so warm and generous, as if we'd known each other for years.

I got in the Bronco and began to cry. There was something about the pace of the encounter, the waiting, the listening, the eventual acceptance she had given me, the graciousness she had shown me, that touched me deeply. I later understood that this early reserve, followed by the consideration of a relationship, and finally a great friendliness was not unusual. And I later understood that it was based on some good sense and probably a lot of painful history. A Navajo encountering a stranger needed to be cautious, to wait, and to rely on good instincts before making a decision. In contrast, I saw myself and other Anglos hustling and bustling everywhere, in a hurry, talking constantly, too enthusiastically, often about nothing, or at least nothing important. All of our "so nice to meet you," "so good to see you," "you look great," "I'm just fine," "how's this? how's that?" began to seem so pointless to me. Or perhaps, beside the point, the point being, here are two people who may or may not have a relationship, and they each need to give it some time and some thought. I was learning about being Navajo.

Still unemployed, I spent my days shopping at the trading post, cooking mutton casseroles, and going to the laundromat in Many Farms, fifteen miles north of Chinle. I was also checking in regularly with my potential employers, the BIA, the local elementary school, and the Tribe. I had gone to Hubbell's Trading Post in Ganado thirty miles away for the day to talk to weavers about weaving and equipment, and I had bought the lumber at the Ganado hardware store for the loom. There seemed to be plenty to keep me busy.

We were still in the apartment, while our house waited for a water connection, and it was now known to all in Chinle where the new lawyer and his wife lived. I had visitors on a daily basis, who were curious or in need, or had something to offer. It was hard to say no to rugs and kachina dolls that appeared at the door, and in fact we usually said yes. We adopted a cat, the beginning of another weakness that flourished in Chinle, and named him Big Fella. We had all Navajo neighbors in the compound, and I spent some time with kids who were fascinated by our household and by us, and wanted to know if we were hippies, or if we knew Kennedy. John F. Kennedy was such a hero to Navajos. His picture was in every home and hogan. I even saw a rug woven in his likeness. It was very touching. We were also beginning to socialize with Bob's staff, and had some enjoyable evenings with David, Lucille, Florence, and others.

I treasured time to be alone as well. I had the feeling that once I went to work, these times would disappear. Some afternoons I chose to be domestic and sew curtains. Other times I drove up to an overlook on the rim of Canyon de Chelly and did some sketching. From there I could look down into the canyon, and as fall came, I could see the cottonwoods turning golden below. I was surrounded by Navajo people and Navajo landscape. I was very content, maybe even beginning to feel at home.

And then one morning in September I woke up as usual, and as I finished brushing my teeth I looked at myself in the mirror. I didn't look well. What was wrong? Maybe I did feel a little feverish, or chilled. What could it be? A bug from the kids next door, probably. We had made brownies together last week, and the bowl and spoon licking had been enthusiastic. I went about my day, and felt better. But the next morning, the same affliction seized me. My skin looked yellowish. Maybe it was hepatitis. My eyes looked pale, not right. Again, the day went well, and again the next morning I looked worse. It was my hair. Once the object of pride, long and straight and thick, now it was limp and lifeless. Surely it used to be thicker, with more luster. Didn't it? Or did it? What was happening to me?

I asked Bob if I looked sick, fearing that I faced a long battle with leukemia and that the sooner I told him the better. To my disappointment, he agreed. Yes, maybe I didn't look quite right. He added tuberculosis to the list of possibilities, and suggested I go to the doctor in Ganado. I agreed to make an appointment. But first I needed to pick up the mail. I drove to the post office, parked, and went inside. I was a little shaky, and now that I had TB on my mind, I was suppressing a brand new symptom, a shallow cough. There was a long line, as usual. I took my place at the end, and fell into a semi-conscious state as I waited my turn. I stared at the heads in front of me in line, men, women and children, all with thick, lustrous, black hair. I stared at the arms and the faces, beautiful tones of golden brown and red. I looked behind me and made quick contact with a set of eyes, deep, rich, and black. And suddenly, I knew at last what was wrong with me. I was *not* Navajo. I wasn't sick—I was just white.

It was a difficult but important realization. I was feeling like the minority that I was. In Chinle, approximately one percent of the population was non-Navajo. Whether we were Lester the African-American at the auto repair shop, or Lucy the wife of the new attorney in town, we were in the minority. I thought I had been in that position before, the position of a minority. I had worked in a Black and Puerto Rican section of Boston as a welfare case worker, and had been in the minority in certain neighborhoods. But I retreated every evening to my apartment in Cambridge, where my co-tenants, my co-shoppers, my co-moviegoers almost all looked like me. The fact that I held a small part of Indian blood in my body was never a factor, except to occasionally cause a little discomfort, the anxiety of harboring a secret, not sure from whom or why. For all purposes I was white, raised white, schooled white, married white. And as such I was in the majority. Minority in fact meant to me someone of a different color, or more accurately, someone *of* color. Anglo America had no culture, no color, no ethnicity to set it apart. Those in the minority had the culture, color, and ethnicity. That's what made them minorities. It was a common, but not excusable, view of the world.

And here I found myself going through the looking glass into that world of being a minority. I was overwhelmed with the feeling of being wrong. I was the wrong color. *I* looked pale, yellow, and terminally ill. *They* looked healthy and beautiful and right. I spoke the wrong language. The Navajo majority could make fun of me and I wouldn't know it. I came from the wrong place. Seattle or Cambridge meant nothing. To be from Kayenta or Chinle, from Flagstaff or Low Mountain, well, *that* meant something. The majority had a way of doing things, an understanding among themselves about how and why things should be done in a certain way. It was important, and it was easy for them. For me it was confusing and embarrassing. I was always in the wrong, always on the outside, painfully aware of my inferiority to those on the inside.

The challenge was to make peace with my situation. I needed to hang onto that insight and those feelings of minority, because they would be important in understanding something about Navajos, and about being a minority in the United States. But I also needed to accept my color, language, and culture (fuzzy as it might be) and find comfort and even pride there. It would be a struggle to overcome a certain loathing of my own cultural identity and give up the illusion that I could become almost-Navajo. It would also be a struggle to relate to those insiders, Navajos, who (like me, ironically) wanted to reject their own culture, that very culture that I coveted. I needed to accept the history that set the stage for some of the strange dynamics in Navajo country, and understand my role in this drama, as a white person, even if I had been in Chinle only three months. I needed to understand that "you people," as Mr. Koontz said, were *my* people, like it or not, and that some of them were good and some were evil, and most were somewhere in between. I hoped to God we would at least be somewhere in between.

❖

There is a story that became legendary in the lore of legal services. It is true, I swear. I know because I met them, a couple, both lawyers, who had arrived in the winter and set up housekeeping in Tuba City. They had shipped all their furniture from their Manhattan apartment to their new quarters, including a large, white—snow white—sofa. There were apparently marital problems, exacerbated by the shock of moving from *The* City to Tuba City, and in the spring the wife fled back to New York. The story was that she had a sort of springtime sandstorm breakdown, and began shrieking, "My sofa has turned red! My sofa has turned red!" referring to the dust that found its way into the very weave of that pure white fabric.

Of course, our furniture turned red, too, and during our seven years in Chinle I thought a lot about the symbolism of that pure white sofa from New York turning red in Indian country. What does it mean to be an outsider? If instead of a white sofa, you are a white person, what happens to you in Navajo country? You do not turn red, no matter how much the wind blows.

FOUR

More Learning than Teaching

The realization that I was not Navajo, and never would be, set me back. I wondered what I really was. White, of course, but did that mean I was like all Anglos, that I was perceived to be like all Anglos? Couldn't I somehow distinguish myself from those others who seemed to me to be unattractive and inappropriate at best, and selfish and malevolent at worst? Could I be a different kind of Anglo, not really *Anglo*, but something else—like "nice-Anglo" or "good-Anglo"? Might people say behind my back "She's Anglo, but..." and go on to enumerate my specialness? I felt myself sinking into a major quagmire of self-doubt, self-loathing, self-anything that would make me feel bad. I decided to fight the temptation to be stuck and chose to keep moving. Maybe if I had a role, was useful and busy, maybe then things would become clearer to me.

By this time I had applied for work with the BIA elementary boarding school in Chinle, with the Headstart Program, and with the

State of Arizona. I had declared myself ready, willing, and able to fill a variety of positions, including teacher, social worker, and clerk-typist. For some of these I was qualified, or at least had some kind of experience that would indicate qualification. For others, like teacher, I was not. I figured that everything at Navajo was so different, so remote, so culturally unique, that "qualified" would never apply to me anyway, and that the best approach would be to plunge in and learn as I tried to swim.

I secretly hoped that the BIA job would not come through. I had a prejudice against the agency, about which I had heard so much. They ran boarding schools that were cruel in many ways. It was standard BIA practice to yank six- and seven-year-olds out of the hogan, away from grandma's well-worn and well-loved skirt, away from parents' arms, and dump them into a boarding school many hours from their homes. Parents were asked the names of their children before they were taken, and reluctant to speak what shouldn't be spoken in Navajo culture, remained silent and deferred to the BIA employee. Children were given first names and in some cases last names by these new guardians, which is why today in Navajoland there are so many Yazzies, which means small, and so many Bias, which needs no translation.

I had heard of heartless BIA employees, Anglo and Navajo alike, who cut children's hair, took their clothes, de-loused them whether they needed it or not, put them under a shower—a terrifying experience for the first time—and gave them new and strange wardrobes. They told them to sleep in beds—another strange and frightening experience—and warned them not to utter one word of Navajo from now on. There were also tales of physical abuse and cruel punishment for infractions of these new strange rules.

I understood that many of these practices were part of a past that the BIA wished to correct, and that many within the agency were sincere. But, I also read in the paper, every winter, of runaways who could not bear it—whatever "it" might be—any longer, and who escaped and headed for home. Sometimes they made it. I suppose we didn't hear about them. Sometimes they didn't, like the three boys who ran away from Lukachukai Boarding School in the winter of 1970 and were found with frozen feet, which had to be amputated. Even if the BIA was mending its ways, it would be a long time before reform was complete.

And so, hoping the phone would ring from certain prospective employers and not from others, I decided to pretend I had a job. I chose a position that appealed to me, and one where I thought I might have something to offer. Headstart appealed because the program was relatively new on the reservation and it was run by the Tribe. I liked the idea that I would be part of a Navajo effort, rather than a tool of the federal or state government, which I saw as colonizing forces to a greater or lesser degree. I knew that any classroom needs an additional adult body, to free the teacher for more important work or to pay individual attention to a child in need. And, finally, as an Anglo and an English speaker, I thought I might be able to offer the kids contact with "my kind of people," contact that I hoped would be unthreatening and reassuring. Almost all of them would go to the local public school as first graders, not the boarding school, but there they would encounter Anglo teachers and administrators. In 1968 there were very, very few Navajos in any positions above cook, janitor, or bus driver in any school system. And in Chinle, as I walked down the hall looking for the principal's office to apply for a job, I saw that every room was led by an Anglo teacher. So I might be a stepping stone for these first-graders-to-be, a relationship with an Anglo that would be positive and encouraging, and give them some confidence with their next contacts.

These were my intellectual reasons for choosing Headstart. But, of course, the real reason was the desire to be with these kids. I saw them with a parent or grandparent in the trading post, or bouncing along in the back of a pickup, or sitting under a piñon tree watching sheep, and my heart responded. They were irresistible, they were lively, they were unspoiled in the terms that I was used to, and their eyes . . . they seduced me. I wanted to be with them, to play with them, to be a helper and a friend.

I waited one afternoon until I saw that the vans had left with the kids, and approached the Headstart "complex." There were two classes, each in its own building sitting in the big dirt parking lot surrounding the Chinle Chapter House. One of the buildings was a Quonset hut painted a dull yellow; the other classroom, a small frame-and-tarpaper room, joined its neighbor at a right angle. Each classroom had its own entrance, and I chose the square building, having no experience with Quonset huts and being reluctant to knock on a door set in the end of a building that looked like half a giant culvert. Mrs. Baldwin opened the door and looked a little quizzical seeing a young, long-haired Anglo woman standing there. She glanced quickly at my vehicle—often a clue as to the identity and purpose of a stranger—but gained no insight from the mud-splattered Bronco. I introduced myself and said that I would like to volunteer and help in any way that I could. I explained that I had applied for work with ONEO in Window Rock, but had heard nothing for three months, and that I wanted be useful. My husband was the new DNA lawyer, I added, and that was why I was here in Chinle.

"Well, I guess we could use some help," she said. I was quietly elated. I had a home, a place I might belong, with a woman I liked immediately. She was small, with gray hair in a bun and a quick smile. And incredibly, she wore a gray dress, a soft gray, long dress with a concho belt. At an unconscious level I connected her with my own beloved nursery school teacher, Mrs. Farwell, whom I called "Mrs. Pussywillow" because it seemed to me, at four years old, that she always wore a long, full, knit gray dress, gentle and soft like a pussy willow.

I learned that Sybil Baldwin was the head teacher of the two classrooms, and that she taught in one of them, with her aide Mae Yazzie. Louise Claw was the teacher in the other classroom, and her aide Edith Bitsui, a Choctaw, married to a Navajo, also drove one of the buses and helped cook. Kee Yazzie drove the other bus and was maintenance person. Although they had different titles, their job descriptions were identical. Edith and Kee both helped in the classroom, both cooked and cleaned in the Chapter House kitchen, and each drove a van. Once I began, I saw that in fact everyone did everything—teaching, driving, cooking, cleaning, and performing minor medical procedures as needed. I quickly learned that to be really helpful, I would need to do everything, too.

Mrs. Baldwin suggested that I begin by helping Louise in her classroom. She indicated that Louise might not be quite up to her standards, and that a little outside expertise might give her a boost. I briefly wondered what kind of expertise she thought I possessed, but was overcome with eagerness and nodded and made noises of total understanding and agreement. I would be there the next morning, I promised. I would do whatever I could to help. She smiled, smoothed her soft, gray skirt, and said, "That will be very nice." I was in heaven.

I arrived as promised the next day, more nervous than I had expected. I was worried that I would not fit in, that Louise would not want me in her classroom, that the kids would not like me. As it turned out, probably all those fears were well-founded. There was a wariness around me, and it took patience on my part and a willingness to sit back and wait. I was determined not to be the typical Anglo, as I saw us, pushy, loud, knowing it all. I would watch for chances to help. I would listen and learn.

Mrs. Baldwin introduced me to Louise and said that I was going to "help with the children." Louise seemed to receive me like a new-fangled mop, something that might be useful, but she couldn't quite see how. I also sensed an automatic reluctance to accept any idea that originated with Mrs. Baldwin. Perhaps there were personnel problems I would have to avoid, if I could. Edith and Kee were curious and pleasant, but clearly had a lot of tasks before them and needed to get to work. There was no orientation program, no small talk, no "let's show you where the break room is," or "here's where you hang your coat," or "here is where you can park your car." There was no break room, no coat hanger, no parking space. In the crook of the "L," where the two buildings joined, were a restroom and a tiny closet for supplies. These I discovered by following Louise around before the kids arrived.

The kids! They poured into the Quonset hut, chattering and laughing. Their boots and shoes made an amazing amount of noise. They seemed small, even for four- and five-year-olds, but they overwhelmed me. I only heard Navajo; I only saw black shiny hair, dark brown eyes. I was in danger of having a "mirror" relapse. I felt so big, so white, so out of place. But Louise quickly drafted me into action. After she had barked the kids into their seats, she said to them in Navajo that this *bilagáana* [white lady] was here to help her, Louise, and that they should do everything I said. Before I had time to ponder how the kids and I were going to pull off that relationship when I spoke no Navajo and they spoke no English, she handed me the attendance list and left the room. Well, I thought, I can read and they know their names, so this may be a place to start. I will begin to match up these unbelievably cute faces with the right names. I started with the first name. "Harrison Ben?" I called out.

A little girl who spoke English and probably for this reason saw herself as the authority in the class when the teacher was gone, piped up "It's not Harrison, it's Harson. His name is Harson."

OK. "Harson?" I asked again, and heard a faint "pressin" from the back of the room. I moved to the next name, "Jerison Claw?" I said, making the same blunder.

"That's Jarson," shouted several kids in unison.

I smiled, and repeated "Jarson." I was rewarded with another "pressin." OK, I thought, here we go. With the next name I would surely be home free. "Lyle Kinsel?"

This time the whole room shouted "That's Loll!"

OK, Loll, I am beginning to catch on.

In a few days, Loll, Harson, Jarson and the others were distinct personalities for me, and the thought of them as Lyle, Harrison, or Jerison was ridiculous. And I quickly became "Lucy!" to them, as in "Lucy! Look!" or "Lucy! Go to restroom!" I began informally to teach English phrases. Only two of the twenty-two kids spoke any English, so my suspicion that I could offer something useful seemed to be true. I could teach them phrases that would help them in those first awkward days of English-only first grade. I could give them a first impression of English and Anglos that was unthreatening and even fun. In return, they taught me Navajo phrases of necessity, about going to the bathroom, about pains here and there, about food and drink, about animals and trucks. They were easing my discomfort with some Navajo and I hoped I was laying a little groundwork for the challenges they would encounter next year.

I soon branched out from the classroom, doing cooking and cleaning in the Chapter House, and, once I got my chauffeur's license, I even drove the school bus, if the roads weren't muddy. Kee was protective of those vans and wasn't sure the new Anglo lady could handle the automatic transmission in deep mud—an art form I would eventually learn. I also became the first choice to take children to the Indian Health Service Clinic across the street. At first I resented leaving the classroom and spending as many as two or three hours in the clinic waiting room. But then I saw my value in that role. I could communicate clearly and firmly with the doctors. I also seemed to be able to get more supplies for the classroom—Band-Aids, gauze pads, tape, soap, antibiotic ointment—than the Navajo staff could. I developed good relationships with the doctors. Some of them we saw socially, and I could take advantage of that instinct to go the extra mile for a friend. Finally, I could use the time with the child—if he/she felt well enough—to look at magazines, teach a word or two, laugh at some of the funny pictures, usually of jet-set types on the gossip pages. And, if the child was really sick, as opposed to the common lice or impetigo problems, I hoped I could be comforting.

Sitting in the waiting room was an education in itself. I saw Navajo life up close, the illnesses, accidents, crises. I began to pick up snatches of conversation in Navajo. I developed an appreciation for waiting that has remained with me. Waiting is like driving in the mud. It must be done. There is no choice if you want to get from here to there. You can panic and flail and send your blood pressure soaring, or you can do it with grace. The graceful driver takes the wheel calmly and firmly, and applies the gas with great sensitivity, not so fast that she spins out, not so slow that she sinks to the floorboards, just the right touch so as to float on the surface. The person waiting can practice the same art—sitting or stand-ing, quietly, alert to the activity in the room and the flow of the people ahead and behind, observant and engaged but not sinking into a mud hole of impatience and irritation. Floating on the surface, with grace. I began to feel comfortable in my role bridging cultures, at least at this preschool level.

My appreciation of Navajo culture and my early childhood philo-sophies soon ran afoul of my co-workers. All five of them were products of BIA boarding schools. All five of them had succeeded by some meas-ure, and were committed to perpetuating at least the core of their educa-tional experience. After I took the attendance that first morning, Louise, who had set up the classroom with rows of tables and chairs, all facing forward, led the class in several nursery rhymes. The first one, Peter Peter Pumpkin Eater, was a real eye-opener. She had a picture, hand-colored in crayon, very carefully within the lines, of Peter, we are to assume, peering in a large pumpkin, looking for his wife, we are to assume.

She held the picture up in front of her and pointed to it as she began, "PEE-TUR-PEE-TUR-PUNG-IN-EE-TUR-HAD-A-WIFE-AN-CUD'N-KEE-PUR." The kids fell right in with her, shouting each syllable in uni-son. It was deafening and mystifying to me. What was the point of teaching Navajo kids English nursery rhymes? This wasn't helping their understanding of the English language. They had no idea what the picture was about or the syllables. All I could see was a room full of little Louises, one generation later, reciting the same meaningless chant that she had done as a five-year-old. I was appalled. This cycle of dysfunctional education must stop, and it must stop here. I had seized a mission for myself.

Already after only three months of practice, Bob was seeing a sad pattern of young Navajos, who seemed to be victims of their school experiences. Some had made it through school and couldn't find a job on the reservation. They got married, started drinking, abusing wife and children, and ended up in jail. Others were taken from a traditional home at six or seven, kept in boarding school nine months of the year, and sent home for awkward summers, where they fit in less and less well on each visit. The BIA sent them off upon graduation to join mainstream American society. Instead, some tried to return to the hogan and regain a role in the family and clan, only to find they were misfits. They had lost the Navajo language; they had missed important ceremonies and milestones; they were used to electricity and showers. They were ridiculed and revered at the same time for their Anglo skills, and they were expected to provide for everyone with any family connection.

Others decided to *be* Anglo, to move to Phoenix or Los Angeles, to fulfill that BIA myth of becoming Americanized. There were special programs in these cities to learn how to be a machinist or a baker, and the BIA was happy to enroll you in your choice of vocational training. This rarely worked either. Hard as the BIA may have tried, it was not so easy to erase the culture from a Navajo child's mind and body, even after twelve years in school. The landscape, the family, the beliefs, ceremonies, and chants were too much to leave behind. Those who left the reservation often returned more detached and desperate than ever. These stories made a deep impression on me, and I villainized the BIA as the root of most of the evil. I was determined to influence, however little, the machinery of education in a direction that would be more sensitive to individual children's needs and would allow a child to grow up secure and competent in both the Navajo and the mainstream worlds.

Having turned my own back on that mainstream world, at least for awhile, and being a product of the 1960s, I was also determined to champion the cause of the underdog, the minority, the abused and the have-nots.

I was in the right place, I was sure. Navajos needed me. I knew I had Anglo skills—speaking and writing English—that could be very helpful. But I also saw that I could help reinforce the value of traditional Navajo ways and culture. I could make sure that Headstart graduates entered the first grade with a sense of clarity and pride about what it meant to be Navajo. As an Anglo, in fact, my endorsement of their ways and their beliefs as important and valid might carry extra weight. Such was the nature of my missionary zeal.

I also had a mission to bring what I believed was sound preschool philosophy to this Headstart classroom. There were some universals, I felt, about early childhood development. These included the freedom of each child to develop his/her own personality, preferences, and strengths, and to make choices. Independence and self-esteem, nurtured with warm and loving support, was the key to competent adulthood. Yes, that was the goal, to produce competent adults. I deduced these truths from my own dim memories of Mrs. Pussywillow and from the popular beliefs among "my kind of people," to invoke Mr. Koontz again. I also had some papers on early childhood education that I had ordered through a friend in graduate school in Berkeley. I was feeling guilty that I was not academically qualified for the task ahead, and I crammed every night trying to glean a little helpful information. My readings re-inforced my approach, and reminded me that concurrent with the value of empowerment and independence was the need for limits and con-trols. But in the case of my Headstart kids, it seemed to me that the self-esteem, not the control, was lacking.

One night I opened a pamphlet from the National Association for Nursery Education called "Let's Play Outdoors." I began to laugh. There was a paragraph on the importance of allowing the children plenty of outdoor space in which to play. There was a section entitled "Nothing Like Sand," promoting the wonders of the sand box. Another section, "Water Play Is Essential," encouraged the teacher to provide wading pools and free flowing hoses so that children could experiment with floating objects and create mountain streams in the sandbox or through the grass. That was the end of my early childhood self-education pro-gram. Even after only a couple of weeks I knew that the Navajo child has plenty of outdoor space and plenty of sand. I also had observed that water was a very precious commodity, and that most of the children in the Headstart classes lived in houses or hogans with no running water. Their families hauled water at least weekly in big drums. For them "water play" would be a very strange—and wasteful—activity indeed.

It was a challenge to try to introduce some of the translatable philosophies relating to independence and self esteem into the classroom. I realized that it was of utmost importance to keep a good relationship with my co-workers. I could be sent home, or I could be undermined with the kids if I became the enemy. I made some attempts to talk to Louise about giving the kids a little more freedom in their art work. Could they have free drawing time instead of coloring inside the lines of mimeographed sheets illustrating suburban life? Could we change the room arrangement so they weren't in rows but rather were in a circle, a more equal and more friendly arrangement? I could see her biting her tongue. She did not like either of those ideas. It was one time when she sided with Mrs. Baldwin. A classroom was a classroom and it should look like a classroom. I think her idea of preparing the kids for the first grade was to introduce them to the format, the attitude, the strangeness that lay ahead, by enforcing it now, during their Headstart years. That's what Headstart was for. Get them used to that other world that lay ahead.

She did allow me to have my way sometimes. We made body-sized self-portraits on butcher paper of each child, cut them out, and "dressed" them with paint clothes. We made big maps, showing the school, the trading post, their hogans, and other points of interest, like where that big oil truck turned over on the road last year, or where my dad's horse got caught in the fence by the highway. I was determined to liberate them from the constraints of the classroom curriculum and the limited resources. Only later did I realize what an outlandish waste of paper these exercises must have seemed to my colleagues.

I encouraged them to draw and paint, and they produced some amazing work. Albert Begay drew in brown and black color crayon three of the most beautiful, snake-like snakes imaginable. They were intertwined, loosely woven, one on top of another, and he had carefully used the colors to show which one was underneath and which one was on top. It took my breath away, as did Alfred Holtsoi's crayon drawing of a sad-eyed buffalo, standing alone, face forward, under a stack of three carefully drawn rifles which floated above the animal like an ominous cloud.

The toys provided by Headstart were few. There was one wooden truck, two small wooden cars, and one set of building blocks (about fifteen pieces). When I first arrived and looked around the classroom, I thought, "This is going to be a nightmare, enforcing sharing of these few playthings among all these kids." To my surprise, they shared beautifully. Not one child seemed to assume that there should be more toys, or that he/she should be first to play with the truck, or that so-and-so had been playing too long with the blocks. Those that didn't get a turn with a "real" toy that day played patiently and with great enthusiasm with whatever else was around. If we were outside, it was rocks and pebbles, sticks and leaves, and maybe a paper cup. If we were inside, a box of crayons became the trading post, an eraser was a pickup truck, a jar of paste was the water tank outside Chinle where your grandpa went to fill up his metal drums every week. I couldn't imagine any group of kids anywhere else, at least in the United States, behaving that way. It was a lesson in Navajo culture, and I appreciated what I saw.

I asked if at story time we could sometimes tell Navajo stories, instead of Goldilocks and the Three Bears. In fact—and here I was rather proud of myself—I pointed out that I knew that the bear in Navajo myth is an important and special character, and maybe the story trivializing bears was not appropriate. Louise blushed and said that she didn't know anything about that. Clearly, she said, I was getting to be more Navajo than she was! Her blush gave her away. I knew it was not appropriate to tell a story about the three bears, but she would not admit it. Mrs. Baldwin instructed me that it was all right to tell the Goldilocks story because it was an Anglo story, and besides she said, it was against Navajo religion to tell certain traditional stories in the winter. I understood that, and backed off until spring time.

I asked what the dances were that were held this time of year, and was told they were squaw dances and social dances. Could the children teach me how to do that kind of dance? I asked. Again, Louise said, she didn't know how herself, but she guessed it would be all right if I wanted to learn from the kids. I could tell that she liked the idea and thought it would be fun, although her aloof expression provided a good mask. So, after lunch one day, on the concrete floor of the Chapter House, I was led around in a circle by twenty-two diminutive dance partners, while Kee banged the beat on the mutton stew kettle. After a few rounds, Louise joined in, obviously not her first time stepping the steps, and in the end we were all laughing.

The holiday season gave me another dose of cultural confusion. Thanksgiving brought with it paper pilgrim hats and bonnets for some and Indian paper feather headdresses for others. After Louise had given instructions for coloring, cutting, and pasting the head wear, I asked her if she would tell the children in Navajo the story of the first Thanksgiving. She told about how white people came from across a very, very large lake to this country where there were only Indians, and how they made friends with the Indians and had a great big dinner together.

She asked the children, "Are there any Indians in this room?" Eyes were wide and heads shook back and forth "no." "How about Navajos?" she asked. Everyone nodded vigorously. She explained that Navajos were one kind of Indian, and that they themselves were Indians. Eyes grew even bigger in disbelief. Then she asked, "Are there any white people in the room?" Heads shook "no" again. "What about Lucy?" she said, "What is she then?" A long silence was broken by a tentative "Indian?" from the back of the room. It was a sweet moment, such racial ignorance. We continued to talk about Indians and whites, we acted out the story of the first Thanksgiving, we played different parts, we talked about where the Navajos were then and how the *bilagáana* came to Navajoland later. I told them a little bit about where I came from and how I came to Navajoland, too.

And then came Christmas. I was hoping that the program Mrs. Baldwin and the aides were anxiously preparing for would be Navajo-based in some way. Perhaps there could be an acting out of a myth, or a dance to keep winter snows away, or something like that. I was imagining bringing in Navajo elders to help the children learn these stories and dances, and design a deeply significant—for me, at least!—program. I was certainly naive. Mrs. Baldwin and crew were furiously working on the traditional Nativity scene, just the way they did last year. Only this year they looked to me, a real Anglo, to help them make this Nativity the best one ever, the most Christian, the most accurate, the most "like regular schools do it," as Mrs. Baldwin said.

I was at a loss. At last they were seeking direct help from me, and I was ignorant, reluctant, embarrassed. I deferred to them, and said that they knew best how to do it, and I would help sew or write up a program for the event, or collect food donations, or whatever they wanted. I couldn't resist asking if the children might wear traditional Navajo costumes, instead of Nativity garb. For the community program, Mrs. Baldwin said that would be fine. But for the program we put on for the parents, no. The parents would want to see the real Nativity clothes. So, we ended up with little black-haired, black-eyed shepherds, wise men, kings, and angels. If you're into Nativities, it was a very special one.

As the months went by, I could see Louise lower her guard ever so slightly. She smiled more, laughed sometimes with the kids. She dropped her automatic "don't-do-that!" voice, and replaced it with a slightly softer "do-it-this-way." But I learned not to be surprised if, on one of *my* mornings when the chairs were in a circle and I was called away to the clinic, the chairs and tables were lined up again in rows when I returned. As I opened the door, I would be met by the deafening drone of "PEE-TUR-PEE-TUR" reverberating off those Quonset hut walls. And Louise would give me that look that said, "You think you're changing things, but I will outlast you."

I knew she was right. I struggled to have my small impact on a handful of kids. I thought I was defending and honoring Navajo tradition. But what was Navajo tradition? How would I know? What was its value? How adaptable was it? Who was the rightful protector of that tradition? I knew less and less as time went by. Things were getting more, not less, complex. It had been so simple. The BIA was evil. Mainstream America was corrupt and corrupting. And yet there were Navajo parents, many BIA graduates themselves, who wanted their children to go to boarding schools, who were grateful that they would be well fed and clothed, who felt it was a tradition to be adhered to. They knew their children would gain English skills and would have more choices in life because of that. They knew the dominant society was going to continue to dominate, and they wanted access to it for their children.

I was part of that mainstream. I came from the dominant society. Who was I to dictate dreams, values, choices for the Chinle community in 1968? I already knew that my college degree in English and French History and Literature was useless. Why did I think I had anything to offer, beyond sewing the Nativity costumes and making sure the mimeo-graphed program had no spelling mistakes? And yet, to complicate things further, many Navajos deferred to me inappropriately, just because I was Anglo. I was never sure whether I was being given some kind of unwarranted credit for something, or whether it was a technique of causing discomfort, a kind of subtle one-upsmanship.

"Shall we give the children milk and cookies now?" Mrs. Baldwin had asked me on that first day. She was the teacher, with years of experience, and an elder in the community. I was a twenty-four-year-old who had just arrived and never taught a day in her life. It made me want to cry.

"Sure," I said weakly, "that sounds like a good idea."

This "doing good" business was getting very complex indeed.

FIVE

Role Models ▟▖

I began to look around at other Anglos in Chinle for clues about how to act, or not to act. There seemed to be several ways of dealing with life as a minority person in Chinle. You could become confused and unsettled, as I had done. You could develop a colonist mentality, as many federal government and school people had done. You could become a savior and protector, like some of my fellow do-gooders. Or, you could just put in your time and pretend you were somewhere else. In their extreme, none of these possibilities appealed to me, and I found myself more and more isolated from fellow Anglos. It was not a bad feeling, but I knew there were inherent dangers in feeling too different, too special, and in living some kind of myth that I was not really Anglo, but some kind of "almost Navajo."

I was careful to remind myself that these were my "Anglo brothers and sisters," and that I should try to understand them, if not embrace them. Many of them were probably feeling like me—wondering how to fit in, how to do good, how to avoid being stereotyped. Most Anglos were stereotyped by Navajos, and each other, by the jobs they held. It was hard for me not to fall into this trap of stereotyping and alienating myself from fellow Anglos. Fortunately, with no "lawyer and wife" preceding us, we may have been harder to fit into a mold.

In the late 1960s and early 1970s, many of the Public Health Service doctors in Chinle had chosen practice on an Indian reservation over going to Viet Nam, and sometimes their attitude showed. "I guess this is better than Nam," muttered one doctor to me as we stood in line at the post office, crunching dried mud under our shoes with every step forward. The medical professionals—the doctors, the dentist, the pharmacist—lived in a row of houses next to the clinic, across the street from the Chapter House and Headstart. There were eight houses, stuck together in pairs. They had amenities few others had, including garages, lawns (front and back), and cyclone fences to protect it all. Without the fences, I suppose renegade sheep and horses, which were not unusual, would have thought they had reached the promised land and might have died of joy and overeating. Most of the doctors came with wives and some came with babies or small children. Some simply stayed put behind the cyclone fence and counted the days until their two-year tour of duty was up and they could return whence they came. They made trips to Gallup every weekend to buy food for their freezers, took mini vacations in Phoenix or Albuquerque—R&R they called it—and generally bided their time. Their relatives showered them with care packages of necessities from the city, and their phone bills were probably astronomical.

It was possible to save large amounts of money living and working in Chinle, even in this lap of luxury. Housing, utilities, and hardship pay were included in the tour of duty. One PHS doctor and his wife focused on amassing enough money to be able to buy a Mercedes Benz when they left. Every other week, when they deposited their paycheck, they calculated what piece of the car they had just bought. After a costly pay period in which they had had to buy a new lawnmower, the wife bemoaned, "Out of this paycheck, all we got was one door handle! Last time we saved enough for the windshield and two tires. Oh, well, maybe next pay period we'll cover the rest of the door handles."

During our time in Chinle a few doctors and other PHS professionals proved to be exceptions. They relished their time spent in Navajo culture, were pleased to be able to help, and spent their paychecks on rugs, jewelry, and kachina dolls, leaving significant portions of their income in the community. They made Navajo friends, regretted leaving, and kept in touch after they were gone. One PHS dentist asked permission to stay in Chinle past the mandatory two years, and was told that he would have to move to Kayenta, or another post, if he were to stay in the military. Who would want to move to Kayenta after you've seen Chinle?! He and his wife were heartbroken and angry, as were a lot of their friends, at the cruelty of such a seemingly meaningless rule. We made some close friends among some of these outsiders who shared our enthusiasm for being where we were.

Another model for behavior was the colonist, and there seemed to be plenty of those to observe. At least these outsiders were content and in a way appreciative of the benefits of living in a colonized country. Many of the BIA employees and the teachers and school administrators were there for the long haul. They had settled in, figuring out how to maximize the experience in every way. They had housing, good salaries, benefits, retirement, overtime, hardship pay, mileage, and sometimes government vehicles to drive. Some had good working relationships with Navajo workers and neighbors; some had real friendships. But there was an assumption that they, the Anglos, were superior. That was part of the contract, it seemed. We Anglos are here, we are giving of ourselves to make this place function as it should, and some day you Navajos will learn these skills for yourselves . . . but not before I retire.

As new Anglos in town, we were welcomed by some of these colonists, although as legal services people, we were also held in suspicion. It was an interesting and sometimes comical little dance that we performed, usually only once. The two worlds—legal services and colonists—came together occasionally in odd ways.

One of Bob's first clients was Frank, an Anglo high school student who inevitably had identity issues more serious than the rest of us. He was a bright, ambitious, rebellious kid who had had a bizarre life so far as a very fair-skinned, blond Anglo in a school that was 95 percent Navajo. In an effort to challenge the power structure, he had written a letter to the editor of the *Navajo Times* that was highly critical of Superintendent of Schools, Jodie Matthews, the Arkansas refugee who had attacked Bob on his first day of work. Frank signed the letter with the name of a movie star of the day, and why the paper published it remains a mystery. But it was in print, it was eloquent, and the superintendent was livid.

Matthews ordered a spelling test to be given to everyone in the high school, a test that included key words from the letter. Only one student in the entire school passed—or in this case, failed—the test. Frank was sent to the School Board for expulsion. He knew what lawyers were for, and immediately sought Bob's help. It was a messy case, and not exactly what Bob had imagined in his vision of helping Navajos better themselves. But here was a client, whose mother, an elementary school teacher with three other children, met the indigency standards, and not wanting to discriminate, Bob took Frank as a client. The consequences could have been serious; Frank might not have graduated and could have lost his college scholarship and ticket out of town. Bob was victorious, and Frank did graduate, as class valedictorian. We were at the graduation held in the Community Center and heard Frank's speech, or at least the beginning of it. The superintendent had his ways, and the public address system went out before Frank had a chance to let loose.

Frank and his mother expressed their gratitude to Bob by inviting us to the Chinle High School Senior Prom that spring before graduation. The theme was "Blue Hawaii," and the gym was decorated accordingly, probably a rather weak imitation of about 10,000 other Blue Hawaii senior proms that year around the country. It reminded me of the attempts of Mrs. Baldwin and her Headstart cohorts to produce a Christmas pageant earlier that winter. Everything was ten times harder to accomplish because of the lack of funds and the great distances, and also because the ritual from mainstream America didn't really fit in this context. It had been an uphill battle, obviously, for the prom committee to pull off this event. And yet it was a symbol for the colonists of the way it was back home, and they did their best to honor the prom tradition. The band, which was coming from Flagstaff, got drunk en route and ended up in jail in Holbrook. They did arrive, finally, at 11:30 P.M., in time for the theme song *Blue Hawaii*. Bob and I weren't there to see or hear it, since we bailed out after about an hour.

The prom was an event where the Anglos were in the majority, a big majority. I counted only six Navajos, out of about twenty couples. The

Anglo parents were in their element. This was a ritual they knew all about, and they were not going to let their kids down. The boys rented tuxedos from Gallup (100 miles away), and provided corsages for the girls, also from Gallup. They took their dates out to dinner, either at Fleming Begaye's Café or the Thunderbird Lodge cafeteria. I suppose there were strong allegiances and opinions about which was the "right place" to be. The girls had on the fanciest long formal gowns, reminiscent of a Miss America Beauty Pageant, and hairdos to match. Again both formal wear and hair were "by Gallup," unless you had partaken of the First Hairpeice [sic] Workshop, offered earlier that fall at the high school.* It had to have been an expensive proposition, and it is no wonder that very few Navajo families chose to take part in this colonial ritual.

The kids stood around in these costumes, ill at ease, particularly with no music. The parents, also dressed up, bustled and scurried around the edges of the gym floor, worrying about the band, looking for the dimmer switch to create a more romantic atmosphere, and making more Hawaiian (naturally) punch. We said hello to Frank and his date, a stunning Navajo girl, and to his mother, and shuffled from foot to foot, wondering how long we should stay. I was worried that I might embarrass myself and Bob by shouting, "This is absurd!! This is like a cricket match in colonial India! It is disgusting!! Go home, all of you!" But I bit my tongue. After about an hour, a parent returned from a rescue mission with a record player and a handful of records. Amid the commotion of finding extension cords and searching for songs that might pass as Hawaiian, we slipped out and sneaked home.

---

*I was a substitute teacher a few painful days at the high school during this period, and ran across a flyer that was put in all staff boxes and sent home with students. It announced that the Chinle High School Vocational Program would be offering the First Hairpeice [sic] Workshop three hours on a Friday evening and three hours again on a Saturday morning. For a fee of $5.00, the instructor, beautician Jewell Hodson, would teach you how to "care for your hairpeice [sic], including shampooing, setting, shaping, styling and attachment." If you didn't yet have your own wiglet, cascade, wig or fall you could order one from Jewell. They were priced by the ounce and the inch—from $2.00 for one ounce and 5 inches to $25.00 for eleven ounces and 24 inches.

My final model for Anglo behavior was the most tempting. There were those who came to Navajoland either intending to save the people and their culture, or they grew into that role as a result of what they saw and how they were treated. The longer they stayed the more credibility they gained, and the more special I imagine they began to feel. Some married Navajos and had children, giving them a level of belonging that others of us envied, although there seemed to be greater numbers for whom this belonging was a threat.

Bob Roessel had arrived in Chinle a few years before us, with a passion for reforming the educational system in Navajo country. He felt the BIA influence was destructive of Navajo culture and permanently damaging to individual Navajo children. The public school offering was little better, in his opinion. He had a vision—personal and professional—of creating a model school that would educate Navajo children in a completely different way. They would be taught the Navajo language and culture in school. Their families would be welcome in the schools and would act as teachers for these subjects, including weaving and jewelry making. The academic standards would be high, and teachers would be well qualified and carefully chosen. They would feel privileged to work at the school and would give 110 percent to the cause of creating an education system that produced Navajo students who were strong, confident, and comfortable in both the Navajo and the Anglo cultures. These children would have choices in life.

The Rough Rock Demonstration School was as exciting and full of hope as other 1960s and 1970s initiatives born during the War on Poverty. It was hailed as the new model for teaching Indian children around the country. Robert Kennedy had visited the school shortly before his assassination, giving it a blessing that meant an enormous amount in Indian country, where the Kennedys were heroes. I was intrigued with the school and its founder, and noticed that he was genuinely liked and admired by almost all Navajos I talked to. Anglos, on the other hand, were highly critical of him, and attacked him personally, accusing him of being overly ambitious and egotistical, and of having an excessive appetite for control. His school would fall apart in a few years, they said, and he would be gone, looking for glory somewhere else. Of course, his school did fall on hard times in future years, but it survives today, and Roessel never left Navajoland and Navajo causes. He married a Navajo, had children, and in the early 1990s he was the principal of a small, remote community-run elementary school at the base of the Lukachukai Mountains. Wherever he was, he continued to spread a philosophy of education for Navajo children that was appropriate and positive and maximized their potential for success in both worlds.

Bob Roessel remains a complex person, and back in 1968 I got a glimpse of that complexity in action. At that time, he was serving as the first president of the newly created Navajo Community College, located on the BIA boarding school campus at Many Farms, just north of Chinle. A young political science teacher at the community college who was a member of Students for a Democratic Society (SDS) had invited the San Francisco Mime Troupe to perform at the college. The teacher had been trying to open his students' eyes to politics, particularly radical politics, with no success. Most Navajos in those days were conservative politically, and deeply patriotic. A high percentage volunteered to go to Viet Nam, believing that was the American thing to do.

The Mime Troupe arrived and gave an afternoon show that was billed as a "puppet show." There was no warning that the Uncle Sam "puppet," a huge and grotesque papier-mâché figure, would at one point give the finger to the audience, thrusting it through an American flag, no less. Mothers had brought young children to see the puppets, imagining something quite benign, and high school students were also allowed to attend. Apparently it was pretty shocking. Girls cried, boys stomped out of the performance, upset and indignant. Mothers grabbed children and fled. From what I heard, only the little kids were disappointed to leave. They enjoyed the flamboyance, the color, and the excitement of it all.

The troupe was scheduled for an evening performance for the college students and community members, and we were looking forward to it. But immediately following the afternoon debacle, President Roessel paid them their fee and told the troupe they had one hour to get off the campus. He insulted them and told them that kind of free speech was not part of Navajo tradition. As a protector of the Navajo way, he could not allow them to perform. Troupe members were indignant and felt that the college students had a right to see the performance, and as a matter of principle they felt they should go on with the show. They attempted to put on the evening performance, but were bodily evicted from the stage by Roessel, who by then was in a rage.

Being red-blooded Americans denied freedom of speech, the troupe headed straight for the nearest lawyer. They arrived at our house later that night to fight the "fascist pig." It was an uncomfortable couple of hours for us. Bob had to explain that DNA was in serious trouble with the tribal government, and that his representing the Mime Troupe would only reinforce the rumor that the DNA lawyers were bringing hippies onto the reservation. It would have been the worst possible publicity for DNA, and besides the troupe members weren't local residents, and that was one of the requirements, along with being indigent, which they were. They were outraged that they had been kicked off the campus "by a crazy man," and that now a "poverty lawyer" wouldn't represent them. A college where freedom of expression was denied should be torn down, they ranted as they stomped out of the house and headed for their vans. We later heard that they had hired an ACLU lawyer and were bringing suit against Roessel for taking a swing at one of them.

Their visit reminded me of our first encounter with hippies in Indian country. In the late fall of 1968 we had gone to Shalako at Zuni. We and the other DNA newcomers were eager to gobble up every "Indian experience" as quickly as possible. After all, the legal services program was becoming more and more shaky since the Ted Mitchell incident and its fallout, and none of us knew how long we could stay, even if we wanted to. Shalako was a must, we were told, an annual blessing of new houses and additions to houses at Zuni Pueblo, open to the public, and guaranteed to be memorable. We left Chinle in order to arrive at Zuni, south of Gallup, near midnight when things begin to happen. It was bitterly cold, and we stomped our feet trying to stay warm, as we waited for the Shalakos.

We heard their rattles before we saw them, medicine men dressed in huge headdresses, coming out of the darkness into the smoky light that came from one of the houses destined for blessing. We spectators were drawn to the Shalakos and fell in behind them, as they moved from house to house, offering blessings, singing, dancing, and praying. In each house there was a feast, and part of the tradition dictates that strangers be welcomed and fed on the night of Shalako. So not only were outsiders like us treated to a remarkable feast of the eyes and ears as we followed the Shalako, we were also fed royally and made to feel completely welcome by people we had never seen before, and probably would never see again. The warmth came from the wood stoves, the fires, the hot food, and the hearts of people whose culture taught them generosity at the deepest level.

Hippies were a rarity in Chinle at that time. The heart of Navajoland was too remote, I suppose, and the Indian experience could be had more conveniently elsewhere...like at Zuni. Shalako was a perfect opportunity to become one with an Indian community, to benefit from the culture, to escape from mainstream America, at least for one night. And in those days, with an uncertain future at home and abroad, one night could seem a very long time. There were hippies everywhere that night at Shalako. I was embarrassed and angry. They seemed to be taking advantage of culturally mandated hospitality, with little sense of gratitude or graciousness.

The Zuni hosts and hostesses were dressed in their finest, and so were their houses. Made mostly of cinder block and concrete, each one was a treasure chest of exquisite pottery, rugs, blankets, and the giant elaborately painted and be-feathered kachina dolls. I was touched to see a picture of John F. Kennedy, draped with turquoise beads, sitting at the center of an impromptu altar. He had become incorporated into the house and the ceremony. That was my first glimpse of the kind of reverence for the Kennedys that pervaded Indian country in those days, a reverence that I found very moving. It was another sign of the allegiance of Indians to this country (in spite of its flaws and abuses) and their capacity to recognize and adopt Anglo American heroes. I wondered what the hippies thought looking at that portrait, and the miniature American flags on either side of it.

Bob and I had learned that the reservation was not the place to "dress down" or "go native." In fact, "native" meant looking clean, pressed, and relatively covered up. It was disrespectful to look otherwise. We were looking as respectable as we could, and still stay warm. The hippies exempted themselves from these norms, and I understood their reasons for wanting to make that statement. But I resented their presence at Shalako, where they assumed a right to take everything, including the food, the shelter, and the precious intimacy offered by the Zuni people and their culture.

I couldn't help but see the San Francisco Mime Troupe representatives against this backdrop of the previous fall. I had little sympathy for them, and was relieved that there was a legal reason (residency requirement) that kept them from becoming clients of DNA. It would have been difficult to feel right was on our side in this particular situation. Of course, they had a right to free speech, but didn't they also have the responsibility to have some awareness of where they were and the cultural appropriateness of what they were offering? The troupe had no idea what the situation was on the Reservation, no sensitivity to the cultural norms. Nor did they have any understanding of how difficult it had been to establish the community college, and how fragile its tenure was.

Roessel, fresh from his success at Rough Rock, had done an amazing job raising money, recruiting faculty, and—the greatest challenge of all—selling the concept to the tribal government and the BIA, which gave up part of its campus to share classroom and dorm space with the college. All that was needed was some kind of scandal of a radical political kind to kill this nascent effort to bring higher education to rural Indian country. For the troupe members to say "better no college at all" was, in my opinion, uninformed in the extreme. But the definition of righteousness seems to include an allegiance to a higher authority, a higher moral ground. The Mime Troupe held that ground, believing that the U.S. government must be brought to its knees. My higher moral ground—just as righteous, I confess—was one of cultural appropriateness and sensitivity.

Although our hearts were with the offended community and Roessel, and we could understand his outrage, there were undertones of paternalism that made us uncomfortable. He acted single-handedly and dictatorially, defending the Navajo sensibilities and culture like a possessed avenger. His passion and drive on behalf of his Navajo students, their families, and the community were intense, and I could empathize. On the other hand, I thought—probably in retrospect—there were other ways of handling the crisis that could have empowered the college, rather than taking on the battle alone. He could have, for instance, let the students or the Board of Regents (community members) decide whether or not they wanted the performance to continue that evening. Probably the answer would have been no, but perhaps the enforcement of that decision could have been by the Navajo Nation rather than by a lone Anglo defender. And perhaps coming to that decision would have been a stimulating and educational experience for the student body and/or the Board of Regents.

There were far more egregious examples of righteous behavior, masquerading as concern for Navajo welfare, to be found right within our DNA ranks. Some critics would have painted all of us with that brush of misplaced zeal. I would apply that brush more selectively, but it certainly would cover a certain VISTA volunteer, assigned to DNA Legal Services, in early 1969. A high school on the reservation had held an appreciation ceremony to honor two graduates who had fought in Viet Nam and returned to speak to students about their experiences. Part of the ceremony included raising the American flag, saluting, and pledging allegiance as a way of thanking the two young men who had risked their lives. The VISTA attorney fired off a letter—an open letter published in the *Gallup Independent*—to the high school principal, threatening to sue the school for forcing students to pledge allegiance to a government that was corrupt and illegal.

Most in the DNA family were horrified. Whether or not we supported our government in Viet Nam—and my guess is that none of us did—we admired Navajos for their fierce patriotism, which they demonstrated in whatever conflict came along. The Code Talkers of World War II had risen to the occasion, and had kept a vow of secrecy that denied them any recognition for thirty years following their service. Young men flocked to recruiting stations to go to Viet Nam from reservations all over the country, and Navajos were no exception. It may have seemed sad and misguided to defend a country that had done you wrong, but their sincerity and courage were undeniable. The arrogant and callous letter, from a righteous zealot attorney, was an embarrassment to DNA, and could have sunk the program. The school principal, his supporters, and the Tribal government protested loud and clear to the powers in Washington, D.C., particularly to the head of the Nixon administration's Office of Economic Opportunity, Donald Rumsfeld.

In an astounding and still inexplicable move, while DNA shook in its collective cowboy boots waiting for the ax to fall, Rumsfeld sent a letter to Ted Mitchell, reprimanding him and the staff. He said that he never wanted to see anything of the kind happen again, and that he would have to levy a penalty on the DNA program. He demanded that Mitchell send in the return mail a money order to cover the cost of the postage on Rumsfeld's letter. We had escaped disaster, but understood that those other outsiders—the teachers, the missionaries, the traders—were not the only ones who could deeply offend Navajo culture and undermine the Navajo way of life

A little later in the spring of 1969, oppressive policies and academic inflexibility were the target of student protests and riots at Harvard. I watched news coverage of students, only three or four years younger than me, shouting down administrators on the steps of University Hall, hurling rocks, faces contorted in rage. I was confused and irritated. I had protested the war and taken part in civil rights sit-ins. I had considered myself one of the revolutionaries. But I had also lived comfortably in dorms and apartments, eaten well, seen foreign films, and had access to an incredible education. From my perspective in Chinle, those students were lucky to be there. They had it so good, and they were griping about student rights. On the reservation I was seeing real poverty, subsistence living, terrible alcoholism, and a truly rotten school system, worthy of rioting. I would have welcomed an uprising in Chinle, against the BIA, the public school, the roads, the bug-infested commodity foods. Those students in Cambridge looked like spoiled brats. I was surprised at myself.

SIX

The Del Muerto
Connection

It was ironic. The longer we were in Chinle, the more we wanted to stay, and the less certain our tenure looked. Although Ted Mitchell had won the right to return to the reservation, that was not the end of either the lawsuits or the controversy over the legal services program. Funding at the national level was in doubt, and locally there was growing concern in powerful places about the desirability of this renegade band of do-gooders. Just who was benefitting, and who was being threatened? It seemed that those in power were being challenged, including border-town businesses, reservation traders, and the Navajo government itself. Particularly nervous was the attorney for the Navajo tribal government at that time, General Counsel Harold Mott, whom we at DNA Legal Services considered to be doing more harm than good in his position. DNA favored the concept of a Navajo Department of Justice, with its own attorneys, rather than the outside general counsel system, so vulnerable to abuse. We delighted in the ability of DNA to challenge Mr. Mott and Chairman Raymond Nakai and to defend the individual Navajo citizen, but there were consequences. The program was on thin ice, and the Chairman and his general counsel were working hard to melt that ice in a hurry.

We were determined to make the most of our remaining time. Bob continued to take clients and move them through whatever maze was necessary as quickly as possible. His staff increased by two more paralegals.* I continued to volunteer at Mrs. Baldwin's Headstart program in Chinle, surviving the Christmas program and subsequent holidays that also required formal recognition by the mystified little students. They cut out black silhouettes of George Washington and Abraham Lincoln and pasted them on white paper. They made Valentine cards for their mothers and fathers, with much supervision by the aides, who wanted to be sure the doilies were placed properly in the middle of each heart.

Before I had a chance to help them with their cutouts of shamrocks and little pipes, but not before I had a chance to worry about how to explain the meaning of those little pipes (having no idea myself), I received word from Window Rock. Mr. Koontz had actually found me a job. There was an opening for a Headstart teacher at Del Muerto, twelve miles up the north rim of the canyon. The school had been struggling with two aides and a bus driver since the teacher had left. He was Navajo, and popular with the community and parents, I was told, but performance reports by Window Rock evaluators said he had little feeling for the children and made no real contact with them. He was a firm disciplinarian and emphasized manners, and that apparently was what counted in Del Muerto. I shuddered to think of filling these shoes, and being expected to enforce good manners among three- to five-year-olds. I was suddenly very attached to my spot with Mrs. Baldwin, and very grateful for the experience that she and her staff had given me. Without that apprenticeship I would have been really lost.

I was thrilled to have a paying job. We were about to move into our new house. The water line had finally been hooked up, and it was ready for us, but we anticipated a steep increase from our $26-a-month rent in the

---

*One was Joe Shirley, a bright, shy young high school graduate, who many years (and lifetimes) later in 2002 was elected president of the Navajo Nation.

BIA apartment. Now I would be able to help, and I would feel more like a contributing member of the community, more official, with a real identity. But I was also squeamish about taking over as a teacher in a situation where the kids, the parents, the staff were all Navajo. What would they think of me? Did they even want a teacher, or were they doing fine without one? Or, worse yet, were they *not* doing fine, and was I supposed to fix things? Would I find myself in the same bizarre position of being inappropriately deferred to as an Anglo, while simultaneously being undermined?

I began at Del Muerto the end of February. That first morning I took Bob to work and drove the Bronco up the twelve miles of dirt road. One curve took me by surprise and I found myself skidding on the washboard created by thousands of sets of tires braking before me. I had been admiring the steep wall on my right, the gracefulness of its natural curve and had accelerated up the incline a little too enthusiastically. The Bronco chattered and rattled, swinging its rear end dangerously near the drop-off on the left where a small canyon, tributary to Canyon del Muerto, paralleled the road. I realized that the road was cut out of the rock wall of the canyon. Blowing spring sandstorms had built up on the rock ledge, and I had nearly surfed right off the edge.

This spot on the drive, both to and from Del Muerto, became a highlight for me. It was an adventure. It held the real possibility of disaster. I learned to honk several times on my way through the turn to alert anyone on the other side to wait. I was even able to smile, fleetingly, as I took a quick glimpse at the stunning beauty of the sandstone walls and cottonwoods below. And I shared with Del Muerto residents' grief when, a few years later, the BIA roads department blasted a particularly spectacular part of the rock wall away to widen the road through that curve. They were undoubtedly trying to save lives. Times were changing. Horses and wagons had given way to cars, trucks, and school buses, and it was time to modernize that dangerous bottleneck. But it was a shock to me to drive up there the next time and find that formation gone. It was a loss, even to me, and I understood from friends that it was devastating especially to the elders in the community. That rock had held special significance. It certainly had for me.

I had another near miss on the way to school that first morning. I didn't recognize the landmark, the Del Muerto Evangelical Church, and cruised past the turn to the school. I foolishly expected to see a building that looked like a church, as opposed to a house or a hogan. This one was a prefabricated house, off the road, with a small sign hidden in the junipers. Retracing my steps, I found the turn and the school building. I parked the Bronco in front, but not too close. I was feeling shy and very nervous. I sat there a few seconds looking around. I was charmed by four big black flower planters, each painted with an Indian motif, and each full of pink and white petunias. It was an elegant touch, and I wondered briefly where I might get planters like that. It was weeks later, when I was more relaxed and able to take in things more clearly, that I realized that these were old car tires, turned inside out. The strain caused them to take a most graceful shape. That was typical of Del Muerto, inventive, aesthetic, and full of surprises.

Like its Chinle counterpart, the Headstart complex was a hodge-podge of structures of various ages. The classroom was new, but not quite finished. The kitchen was old, and there was electricity but no running water. There were outhouses and the bus driver had to bring water in giant metal coolers every morning with the children on the bus. But all this was minor. It was the people I was interested in. I was greeted by Irene Teller, who smiled, a little shyly, and welcomed me to the school. She had a certain look in her eye that was playful, but I couldn't tell whether I was going to be a playmate or be played with. Irene was getting ready for the children, fixing breakfast. The poverty level in Del Muerto made Chinle look like a gated community, and there were extra funds for breakfast as well as lunch for the kids. Irene introduced me to Eleanor Hardy, in her late teens, who was attending to the academic side of the program, setting out a box of color crayons and mimeographed papers with large alphabet letters on them at each place. She looked up with what felt to me like cold curiosity. The third staff person was Kee Lagai Begay, the bus driver, who was still picking up kids. I hoped that he would be the warm, jolly type.

No such luck. Kee arrived in the bus, stepped out, opened the door for the children, and stood by as each child got out, scrutinizing clothes, hair, attitude, behavior, and making "shape up" type comments as necessary. When we met and shook hands, he looked at me briefly and seriously, and then turned to his chores. Given the options, I stuck to Irene like glue, and was grateful that she allowed me into her world. She explained the routine of the day, showed me where to find supplies, and which outhouse to use. She told me a little about each of the children, two of which were hers, Adam, five, and Eva, three. "Like in the Bible," she said "Adam and Eve."

This was an important piece of information, for it turned out that religion was a major part of life in Del Muerto. Kee was a lay preacher in the Navajo Bible Church, and both Eleanor and Irene were devoted members of the congregation. Part of the school routine, I quickly saw, included an opening prayer before breakfast, a long grace before lunch, and a closing prayer before the children got on the bus. I was disturbed by this merger of church and state. Headstart was, after all, a federally funded program, and there was no place for religious practice in the clasroom. Although I had faced similar moral dilemmas with Mrs. Baldwin's staff in Chinle, this seemed more serious. If I was to be the teacher, the one with authority, I shouldn't be acting in an unconstitutional manner. I was determined to go slowly and not rock the boat, but I needed to do what I thought was right.

At our first staff meeting, I explained that prayers in school were against the law, and that I was sorry but that we would not be able to do that anymore. It was certainly awkward, and as confusing for me as it was for them. I was choosing to enforce—with a feeling of righteousness—certain laws from the outside world that I believed were important and worthy. But at the same time I was denying the local community—or at least the majority of the local community—their ability to determine how their children would be taught. If the staff had wanted a medicine man to come in every morning and bless the school day for the children, I would probably have been deeply moved that the Navajo culture was intact and that I could support it in this way. I doubt I would have considered this a time to separate church and state. I also was haunted by the incident a few months earlier when the VISTA Volunteer attorney had threatened a civil rights lawsuit against a reservation high school for holding a patriotic, flag-saluting, veteran-honoring ceremony. How confusing it must be to be raised with instructions to be part of the American mainstream, and then to be criticized for plunging in with enthusiasm.

The staff seemed to understand, or at least accept, what I was saying, but I am sure that it contributed to a coolness in my reception. At least I left the Pledge of Allegiance intact and allowed that saying grace before meals would be ok. Oh well, I can imagine them thinking, let's see what she has to offer. An outsider brings good and bad. What else is new?

Also at that first meeting we talked about ways to raise money for the school. We were in desperate need of furniture, supplies, and winter coats for the kids. I suggested showing a movie at the Catholic Church or the Community Center in Chinle, the two biggest venues. There was no movie theater within 100 miles, and people flocked to the monthly movie night sponsored by the public school. Kee was enthusiastic. "Oh, yes," he said, "if we had a really good movie—like *The Bible*, or *The Ten Commandments*, or *Christ the King*, then I know a lot of people would come."

Kee and I negotiated. I think he won. Stapled to the back of the next mimeographed newsletter *Dine Bizaad* put out by the Chinle Boarding School was an announcement of a not-to-be-missed double feature. The flyer read: "Don't Miss It! Two Big Movies—*David and Goliath* and *The Daltons Ride Again*, Saturday, March 15, 7:00 P.M. at the Catholic Mission Hall—A fundraiser to benefit Del Muerto Preschool." After expenses, we cleared $110, and a good time was had by all.

I had expected that moving to a school farther out of "town," in an area less in contact with the outside world, would mean working with people who were more traditional. In a way yes, in a way no. There was less English spoken, the life-style was more rural, the diet more traditional. Many of the parents had never been to school. Before the bridge was built across the mouth of Canyon de Chelly in the 1950s, there was no reliable way to reach Del Muerto. You had to cross the wide wash, difficult and sometimes impossible in the quicksand of spring, the deep, dry sand of summer or the ice of winter. As a result, children in Del Muerto were often left undiscovered by the BIA in its quest for boarding school candidates. Irene and her husband, Ben, had finally been "found" when they were twelve and had been sent to a special program for older children at Brigham City, Utah. Having missed the early years, they were pumped full of English, reading, writing, and math for an intense five years, and then released back to the reservation. They both returned to Del Muerto, where they carefully placed one foot back in the old ways, and the other in the modern. Irene worked off and on at the trading post in Chinle. When Headstart came along, she pressed for a school at Del

Muerto. She had two small children by then, and saw that she could have an income and take care of her children at the same time. Ben had a job in the maintenance department of the public school system in Chinle.

The community was used to being ignored by Chinle, and had developed a proud—some would say arrogant—self-sufficiency. When Chinle turned its back on the request for a satellite school in Del Muerto, and Window Rock said there were no funds for a building, the parents simply set about building a classroom. They were incredibly industrious and ingenious, and managed to build a handsome classroom, furnish it, and provide electricity by tapping into a utility pole a hundred yards away on the main road. They relied on their own hard work, and I'm sure on help from God, who they knew was on their side. Other Headstart classes around the reservation were plagued with building and utility problems. Mrs. Baldwin's buildings in Chinle were left without heat for several weeks because the Headstart Office in Window Rock seemed unable to figure out how to pay for utilities. No such problem existed in Del Muerto. In fact they had hired their own teacher and aides without help from Window Rock, and had it not been for the dependence on Window Rock for salaries they would have completely ignored any direction from the capitol.

The staff tolerated my presence as a necessary hoop to pass through in order to satisfy the wishes of the funding agent. Eleanor remained cool and moody. She did nothing unless asked, and when she completed the task, she did nothing again. She read magazines and seemed intent on being in some world far away, or at least as far as California. I decided that it was possible that she hated me, but I would never know if that was true, or why. I confided in Irene, and asked if I could do anything to help Eleanor feel better about work. "Oh, she's like that," she explained, and that was the end of the subject. Kee was clearly a powerful character in the community. His son Roddy was in the Headstart class, and was being groomed to be a powerful character as well. There were many rumors about Kee that I didn't understand, or want to understand, but it seemed that his powers were considerable. Not long after we left Chinle in 1975, Kee Lagai Begay was murdered in the canyon. With me, he was kind, hard-working, and honest, and I felt a personal loss when I heard the news.

I was cautious as Easter approached, hoping to avoid a conflict over some religious program during school hours. I feared that the staff might be plotting a re-enactment of the crucifixion or the resurrection when I came in one morning and found them in a huddle around a low table, speaking Navajo and turning pages on the calendar. It turned out that they were choosing a day for the community Easter egg hunt at the school. Eleanor came to life around this event, and spent hours dying eggs, making baskets out of woven strips of paper, cutting out and coloring paper rabbits and chickens, and creating crepe-paper flowers that I have never seen the equal of since. I was glad she was excited about something, and I was happy to help however I could with the preparations. Because I drove from Chinle every morning, I was designated to bring up the Easter candy, and the sodas, bread, baloney, and cheese for the lunch that day.

I pulled up in front of the school with the supplies and saw Eleanor and Kee outside hiding eggs. The spring wind was horrendous that day, blowing dust horizontally from west to east. And it was surprisingly cold. I joined them, tucking foil-wrapped chocolate eggs and little bags of jelly beans under clumps of weeds, next to rocks, and in the lower crooks of tree branches. All of us had to be on the lookout for hungry dogs, for whom neither the cold nor the wind was a deterrent. It was a bizarre scene, and I couldn't help but think about the Easter egg roll on the White House lawn that would be happening in a few days. The kids were having breakfast in the classroom, and Irene would keep them busy until the grownups arrived, and then the egg hunt would begin. I assumed that the parents and grandparents would be there to watch and cheer on their children, just like on the White House lawn.

Once again, I was surprised. The Del Muerto community took holidays and holiday activities very seriously, and this particular event was a fully participatory one. When a sufficient number of adults had arrived, the children were brought outside, their little paper baskets straining against the wind. At a signal that was beyond my detection, everyone took off in the direction of the area where the goodies were hidden. Moving fastest were the grandmas, bundled in wool coats, heads covered with scarves. Close behind were parents and others from the community. The children were being herded, a little too quickly, by the staff, who didn't want to lose out. It was a strangely silent affair, except for occasional wind howls. No one talked or joked or exclaimed. No one cried and no one comforted. They were all—young, old, small, big—moving methodically and rapidly over the dusty landscape, isolated from each other, taking care of the business of gathering. Grandmas snatched eggs from under the noses of preschoolers, and dropped them mechanically into their purses or flour-sack bags. Young men edged out nieces and nephews for bags of jellybeans. All in silence, all squinting against the sand. It was a very serious business. As I left school that day, two dogs were sniffing the disturbed terrain, hoping for a remnant from the hunt. They were disappointed. I drove home knowing I would never see another Easter egg hunt to match that one.

❖

The greatest gift from my time at Del Muerto was the friendship of the Tellers. Ben and Irene became some of our closest friends. Thanks to them we experienced both canyons—De Chelly and Del Muerto—in ways not common for most Anglos not associated with the Park Service. I once asked Irene if she had ever been to Grand Canyon. "Oh, I went there once," she said. "But it's not a canyon, it's just a big hole in the ground. Not like Del Muerto—that's a canyon." I had to agree with her.

We spent dozens of weekends with them and their families, helping plant or harvest, gathering firewood, and eating mutton ribs and fry bread. Those were amazing, memorable times. On Saturday morning we would meet at the Park Service Visitors Center at the mouth of Canyon de Chelly. We would sign in as visitors and receive a day permit to travel into the canyon with a named guide, either Ben or Irene. Non-Indians were not allowed to roam the canyons without a Navajo guide. Although the area was a national monument operated by the National Park Service, there were special conditions because it was on Indian land, and because there were Navajos still living and working in the canyons. It was important to protect these families from intrusive, camera-wielding tourists. If you did not have a private guide, as we did, you were able to sign up for a "jeep tour" of the canyon, provided by the concessionaire, Thunderbird Lodge. The "jeep," apparently used in World War II to transport soldiers, was a big open-bed truck fitted with rows of bench seats, enough for about twenty people. Navajos called the jeep tours "shake and bake," an abbreviation for the bone-rattling trip for Anglos under the blistering sun. The only way to see the canyon without a guide or a tour was from the overlooks above, or from the White House Trail that led from the rim down about 800 feet to the floor of Canyon de Chelly and a spectacular ruin.

With our precious permit in hand, we (Bob and I, and later three and then four of us) piled into the back of Ben's pickup. We wedged ourselves between coolers, shovels, ropes, quilts, kids, and grandmas and prepared for a race across the canyon floor. There were probably many reasons for the race. At least two were clear. Sometimes it was necessary to step on the accelerator and fly forward in order not to sink in the deep sand. Other times it seemed equally critical to beat a competitor in another truck who was trying to pass on the open sand, or sneak through a shortcut between the cottonwood trees. No one sat on the edge of the pickup bed, or at least not for long. The bounces and the swiveling of the rear end were as effective as a bucking bronco at unseating a rider. I squealed and gasped and held onto anything that was heavier than myself. Often I found a child clutching my leg.

There were different routes along the canyon floor, and both Ben and Irene were like the finest ship's captains, choosing the right course depending on the look of the tire tracks ahead, the nature of the sand that day, or rumors heard at the gas station about where the bad spots were. Whatever the route, it criss-crossed the canyon, leading across the sandy bottom, where the water flowed in the late spring, then bumping up onto hard ground where the cottonwoods and salt cedar grew, then dropping down into the sand again and across to the opposite side. It was like tacking against the wind in a sail boat.

The most exciting time of year for these trips was late spring, when the water had been flowing through the canyon for several weeks. As it slowed and swirled around the sharp bends in the canyon walls, and dallied under the deeply cut overhangs, it created the most terrifying of phenomena for the pickup truck driver—quicksand. I loved the idea of it. I was addicted to the excitement of it. You never knew where it was lurking, or when you might suddenly feel that drop as the wet sand simply gave way underneath, and you found your tires half gone, floor boards resting—but not for long—on the quivering surface. The good drivers never got caught; they could somehow sense it in time and swerve away, delicately, not disturbing that sucking monster that might reach out and grab them.

A few years before our arrival in Chinle, a driver of one of the "jeep tour" trucks had driven into the quicksand and lost the vehicle. There were pictures of it at the Thunderbird Lodge, listing to one side, clearly in the act of capsizing. They said it took days to completely disappear. These events didn't happen often, but when they did word traveled quickly. In 1973 a brand new red four-wheel-drive Suburban was caught, just up from the bridge to Del Muerto. We jumped in our Bronco and drove to the bridge, where a crowd was watching in excitement. It was sinking fast. We could still see the roof, like a shiny red lily pad on the sea of ooze. In the morning, I went back, just to check out the progress. It was gone.

Ben and Irene had a land use permit for a few acres between Antelope House Ruin and Standing Cow, on the north side of Canyon del Muerto. That was where we spent most of our time. Irene's family had a hogan and grazing area a few turns farther up the canyon in an offshoot called Black Rock Canyon. This was where great-great-grandparents of Ben and Irene had fought off Kit Carson's invasion in 1864. Carson had entered the canyon in order to round up Navajos for the forced march to Fort Sumner. The plan had been to relocate them from there and integrate them into mainstream America. But the families in Canyon del Muerto had no intention of being captured, and Carson was no match for them. They climbed the walls of the canyon and established fortresses on the area between the two canyons. Carson was unable to get at them from above or from below. They pelted him with boulders, and he had to retreat, although not before burning all the fruit trees along the way. It is a bitter and proud memory, and we heard the stories many times. We also saw Massacre Cave, and from below Ben pointed out bloody hand prints on the pock-marked wall of the cave where hiding Navajos were shot by Spanish conquistadores in the winter of 1804–1805. I thought I could see what he was pointing at, but I hoped it wasn't true.

In the shadow of this history, we felt incredibly lucky to have Ben and Irene as friends. Time spent together in the canyon was always an adventure, of either a physical or a cultural kind. We planted dozens of fruit trees donated by the Mormon Church on their land. On a quiet day we would putter together, walking, talking, examining plants, rocks, animal scat. Irene and I would build a fire and cook lunch—mutton ribs, burgers, hot dogs, squash if it was ripe. Sometimes there was a melon ready to pick for dessert. On a more adventurous day, we would go in search of a lost horse, or visit a neighbor who needed a tractor fixed, or look for a certain plant that Irene's mother needed to make a certain dye. A *seriously* adventurous day might include exploration of the canyon walls. Ben was always eager to take us up or down trails that connected the rim of the canyon with the floor. These expeditions were always preceded by much teasing.

"You guys should come down Baby Trail with me next Saturday. I'm going to go down that way."

"I don't know, Ben. I've heard that one's too hard for Anglos. It has little handholds in the wall, doesn't it?"

"They call it Baby Trail—babies can do it!"

At this point, Adam, now seven, interrupted. "That's not why they call it Baby Trail! They call it Baby Trail because those ladies a long time ago carried their babies up the trail to get away from Kit Carson, isn't that right?"

His father conceded that was true, and that a baby couldn't maneuver the trail alone.

"Well, I think Bob should only go on trails that babies can go on," I suggested amid much laughter. "You know he doesn't like heights."

But Bob was humiliated at the thought of not being able to go down a trail that a woman could scamper up with a baby in her arms, and so it came to pass that the next Saturday we descended Baby Trail. We drove to the Tellers', picked up Ben and Adam, and drove to the edge of the canyon about a mile from their house. Beginning Baby Trail was like stepping off a cliff. In fact, it *was* stepping off a cliff. If Bob was terrified—and I knew he was—I was only scared to death. It took complete trust in Ben to take that first step downward. He went first, then Bob, me, and Adam. Adam was an enormous help to me, chattering away about this and that, pointing out obstacles along the way. "Look out for that little rock. That kind of rock can make you slide."

"OK, Adam, you keep watching out for me, OK? Make sure I do this right, OK?"

"Don't worry. You can do it," he said cheerfully. And I believed him.

In the meantime, Ben was descending almost backward, watching Bob's every placement of the foot and the hand. In the beginning it was not too challenging. We skirted the canyon wall on a little ledge, generous enough for a woman and a baby, or a lawyer and his wife, I observed. We had to be alert and lean in toward the wall, but it was doable. Blessedly, the view downward was of descending levels of rock, stair-stepping down, and dropping off below, so that we could not see the canyon bottom. We made a few switchbacks, the final one moving us around a corner of the wall, and giving us a new perspective. We were looking straight down at the canyon bottom. It seemed miles below us. I suppose it was only a few hundred feet. I was trying to figure out how to keeping moving downward while only looking upward—a strategy that clearly was not going to work.

"Now you can see the water in the bottom!" shouted Adam happily.

"Yeah, that's neat," I managed weakly and without a shred of his enthusiasm.

Ben was attending to Bob more carefully than before. I could feel Bob's terror. I wished we hadn't come. This was too scary and there was no point in being this terrified. There was just no point. What were we trying to prove? That two Anglos were stupid enough to do something that petrified them? Or were we doing it for Ben? And if so, what was he getting out of it besides terrifying two Anglos to death? Oh dear, best not to think about it. We were moving through an area of loose rock, stepping with great care to avoid gravel-surfing to our deaths. And then there were a few yards of rock wall again, with a ledge for creeping. We were on our hands and knees when I saw that Ben had disappeared ahead of us. I heard no scream; he wouldn't scream, not him. He would just sail to his death, quiet, stoic.

"Here comes the ladder part!" announced Adam. "This part's hard! My dad'll help you."

Oh great, this part's hard. And, tell me then, what has this been up until now? "Chopped liver?" I heard myself mutter. And then, more coherently, "Adam, what kind of ladder? What do you mean?" I couldn't picture someone dragging a ladder all the way down here, although I would have been glad to see it.

"It's a log, just a log with these cut out parts on it," he explained.

It was just like Ben never to mention the log ladder, the absolutely most frightening part of the trail. I inched toward the spot where Ben had disappeared over the edge. There he was at the bottom of the "ladder," on a very narrow ledge about fifteen feet below us. Fifteen feet is certainly not a long drop, but if you missed a step during that descent, the rest of the trip down to the canyon bottom would be very fast indeed. The log was propped up, almost flat against the wall, connecting two ledges. There were notches cut in the sides of the log for hands and feet—hands and feet belonging to people much braver than we were, with much more skill than we had, and with the force of a powerful culture behind them. This log was not built for us, but it was the only way down, the only connection between the upper and lower ledges. Bob said in all seriousness that he thought he would go back up to the top. I screamed at him that he couldn't, that I was in the way. There was no way to get past me, and I wasn't going back up. We were closer to the bottom than the top at this point, and besides I couldn't stand to think of Ben teasing us for the rest of eternity. I would rather die after all.

I was proud of Bob. He did it. Ben helped him place his foot on each notch in the right way, at the right angle, and talked him down. I watched impatiently. I wanted to get it over, whatever the outcome was. My turn came. The log wiggled. I panicked and froze midway, imagining myself on this ancient sled, rocketing toward the canyon floor. Bob was elated by now, and encouraged me. I kept moving and joined him on the ledge below. Adam scampered like a squirrel down the log. The next challenge was to traverse and then descend a face of sandstone wall. There were hand and foot holds, carved into the wall. Just when you thought there wouldn't be one for you, there it was, in just the right place. "How did you know," I asked the ancient ones, "that I wanted one *right there*?!" I was high on having survived the ladder, but this was very scary in its own right. It helped me to remember that I was only one in a thousand or more who had placed one foot below the other, one hand under the last, on the way down Baby Trail.

We were within a few feet of the sandy canyon floor, when the wall sloped gently outward and downward. The handholds disappeared, no longer necessary, and we were able to scramble and slide on the sand-covered incline and then jump to the bottom. We turned around and looked up. The log ladder looked like a toothpick, the handholds like dots. The treacherous ledge above that, where we walked hugging the wall and eventually crawled, was not even visible, lost above the canyon's bulge.

Ben was shaking his head and chuckling. "You guys did it! That's pretty good. You did it!" Adam had raced off to play in the sand.

"Wow, that was hard, Ben! It really was!" I said. "It's unbelievable to look up there and see what we did. Thanks, Ben, thanks for helping us . . . for *making* us do it." Bob was speechless.

"Do you want to go back up that way, too?" Ben asked, a twinkle in his eye. "I don't know if Irene's coming in after or us not. Maybe we'll have to go back up Baby Trail." He laughed at our expressions.

"No, thanks," Bob had found words. "I'll be happy to walk out, on the ground. No problem, Ben."

Irene and her younger sister Charlene showed up in a couple of hours, with food. We ate and reenacted the adventure for them, step by step, the first of many storytellings by us, and by Ben, I'm sure. When it was time to go, Irene and Charlene decided to go up Baby Trail instead of riding out in the truck. Ben got in the driver's seat, Bob in the passenger seat, and Adam and I in the back. As we pulled away from the wall, I saw the two women scramble up the gentle incline, and reach for the first set of foot- and handholds. As I recall, Irene wore Keds, the kind with tan, smooth soles, and Charlene was wearing Capezios. She was always very fashion conscious.

SEVEN

Wildlife and Women's Lib

Surely it was one of the strangest landlord-tenant arguments ever. Frank and Galena Dineyazhe worked for the BIA and lived in a BIA house in the New Compound, not far from our apartment. With much foresight, they had built a house for their retirement, which was many years off, and in the meantime, they had agreed to rent it to the new lawyer and his wife. The house was a Jim Walters Home, costing $10,000 and brought in numbered pieces from Albuquerque on a big truck, to the Dineyazhes' home-site lease just east of the Chinle Wash and just west of the post office. It was in place, ready except for water, that first day we pulled into town. Now, nine months later, the faucets produced water and it was ready for us.

It had three small bedrooms and one bathroom, a living and dining area, and a kitchen. It had white siding with brown trim and a shingled roof. The floor was blue-and-brown-streaked linoleum tile. The ceiling was a blown-on foam material, embedded with sparkles, which turned out to be a distinguishing, and enviable, feature for most Navajo visitors. It was a palace by Chinle standards, and we were thrilled to be able to have a new, functional home, outside of a compound. We would be living among the cottonwoods, just off the road, in an almost fertile— by Chinle standards—area between the main road and the wash a mile or so downstream of the canyon mouth. We would be by ourselves. Our closest neighbors were all Navajo, in hogans and log houses a few hundred yards away. We could walk easily on a dirt road to the post office and to the Martinez store, ironically named Imperial Mart. And—here we were in trouble—we could have any kind of animals we wanted.

Bob's salary was minimal, and my Headstart pay was less. We were worried about what the rent would be on this little piece of heaven. The Dineyazhes started the negotiations at $26 per month.

"That's ridiculous," I said. "That's what we're paying for our tiny BIA apartment. This house has to be more than that."

There was silence from Frank and Galena, so we countered with $50.00.

"No," Frank said, "that's too much." Galena smiled in agreement. More silence. "Maybe $28 would be all right."

"What about $38?" Bob tried.

"No, $28 is fine. Twenty-eight will be plenty. We don't the need the house for a while, and you can use it." The best we could do was $30. Every year thereafter we tried to raise the rent, and every year we failed.

Our presence in the house drew attention from the community, and we began to have visitors. They came to admire the sparkly ceiling, to see if we wanted any help with a falling-down barbed-wire fence, or if we wanted to buy a rug or two. Buying rugs became a real problem. They were beautiful, and each one was so different. If the weaver, or her irresistible granddaughter, unrolled it or unfolded it on our linoleum floor, and stood there quiet and smiling, then the purchase was a sure thing. After a while we justified purchases by telling ourselves that we were going to find other buyers for them, among friends or relatives. But when it came time to give one up, to open the stock to someone who was eager to take a handwoven Navajo rug back to wherever, somehow we could never part with one. It was a very enjoyable vice, and after all we were contributing to the local economy.

I also entertained the visiting weavers who stopped by, showing them the rug I was weaving. Now that we had more room, Bob built me a standard Navajo upright frame, and my contact from the Arts and Crafts Guild helped me set it up. I had started learning to spin, card, and weave at the Community College, and I was ready to begin. I had three colors, gray, white, and tan, and I had a design, simple rows of linking diamonds, alternating colors for each row. I had it measured out so that there would be fourteen rows. The length of the rug is predetermined at the time of set up because the warp is one long thread, wound up and down and tied to horizontal bars at the top and bottom. There is no such thing as getting tired and deciding to stop and tying off the warp.

So the die was cast, and I began to weave. It was fun for about twenty minutes, and then the impatient Anglo in me came rushing out. It was a slow and tedious process, moving the yarn by hand through a few warp threads at a time, and then tapping it down with the wooden weaving comb. It took me so long to finish it, that by the time I was half-way done (in terms of my pattern—seven rows complete), the warp had stretched and there was much more than half left to weave. I adjusted my pattern so that each row became a little wider to try to make up the difference. Weavers would stop by every few months to chuckle and cluck over my progress. They needn't have been in any rush. The rug was in progress for almost a year.

Our new home allowed us to indulge in other weaknesses, including dogs. We immediately adopted a reddish-brown short-haired dog with one ear that stood up and the other that flopped over. He was a wonderful friend, perky and loyal, always ready for a walk, always ready for a meal. Navajos laughed at him and called him a "Hopi dog." I never could see the Hopi-ness in him myself, and of course even if I had, it wouldn't have seemed funny to me. We named him Harold Mutt, after Harold Mott, the tribal attorney who was cast in the villain role opposite the heroes of DNA. Harry was soon joined, appropriately, by his bride Louise, after Louise Mott, Harold's wife. Louise outweighed Harry by quite a bit—a big-boned girl, we used to say. She was lovely, with long black hair, and brown dot eyebrows over her deep brown eyes. Both dogs had expressive tails. Harry's stood taller than Louise's. Hers was fringed and swayed as she trotted along. They were a great pair, and we loved them dearly. In retrospect, we were probably rehearsing for the time not too far in the future when we would have babies. At the time, it seemed quite natural to dote on our dogs, to take them to the vet, to buy them dog food, and to let them sleep in the house on a cold night. Many Navajos considered these activities bizarre cultural practices.

I realized after only a few weeks in Chinle that the value of an animal's life was primarily economic. A sheep or a goat was worth a lot, for wool and for food. A calf, too, could bring a good price. A horse was useful for travel, for herding, for the rodeo, and for prestige. A good herding dog would be fed and bred. But other dogs and all cats were expendable. There were always plenty more where they came from. I was shocked at the sight of a mangy, starving animal, walking along the highway, or through a parking lot, or school ground, and more shocked at the reaction of people, children and adults both, who ridiculed or tormented it. Animals hit on the road were left to die, bloating in the summer heat, or stiffening under snowfall in the winter. I told myself that it was a luxury to be able to worry about animals, and that in a society where survival of people is the focus, it is inevitable that the care of pets will not be a priority. I understood that intellectually. I tried to accept this new reality, and not let my tenderness show, but I had to speak up in defense of a dog being pelted with rocks by one of my preschoolers. And I had to take in strays that wandered—or were dropped—into our lives.

Word spread, I can imagine, that the lawyer and his wife took their dogs to the doctor in Gallup. They snickered in disbelief that someone would do that, waste all that gas and money on a dog or cat. But I persisted, and made countless trips to Gallup or Cortez (Colorado) as I shopped for the most compatible veterinarian, cursing the reservation for not having one animal doctor, anywhere, except BIA range management specialists, who only cared for the animals listed above with price tags. Bob and I took Harry and Louise, of course, for shots and check-ups, as well as dozens of successive cats and dogs. There were sad, one-way trips, with terminal patients—probably particularly mystifying to Navajo neighbors. There were dangerous trips, like the spay-neuter mission to Gallup with Mamu, a very weary, mid-sized dog who was in heat, and Big Red, her large and energetic suitor. Bob drove and I rode in the back of the Bronco, throwing my body repeatedly between the two of them, trying to prevent the inevitable. Finally, realizing that I was putting myself at risk, I gave up, and climbed back into the passenger seat. Bob and I stared straight ahead, pretending not to notice the bedlam in the back.

And there were thought-provoking trips. Our big orange cat named Walter Kitty developed a high fever suddenly one afternoon, and he seemed about to go into a coma. I called Bob at work and told him that I was headed for Cortez, where the vet had said he would stay open until 6:00 for me. I put Walter Kitty in a box, placed him on the seat next to me, and took off. I made good time, arriving just after 5:00, and carried the box into the examining room. The vet made a quick examination and declared that the cat was seriously dehydrated and probably had an infection. He would hook him up to an IV and if I could wait an hour or so, I could take him home. I was delighted, and spent the time reading rodeo magazines.

Walter Kitty looked re-born when the vet returned him to me. He was pumped up with fluids and antibiotics, and was clearly going to make it. It was a much happier return trip, and I congratulated myself on a successful and noble mission well executed. The sun went down as I turned right at Round Rock, and I traveled south through Many Farms in the dark. I was about eight miles from home, halfway between Many Farms and Chinle, when a big jack rabbit bounded in front of me. There was no way to avoid it. I slammed on the brakes but it was only for show. The rabbit was dead, and I knew it. Walter Kitty awoke and lifted his head over the edge of the box.

"It's okay, Walter. I just hit a rabbit." I heard my voice crack, and knew what was coming. I sobbed the last eight miles, and staggered into the house clutching the cat and feeling like a killer. A savior of a cat, a killer of a rabbit. How does that work? If I hadn't been on the road at that moment, the rabbit would be alive. My cat might have died, but that rabbit wouldn't have.

There were other animals in our life under the cottonwoods. Our friends John and Leslie Silko had arrived in Chinle a year after us, and had found housing in Low Rent. The price was certainly right, but there was no way to have horses there, and Leslie, whose home was Laguna Pueblo, had two horses, Molly and Sparkplug, that were part of her family and needed to be with her in Chinle. They built a corral next to our house, and we became foster horse parents, feeding and watering them, and occasionally riding with John or Leslie. We never became comfortable enough to ride by ourselves without them. The gear was complex, the horse personality seemed inscrutable and unpredictable, and Leslie's vivid stories about horseback disasters didn't help. Leslie and I became close friends. We spent a lot of time together, over iced tea or wine, talking, laughing, speculating about the gossip of the day. And sometimes we rode the horses together. Eventually she even bewitched me into riding bareback.

"It's so much fun, and a lot simpler, Lucy," she convinced me. "None of those stirrups to get caught up in! You'll love it!"

We struggled to mount the horses, leading them from one stump to another, and just when we were about to leap aboard, the horse would shift ever so slightly and we would miss. We were laughing so hard, it was getting less and less likely that we would ever succeed. Then Leslie lined Molly up next to a rail fence, and with her holding the reins, I climbed to the top rail, and vaulted onto Molly's back. It was huge, as vast and wide as Black Mesa off in the distance. I couldn't believe it. My feet stuck out on each side like little ears popping out of her back. I grabbed for the reins, clutching with them a chunk of mane for good measure. I tried to grip with my knees, but the expanse was much too wide. I was flabbergasted, and couldn't imagine how this was going to work. Leslie had hopped on Sparkplug and I found myself following them down the dirt road toward the wash. I had no choice. Besides my pride stuck me in place like glue. I swayed and lurched with every step, and eventually began to feel almost cocky. I was riding bareback. How cool was this?

Leslie turned around and beamed at me. "Isn't this great?"

I shouted, "Yeah" and was about to add something about how nice it was to be so close to the horse's hide. But the breath vanished, sucked into my lungs as Molly took off. Leslie had broken into a gallop on Sparkplug, and Molly was clearly following orders from someone other than me. I was pulling on the reins to slow her down, but when she reverted to a trot I found that I bounced around on her back like a piece of popcorn. Each time I was jolted upward, I had no idea where I would land on that broad back, or if I would hit the back at all. I let her return to the gallop, which was blessedly smoother, but frighteningly fast. I was rocking on a violent sea. My inner thighs were at peak performance, gripping where there was nothing to grip. Everything rushed by, branches, fences, hogans, and then we were in the wash, where the deep sand called invitingly. At least a fall here would be softer. But miraculously, I held on, by terror and by shrieking, in the belief that if I was still making noise—a lot of noise—then I must still be alive. The horses tired of the sand, and slowed to a walk. Leslie and I fell into a laughing fit, from excitement and exhaustion—and, for me, from relief.

Leslie and John also brought goats into our lives, a mixed blessing, or on second thought, no blessing at all. They were beautiful exotic creatures, some Nubian, and they lived in a pen adjoining the horse corral. But their crazy slitted eyes set me on edge every time I went out to feed them. Leslie milked them, except on rare occasions when I would have to muster all my courage, put myself in a very vulnerable position on a stool next to the hindquarters, and pray I would survive. I suffered butts from the big ram, and lost buttons off shirts. They were like magicians, or witches, hypnotizing you with those eyes, and then playing some devilish trick on you. The next thing you knew your shoelaces were in shreds.

And there were chickens. In a supreme effort to live the genuine rural life, we slaughtered our own chicken that first Thanksgiving in the new house. John, who was a hunter first and a lawyer second, and above all was from Alaska, was nominated to do the deed. Bob held the fellow upside down by the feet, and John chopped off its head. It was a shock, but I had prepared myself for it, and acted as heroically as I could. My job was plucking. I learned the hard way that the million or so mites that live on poultry leap to the closest warm body as soon as they find their host is deceased. I should have dunked it in boiling water first. Live and learn.

In fact, we were learning all the time about life among the cottonwoods. That first spring, as soon as the ground warmed, produced vicious red ants—"Fire Ants," my Headstart kids would say, with big eyes. They built mounds, and traveled throughout their territory biting anything that came in their path and seeking out things that weren't in their path. The bites were very painful, and stung for hours. The best medicine, we were told by a paralegal of Bob's, was Adolf's Meat Tenderizer. Just spit in your palm and shake the powder onto the spit and mix it up with your finger. Apply generously to the bite. Adolf's is still on my pantry shelf.

And, one more helpful hint from Navajoland, on the destruction of red ants. We learned it was impossible to move them, and in fact the effort simply enraged them, and seemed to double their viciousness. In desperation one day, Bob dug up the hills and threw shovelfuls of dirt and ants across the road. Before he was done, several of the ants had crawled up his leg and were wreaking vengeance on tender parts. As he cursed and gyrated, an old man from Rough Rock drove by in a pickup. He stopped and gave Bob a little advice. The best thing to do was to leave the anthill in place, and bury a Coke bottle in the ground within a few yards of the mound, just so the neck is flush with the dirt surface. Leave a little Coke in the bottle, he said, and the ants will "drop by" for a taste, never to return. That advice says something about the Navajo approach to the world and the challenges it poses.

Leslie was a writer and was struggling to be published. She railed against the male publishing world, and the white establishment, and she was right. It was unfair how hard she had to work to be recognized. Her friends were all indignant on her behalf. And besides this was 1970, women's liberation time! We were all in touch with women in other parts of the country, friends from school, sisters and cousins, and we were all reading accounts in the press about the growing movement for equality of the sexes. The Public Health Service wives brought with them all manner of imports from the outside world, both material and intellectual, and in 1970 some of them were bringing eight-track cassette tapes, pet rocks, and an uppity attitude. Leslie and I were intrigued, and not wanting to be left out, agreed to join a Women's Consciousness Raising Group in Chinle. We convinced Linda Thelen, a friend who also lived in Low Rent, to join us. Linda and her husband, George, were teachers and VISTA Volunteers from southern California. The three husbands may have been nervous, but they didn't dare show it.

The group lasted a year, and try as we might, we never succeeding in recruiting a Navajo woman to join us. They were probably too busy making a living, driving to town, changing tires, tending animals, and generally being liberated. It did strike me funny that a bunch of Anglo women in the middle of an Indian Reservation were getting together to talk about being oppressed. Anglos, men or women, in Navajoland were a privileged lot, and Navajo women didn't seem oppressed, at least not by their husbands, who were often left home to babysit. We may have all been *de*pressed, but we were not *op*pressed. Our group floundered, wondering who we were, what we were trying to accomplish by getting together, and how we would know if we succeeded. In the end, it was probably like any gathering of women who find themselves in a foreign situation. We supported each other through hard times. We confided in each other, and never failed to have at least one person cry at every meeting. We talked about our pasts, our childhoods, our family situations, and our marriages. We sometimes stumbled on an issue that related to women's liberation, but this usually brought more dissension than unity.

I was often in a minority that was unsympathetic to women's outrage over unequal treatment. Being on the Navajo Reservation, where an entire people and culture were under attack from bureaucratic mismanagement at best and an ongoing extermination policy at worst, gave me a perspective on the complaints of upper-middle-class white women. I resented them, and I felt little in common with them. They seemed like a spoiled lot, without a clue about what real discrimination was like. I remember shocking my own mother, living in San Francisco and not one to be left behind, with such talk.

I used my righteous indignation to support the rights of Navajos against the government and all oppressors everywhere. I was dismayed at the lack of anger and outrage among most Navajos at how they had been treated and were still being treated. There was a complacency that made me very sad. I acknowledged that I was a beneficiary of this complacency, that after two years in Chinle we had been attacked only once for being Anglo. A client of Bob's was eight months behind in his truck payments, and the company repossessed the vehicle. The client wanted the axle back, which he said he had put on himself. Bob said that given the large amount the man owed, he didn't think it was reasonable to demand the axle back. The man stormed out of the office and said that Bob wouldn't help him because he was an Anglo and didn't care about Navajos. Bob was angry and hurt. I had mixed feelings. I, too, was hurt for Bob, but I was also relieved to hear some anger, some bitterness. We knew it was there, it had to be there, and it was unsettling never to see it expressed.

In contrast to uprisings in the late sixties and early seventies in other parts of the country, Navajoland was peaceful. I marveled that in these times of bombings and attacks against the establishment else-where, it was rare for a Navajo to go after the BIA, or the Indian Health Service, or the county or state government for countless abuses and neg-lects. What might have come out in hostility and aggression was for some Navajos being expressed in what we now call an internalized racism. They were hostile to their own culture, to themselves at their core. They aped Anglos, ate Wonder Bread instead of fry bread, ham-burger instead of mutton. The women curled their hair, wore light-col-ored makeup, and refused to breast feed their children. Parents were proud that their children spoke no Navajo and could recite "Hey diddle-diddle, the cat and the fiddle" at two years old. They turned up their noses at Navajo traditions and beliefs, eager to be the first to show those old ways meant nothing to them. It made me very sad, and I was secretly pleased when I saw some outright outrage against the dominant culture, long-time enemy of Navajo culture.

And how curious it was that part of my response was to turn on *my* own kind, the middle-class liberated Anglo woman. In a February 1970 letter to a college friend, I wrote:

> When I see wild-eyed women on TV screaming that they are being discriminated against just like the Blacks, and when will they be recognized as a minority group with rights, it just makes me laugh. Women are not a minority group in any sense of the word—not even numerically. It seems very unattractive [sic!] to be screaming that women are being persecuted, deliberately, by men in this country. It may be hard for women with law or medical degrees to break into those professions, but any woman with that kind of education, I just can't feel sorry for. She'll get there. With all the discrimination that is going on in this coun-try, including right here, I just can't get too excited about women's rights. Also, I like men too much. I hate to see women viewing the male as an enemy when I don't believe he is.

Bob, to his credit, had urged me to get out in the world, to become some-thing more than the "lawyer's wife." Ironically, he was more interested in my liberation than I was. I had no particular career and didn't feel the need for one. Graduating from college in 1966, I was on the cusp of the revolution. Some were out ahead, leading the charge. Some were hanging on to the old model of the little lady, the homemaker, the supporter of the breadwinning husband. In a way, I had jumped off the train entirely. I had expected to get married and have children, and that seemed feasible. We needed money, and so I found work.

I was quite content as a Headstart teacher, and in the fall of 1970, I was assigned to teach in Chinle, almost across the street from our house. How lucky could I be? I spent the day with wonderful kids whom I adored. I was co-teacher with Mrs. Baldwin, my original mentor. I became acquainted with the families of the children, and with the political leadership in the community. Being next door to the Chapter House, and with the influential Mrs. Baldwin ever present, Headstart was a kind of hub of activity, the place where rumors began and were later brought for confirmation.

I settled into a routine with the kids. The kids taught me Navajo and I taught them English. One day we sang *Shi Naashá,* a traditional song about walking in beauty. The next day we worked on a square dance. I taught them *Frère Jacques* in English, Navajo, and French. I relaxed about the cultural anomalies inherent in being an Anglo teacher of Navajo children, in a setting defined by Navajo adults who often wished they were Anglo. At Thanksgiving, I found myself happily directing the children in the construction of paper-plate turkey centerpieces for the big meal at the Chapter House. I didn't dwell on the strangeness of dressing the kids as Pilgrims, or as three Wise Men a month later.

And when one crisp morning the Yei Bi Cheis came to carry off the children in their gunny sacks, I shrieked and hid with the children. We covered our ears and our eyes, terrified of their threatening rattles, guttural sounds, and grotesque masks. Only dimly did I realize that Mrs. Baldwin probably sent for them, to scare the living daylights out of the naughtiest children, and put them on a straighter path for the rest of the year. And, even more dimly did it occur to me that this might not be a technique approved by the Association of Nursery School Teachers. This event was all part of the scene, and I was a player—for better or worse.

Being bus driver was one of my favorite roles. If Edith, our cook and bus driver, was busy, I eagerly volunteered. I rode the light blue Ford

Minivan like a bucking bull over the rutted roads with the kids laughing and bouncing around on their seats. I practiced Navajo pointing to *tł'ízhí* when I saw a goat, or *chidí* when I saw a truck. And I tried to trick them in English.

"Do you see a horse?" I'd ask.

"Yiss, Yiss! over there Lucy."

"Do you see a dog?"

"Yiss, Yiss! There! A dog."

"Do you see an elephant?"

The one or two "yisses" were drowned out by "Noooooooo! No elephant!"

I came home one day so happy. I had gone through our routine, many times, and finally decided to branch out with the pronouns. I had said, "*I* see a giraffe!" instead of "Do *you* see a giraffe?"

There was a pause while it registered, and then Lyle Kinsel, so shy and with no English at all, piped up "Where? Lucy, where?" It was a great moment.

EIGHT

A Career Appears

I couldn't believe it. Yes, I probably had been speeding, but after all, I was pregnant, and I had become obsessed with the thought of a bowl of mutton stew at Fleming Begaye's. As I headed north from Burnsides on that long straight stretch I lost track of the speedometer. And, as is so often the case, haste made waste, and I spent precious minutes stopped by the side of the road while the State Highway Patrolman wrote out the ticket. He handed it to me, saying, "You can mail in your money, or you can protest the ticket to the Justice of the Peace in Mexican Water."

"Mexican Water? Why Mexican Water? Why not Chinle?" I didn't see why I would have to travel an hour and a half north of Chinle to protest a ticket.

"That's where the J.P. is, in Mexican Water. If you want, you can go to St. Johns instead," was the helpful reply. St. Johns, county seat of Apache

County, was at least two hours to the south. This county, like other counties that included the reservation was long and skinny, with the bulk of the land and the population on the reservation in the north, and the county seat in the small non-Indian portion of the county in the south.

I knew I was getting nowhere, but I couldn't help myself. "Why is the J.P. in Mexican Water? Why isn't there an office in Chinle? That's where most of the people are."

"The J.P. lives in Mexican Water, that's why. He's the trader there. If he lived in Chinle, well then, I guess the office'd be in Chinle. But he doesn't. He's in Mex—"

"Okay, I understand. I'm sorry. I just don't see . . . but that's okay. I'll send the money in. Thanks," and I put the ticket in my purse.

As I drove on, my appetite a little dampened by the stop, I mulled it over. We had been in Chinle two years now, and we were developing a fierce loyalty to this spot in the heart of Navajoland. How could it be that the two places to do state judicial business in Apache County were both as far from Chinle as you could get—St. Johns in the south and Mexican Water, hugging the Utah border, in the north? Chinle was clearly the county's center of population, commercial activity, and cultural richness. Why wasn't there some kind of county judicial office in Chinle?

Over the mutton stew at Fleming's, I posed the question to Bob. He retrieved the Arizona Statutes from his office upstairs, and we pored over the section on Justice of the Peace. The J.P. was the officer of the court throughout Arizona. It was an elected position, and the qualifications were only that you be a registered voter and that you obtain a certain number of names on a nominating petition. Each county was divided into precincts and each precinct had a J.P. who served an unbelievable array of functions, including marrying people, collecting fines, registering voters, inspecting agricultural products, with specific reference to substandard pecans, serving as coroner for the body of anyone who had died outside a medical facility, holding trials and delivering sentences in misdemeanor cases, and holding preliminary hearings for felonies. (With this last one, Bob turned a little paler than usual at the thought of someone with no legal background or knowledge handling felonies.) All of these duties applied to non-Indian defendants or subjects—or pecans, I suppose—on the reservation. The justice of the peace was the equivalent of the Navajo Tribal Court Judge, who had jurisdiction over all Indians. A speeding Navajo went to the Tribal Court; a speeding Anglo went to the J.P. It was all very interesting. I would write my check and send it to Mexican Water.

But returning to the location of the J.P. office, I said to Bob. "Why can't it be in Chinle?"

"Call St. Johns in the morning," he suggested. "And don't use your real name." He was joking, and I laughed, but it was true that he and all the DNA attorneys were gaining reputations. They were heroes to many Navajos, but they were deeply hated by many Anglos, especially those whose power base had been threatened, like car dealers, traders, or county officials. Bob had taken on the county school board more than once, and frequently crossed legal swords with the County Attorney, Kendall Hansen, over jail conditions off the reservation. We drove home to a leaping and bounding welcome from Harold and Louise Mutt.

In the morning I called the county administrator in St. Johns, and asked about the numbers and boundaries of J.P. precincts in Apache County. She explained that the county was divided into seven precincts, and that Chinle was in the Teec Nos Pos precinct, which covered the whole top third of the county, the northeast corner of the state in fact. There was another precinct that included Window Rock, St. Michaels, and Ganado, and the other five were all off the Reservation. With great diplomacy I asked her how it was determined where the Justice of the Peace office would be in each precinct. She seemed a little mystified by that question.

"Well, it's where the Justice of the Peace lives. I guess that's how they do it," she finally said. "The Teec Nos Pos Precinct, well, he lives in Mexican Water, and so . . ." I stopped listening. By now, I knew the rest of that sentence by heart.

"And can you have more than one J.P. in a precinct, or can there be branch offices for a precinct that's as big as this one?" I pressed on.

"Oh, I don't think so. I don't see how that would work. There's no money for that. Oh no, I'm sure that's not possible." She became more sure of things the more she talked about them.

"Hmmm." I bought time while I figured out how to phrase the next question. "Well, what if someone in Chinle wanted to be the J.P.?"

And here she reverted to her bureaucratic core. I even wondered if she began to suspect what my last name was. "Well then, they'd just have to run in the next election, wouldn't they?"

"Oh, yes, I see. And when is that election?"

"November, along with the rest of it. Filings are coming up, due in August." She was very curt by now. I thanked her very much and hung up, feeling rather sneaky and wondering if she was trying to trace the call. Had she kept me on the line more than three minutes, like in the movies?

I realized that I felt more than sneaky. I felt excited. It was not unlike the moment before I jumped onto the saddle-less wide expanse of Molly for that hair-raising bareback ride. What if I took on the trader in Mexican Water? What if I became the justice of the peace and moved the office to Chinle? I called Bob at work and told him about the call. I asked him to get out that statute and read me that list of duties again. Coroner had me worried. Preliminary hearings for felonies had Bob worried. The marriages, the substandard pecans, the speeding tickets, all that sounded like a lot of fun. And besides, I said, remember the higher purpose I would be serving: "That office should be in Chinle, not Mexican Water." It was important for me that I would be representing the state court system. That seemed legitimate for an Anglo on the reservation. I certainly did not want to push my way into a position that ought to be held by a Navajo. Of course a Navajo could be a justice of the peace, and would be in later years—but that is jumping ahead.

Bob was supportive, but warned me that the county might be antagonistic to my running with my close connection to DNA, and that they might resort some kind of nastiness. It may not have been the career he had been imagining for me, but it could be an adventure for us both and might be compatible with being a new mother. The baby was due in January, and I was planning on leaving Headstart before Christmas. We talked about what it might be like to hold the office with a new baby. We read more about the duties and determined that there would be little travel involved, and that with an office at home, it might work out just fine. Why not give it a try?

I drove (slowly) to St. Johns to pick up the petition for nomination, and to get a look at the folks that were running Apache County, and I guess to let them get a look at me. Obviously pregnant, I was twenty-six years old, with long hair, sandals, and wearing a shift that stopped just above the knees. In Chinle I looked decent; in St. Johns I looked like a raving hippie. And when I introduced myself, with the same last name as the troublemaker attorney, eyebrows raised and eyes narrowed. I picked up the petition, a map showing precinct boundaries, a list of voting places, and the Directory of Arizona County Officials. I also bought the list of registered voters for my precinct. The deadline for the petition was only two weeks away. Maybe I wouldn't get the names, maybe this was a crazy idea. Who did I think I was? I wasn't a lawyer, I was a newcomer, I was a woman, and about to be a new mother. Perhaps the hormones were getting to me. Perhaps I should give up this idea. But as the miles and the minutes crept by, I was seized again by indignation. Chinle deserves a state judicial office. We citizens of Chinle, Indian and non-Indian alike, should not be forced to do our state business two hours to the north, or two hours to the south. Yes, it was up to me to defend the homeland, to bring the seat of power to its rightful place. Justice would be done!

The 1970 census for Apache County showed 32,298 total population. Almost 29,000 of the total population were listed as living in areas with fewer than 1,000 people each. One can imagine that many, many Navajos were left out of that count. To be on the ballot required a petition signed by 10 percent of the number of voters who voted in the last election in that precinct. Because it served the interests of Apache County officials to have the majority of voters off the reservation, they had done the minimum toward registering Navajo voters. Each Justice of the Peace was a registrar of voters, and again, it was not in the interest of the trader at Mexican Water to drive down to Chinle and hold a big voter registration drive. Those on the rolls to vote in the Teec Nos Pos Precinct were divided into "districts." Each district included satellite communities as far as fifty miles away. Chinle, for instance, included Many Farms, Rough Rock, Nazlini, Del Muerto, Cottonwood, and more. Eligible voters in the Chinle voting district must have numbered nearly 4,000.

Registered voters in Teec Nos Pos Precinct, as of November 3, 1970:

Chinle District	831
Lukachukai District	127
Teec Nos Pos District	63
Dennehotso District	145

The voting records from the 1968 election showed that 312 voters voted in the precinct. The good news was that I needed only 32 signatures on my petition. If I couldn't manage that, I certainly didn't deserve to be on the ballot. The bad news was that only 312 people voted, out of 1,166 registered voters, and out of a population of several thousand in the precinct. I was outraged. Navajos should be voting, locally and nationally. Their voices must be heard. If I were elected, I would register voters aggressively. I could see myself driving the Bronco out to Blue Gap, up to Rough Rock, over to Lukachukai, baby in a car seat next to me, card table folded in the back, a sign "REGISTER HERE," a box of registration forms, and a brochure about voting rights—I might have to print that myself—but wait, first to get elected!

Given the registration figures above, and given my platform of bringing the office to Chinle, it made sense to concentrate on the greater Chinle area. I visited with community leaders, and my idea was received with a few smiles and chuckles. I understood that. I knew I was setting out on unfamiliar waters for a twenty-six-year-old Anglo woman. But, I explained, there were a lot of reasons why Navajos should vote in this election and should be interested in the quality of state government located on the reservation. There were services that a justice of the peace could offer both Navajo and non-Navajo residents, like marriage licenses and ceremonies, voter registration, notarizing documents, and pursuit of justice where a non-Indian defendant was involved. A Navajo could sue a trader—just for instance—or bring a complaint against a teacher or a highway patrolman—just for instance. All this could happen in a justice of the peace court.

Besides, Navajos could have an influence over the results of state and national elections if they were registered and became informed and active voters. U.S. Representative Sam Steiger, running for Congress representing the 3rd District, which included all of Navajoland, had never set foot on the reservation and didn't seem to be planning on it. Clearly there were too few votes to make it worth his while. If more Navajos voted they could surely influence county elections and elect school superintendents, assessors, judges, clerks, sheriffs with more sympathy for Navajo needs. They could even elect a Navajo to the County Board of Supervisors. Five out of seven county residents were Navajo after all. I got twice as many names as I needed on the petition, just for good measure, and sent it by registered mail to St. Johns well in advance of the deadline. I called to make sure they had received it. "Yes, it's here," was the chilly response. The campaign was on, but not without hurdles from St. Johns.

At the Board of Supervisors meeting following receipt of my petition, the board formally designated justice of the peace office locations for all seven precincts. Mexican Water was named the official location for the J.P. in the Teec Nos Pos Precinct. If I won, I would have to serve in Mexican Water. I sent a letter of inquiry to the County Manager C. L. Haws, asking where in the statutes the board found the authority to name the office location. The location, as I understood, would be chosen by the voters on election day. Mr. Haws referred my inquiry to Kendall Hansen, county attorney, who wrote me a letter affirming the right of the board to designate the location. Although the statutes did not specifically give that authority to the Boards of Supervisors, he said, the Boards were granted general authority for supervising the official conduct of all county officers, and this action fell under that authority.

I made one other attempt to defend myself, asking the Board of Supervisors to refer the question to the attorney general or to withdraw the designation because it had been made following my petition filing, and it clearly favored my opponent in Mexican Water. Lacking a response, I called Mr. Hansen. He said he had nothing more to say on the subject, having given his opinion in his earlier letter to me, and that the board was not referring my request to the attorney general. I was as diplomatic as I could be, knowing that I needed a working relationship with this person if I did by some miracle make it into office.

"You know, there are a lot of non-Indians in Chinle, a lot more than in Teec Nos Pos or Mexican Water. I just want to be able to serve them if I am elected."

"It's a practical matter," he said. "Along Highway 164 through Mexican Water and Kayenta, there's a lot of business for the J.P. that comes off that highway."

"There might be a lot of business off the road through Chinle and Many Farms. We just don't know, because there's never been a J.P. there."

"That may be, but those people seem to be law abiding. We never have much trouble from them."

I was frustrated and angry. I held out hope that the Board would ask an opinion from the attorney general. It was risky, but I was going to campaign on the basis of moving the office to Chinle, something I couldn't exactly promise. Well, I thought, I guess that qualifies me as a real politician.

Bob and I decided that a targeted campaign letter sent to all the registered Chinle voters would be the best strategy. Mail was taken very seriously in that time and place, as we learned with the sewing machine raffle postcard that was treasured long after the raffle took place. I wrote the letter carefully, trying to hit a note that was on the one hand competent and forceful, and on the other hand respectful and non-threatening. I was touched by those who agreed to be on a list of endorsements at the bottom of the letter. They included the Chinle Chapter president, vice-president and secretary, the councilman from Chinle, the BIA superintendent's wife, the superintendent of schools (successor to Jodie Matthews), the Navajo Community College president, and many respected leaders of both modern and traditional Navajo society. I hoped that with a good turnout, and those endorsements, I would make it.

The printed letter and postage were my big expenses. I also indulged in bumper stickers, chartreuse on dark blue, HILGENDORF FOR JUSTICE OF THE PEACE. I remembered that my father had lost a bid for the Seattle City Council when I was in high school, and that a printing error had hurt him badly. The printer left the union "bug" off his brochures, leading to accusations that my father was anti-union, which was far from the truth. I was scrupulous about the placement of that symbol on my bumper stickers. You never knew what might make the difference! I kept careful track of my expenses:

Quik Print (printed letters)	$10.35
Postal Service (stamps)	$30.00
Reflective Advertising (bumper stickers)	$26.46
Diné Baa Hani (newspaper ad)	$5.00
Apache County Recorder (voter list)	$11.76

My contributions, embarrassingly, were all from out of state:

Eleanor Hilgendorf	$25.00
John Hilgendorf (Bob's grandfather)	$5.00

LUCY HILGENDORF
for
JUSTICE OF THE PEACE
Box 888
Chinle

Dear Voter:

We residents of the Navajo Reservation are easily forgotten by the state and county government. The Apache County seat is at St. Johns, 140 miles away, and if you have ever had to travel there on a county matter you know the great inconvenience. In Apache County, Reservation residents make up two-thirds of the population, and all of us, Navajo and Anglo alike, should express ourselves at election time. There are more than 830 voters in the Chinle-Many Farms area alone, and these votes can be crucial at the county level. I urge everyone of you to go to the Chinle Community Center on November 3, and exercise your right to vote.

In order to bring Apache County services to Chinle area residents, I am running for Justice of the Peace in this precinct. A Justice of the Peace on the Reservation hears cases where a non-Indian is the accused. Most of the cases that come before the J.P. are traffic viola- tions, and now that the state of Arizona has taken over maintenance of Route 8, connecting Ganado and Round Rock, we in this area will be watched more closely on the road. A Navajo would appear before the J.P. to bring a case against a non-Indian -- a trespassing case, for instance. The Justice of the Peace is also empowered to marry people, and serve as Notary Public.

Chinle is now part of the Teec Nos Pos precinct -- we can no longer go to the Justice of the Peace at Ganado. If my opponent is elected, he would establish the Justice of the Peace office at his trading post in Mexican Water, 70 miles from Chinle. Since Chinle- Many Farms is the center of population for this precinct, the Justice of the Peace office should be in this area, and if I am elected, the office will be in Chinle, where it can serve the most people conveniently.

I am a college graduate, and have had several law-related courses. I would welcome the opportunity to serve this community as Justice of the Peace. Your vote on November 3 would be appreciated.

ENDORSEMENTS

Jay Armer	Henry Gatewood	William Morgan, Sr.
Thomas E. Atcitty	Joseph W. Gray	Sam H. Reed
Daniel Bahe	Betty Hand	George M. Sayre
Jimmie D. Begay	Ned A. Hatathli	Glenn Stoner
Fleming Begaye	William Leupp	Ida Tayah
Kathy Donlon	Maybelle Little	Ben Teller
Teddy Draper, Sr.	Felix Martinez, Sr.	John Dee Wallace

VOTE FOR HILGENDORF AND VOTE FOR CHINLE-MANY FARMS

NOVEMBER 3

Not long after I sent the letter out in late October, one of Bob's paralegals received a campaign letter from Don Reeves, my opponent. Not surprisingly, he emphasized the importance of experience, and likened holding public office to building a house. When you build a house, you hire a builder with experience. When you vote for justice of the peace, you should vote for someone with experience. Having been J.P. for six years, Don Reeves was the experienced builder. The letter closed with: "Don knows the job and knows how to do it well. We NEED to support people who have proven they 'have what it takes!' Remember it's experience that counts!" My letter was much classier, printed and with those endorsements at the bottom, but my opponent's handwritten, personal appeal might work on a lot of people, particularly Anglos hostile to DNA. A small turnout would help him; a big turnout, which would imply a high percentage of Navajos, might go in my favor.

On election day, I had planned to stop by and offer rides to a few people who wanted to vote but might not have transportation. The first stop was a hogan behind the Navajo Tribal Arts and Crafts Guild. I picked up the grandmother and aunt of one of my preschoolers. They squeezed together onto the bucket passenger seat, and we took off, slowly because the road was badly rutted and I was hugely pregnant. A dog came out of nowhere and chased the car, nipping at the front tire on my side, and barking wildly to let the world know he was doing a most important job, chasing this evil intruder off his property. I was irritated and wanted to speed up to lose him, but I couldn't or I would risk delivering my baby early. As I came to the intersection with the highway and the road smoothed out a little, I stepped on the gas and, seeing no traffic coming from the left, turned right onto the pavement. Thank God I would be rid of that dog, I thought. The dog must have been excited by my acceleration, and sped up to stay with me, racing out into the oncoming lane. He was struck immediately by a truck, and I saw in the rear view mirror his limp body flop onto the shoulder. I felt terrible. That was my last voter pickup. I went home and hid out the rest of the day.

I was pessimistic about my chances. It seemed like a ridiculous idea. I was young, a woman, with no experience, and connected to DNA. I told myself it had been a fun exercise, and I was glad I tried, and that maybe I had aroused some interest in people about the state judicial system and the inequities on the reservation. The votes were counted by a computer in Window Rock, and I wouldn't know until the next morning.

I made an apple pie and focused on my baby. That was something that I was going to do for sure, have a baby. And that was the most thrilling event and rewarding job I could imagine. I had my wicker laundry basket ready for the trip home from the hospital. The baby would be born in Farmington. The closest obstetrician was in Gallup, but we chose the one in Farmington because of the potential for getting stuck at the railroad crossing just north of the Gallup hospital if you happened to coincide with one of those slow freight trains passing through, or worse yet, unloading for as long as an hour. A client of Bob's had delivered her baby in the truck as the train crawled by in front of her.

Of course, most Chinle babies were born at the IHS Hospital in Fort Defiance, or the Project Hope Hospital in Ganado, or at home with help from grandma. By law, the federal Indian Health Services facilities served Indians only, and non-Indians were turned away except in the direst emergency—and it had to be very dire indeed. This left us with the option of the tiny Project Hope Hospital with no obstetrician on staff. As new parents-to-be we were nervous and it seemed worth the monthly checkups in Farmington to be in the hands of a real obstetrician and to have access to a more modern hospital. My doctor insisted that there would be plenty of time to drive two and a half hours from Chinle to Farmington for a first delivery. But being Anglo, and doing this for the first time, we were nervous, and asked what we should do if there was not enough time, and we found ourselves between Round Rock and Rock Point needing help.

"Well, just pull off the road and head for the nearest hogan. Someone there'll know what to do," and we knew he was right. But what if there was no hogan in sight, and Bob was forced to be the midwife?

"Well, you should have something with you to tie off the umbilical cord," he offered.

Our eyes widened. "Like what?"

"Oh, something like shoelaces. Shoelaces would do fine. Just be sure they're sterile."

"How? How do they get sterile? What do we do?" both of us fumbling for instructions.

"No problem, just stick them in the oven, bake them at 350 for twenty minutes or so. Then keep them wrapped in something clean. That's all. You'll be fine, and besides you'll be here in plenty of time."

Needless to say, we left the doctor's office and headed straight for the shoelaces. We bought two pairs—white seemed the appropriate color—and we decided on the longest. Back in Chinle, we set about the sterilizing process. Oven on to 350. Preheat. Set shoelaces on rack. Leave for twenty minutes, better make it thirty minutes for good measure. Reach in, take out laces—wait a minute! We are touching them, they are contaminated by our hands. Wrap the shoelaces in a handkerchief, clean, white, put the packet back in the oven, cook another thirty minutes. Reach in to take out the packet. Oh no, now we are contaminating the handkerchief. Wrap the handkerchief in a small towel. Back in the oven, another thirty minutes. Take out the bundle . . . wait a minute! Get a grip on ourselves. Stop this nonsense before the bundle is so big it won't fit in the oven. Put it by the front door, in the laundry basket, and forget about it.

It gave me comfort to see that basket and its bundle, as I left the house to walk to the Post Office later on election day. Harry and Louise led the way, down the dirt road, happy for the outing, unaware that the household was about to expand by one, and the living room was about to become judicial chambers.

❖

I won the election, 313 to 230. I was sorry that my Democratic Party sweep wasn't enough to make the difference for Raul Castro, who was running for Governor. He lost by only 7,300 votes out of over 410,000 cast. A few more Navajo voters could have made a big difference. I was getting greedy already, eager to get out and register voters. I made another trip to St. Johns. We already knew what to expect from each other, and the reception this time was very cool indeed. The clerk of the court signed me up to become a notary public, gave me the Justice of the Peace Handbook, a blessedly thin volume, and a certificate of election to hang on my wall. It all was frighteningly simple.

The issue of the location of the office was still not resolved. I never received an opinion from the attorney general, nor did the Board of Supervisors reverse their decision, although they did revise it, following the defeat of the incumbent. The board established the office in Tes Nez Iah, a tiny community just west of Mexican Water on Highway 164. They were planning on moving a trailer up there for me, and they had also decided that a forty-hour work week would be necessary. This was looking very grim indeed.

I decided to make a deal. I wrote a very conciliatory letter to the Board of Supervisors, emphasizing that in no way did I want to ignore any part of this large precinct I was now responsible for. I had talked with two other J.P.'s and with the highway patrolman on 164, and they supported my plan. I offered to travel to Tes Nez Iah once every other week and hold office hours there in a room at the Navajo Trails Motel. The rest of the time I would operate from my house in Chinle. The county would have to pay for my "office" up north, since that was spelled out in the law. While I was performing my duties in Chinle, they would not have to pay for office space. The Board of Supervisors agreed to the proposal, probably surprised that I was willing to compromise and perhaps a little disappointed that this particular aspect of the battle was over. That was how I happened to rent a motel room every other Monday in Tes Nez Iah. It was a very boring work day. In spite of my notices at gas stations and in the windows of trading posts (including Mexican Water) in the northern part of the precinct, announcing my regular office hours, no one ever came to visit with any kind of business.

But it was a great opportunity for mother-son bonding. Matt was born January 9, 1971, and yes, we made it to Farmington in plenty of time and without use of shoelaces. He was a wonderful companion as I began my new career, and he joined me for those trips north to the motel room once a week. He traveled on a cradle board, which was probably safer than any infant seat of the day, and we spent the day in the dingy room together, him nursing and burping and filling diapers, me cooing and marveling at this little being, so sweet, so innocent. I felt so lucky to have such a robust, handsome, and healthy baby. He even had an impressive head of hair, considering he was Anglo. It started out brown, then turned blond. Navajos who knew us called him "Little White-Haired Man in the Cottonwood Trees." The Navajo word for cottonwood included reference to white hair, because of the fluffy white cotton spewed by the trees in the summer, and so the name in Navajo had a very poetic sound to it, with lots of "*-itsis*" syllables.

It was a wonderful and easy environment in which to be a new mother. All around were mothers and grandmothers and aunties, young and old, doing what came naturally. They fed their babies when they were hungry, they jiggled them on their cradle boards when they were fussy, they smiled at them, they took them everywhere, they indulged them in every way, and they were for the most part calm and happy little creatures. I followed suit, with occasional consultation of Dr. Spock's *Baby and Child Care*. He was not out of line with Navajo practices, or at least I read him that way, and as time went by, I relied more and more on what I saw around me.

At the end of March, I wrote the Board of Supervisors suggesting that we abandon the office hours in Tes Nez Iah, at least until the summer tourist traffic picked up. My only visitors had been highway patrolmen, stopping to offer me a soda or a bag of chips. And the county could see by then that I was bringing in more money in fines than my predecessor. They finally withdrew the requirement and let me hold court in Chinle. We had converted the living room to an office, put a hollow-core door on four legs, slipped a two-drawer filing cabinet underneath, hung the certificate of election on the wall, along with my Harvard diploma just in case that meant anything to anyone, and I was in business.

My first official function was a marriage. A DNA lawyer was marrying his girlfriend, and they were very excited to think that I could make it legal, on the edge of Canyon de Chelly, no less. The bride was from Cleveland, and her mother called us a week before the event to ask about wedding arrangements, food, music, flowers, and so forth. Well, I said, I hadn't really planned on much. I was just the J.P., and the reservation was dry, and there was no bakery here, and flowers... well, in January Chinle is pretty bleak, she would have to understand. She was crushed. Couldn't I get the caterer involved? Surely there was a caterer in the area? It was a painful call, and I told her that she would have to bring in the champagne and the flowers, and I would try to pull together the rest of it, that is, the food and the music.

Thank God we had picked up a "Wedding Marches and Songs" record last time we were in Gallup. It was mostly a joke, but after all, now I was in the wedding business and I had better be prepared. As for the food, there was no time to order anything special from Fleming's for delivery in two weeks. We would have to figure it out with what was on hand. We served a lovely spaghetti dinner for twenty-five people, with salad, Chianti (from our last trip to Gallup), and French bread, and played the record while the couple cut the carrot cake I had made the night before. With a glass of wine in one hand and a piece of cake in the other, the bride's father whispered to me, "What size are you?"

"Excuse me?" I looked at him a little quizzically.

"I'd like to send you a little something when we get back to Cleveland," he said. "This has been just great. We really appreciate it." Afterward, his wife, in a fur stole and high heels, picked her way through the mud to their rented car, clutching my arm for support.

"This was so wonderful! You are just darling, just darling, and everything is so . . ." glancing at the mud on her shoes, "quaint, so quaint."

Bob and I laughed when it was over. We had done a great job, but we hoped that this was not setting a precedent for weddings to come. It was a lot of work, and not cheap. But we *really* laughed when the package arrived from Cleveland in a few weeks. The box was big enough for a mink stole, a designer dress, or perhaps a lovely cashmere sweater. We ripped it open. Inside were six pairs of duo-fold long underwear, three dark blue for Bob, three light blue for me. The bride's father was the owner of a large line of sports clothing.

Within a month of taking office, I had handled several traffic citations, performed the wedding above, and had a felony charge filed in my court. It seemed as if now that there was a J.P. in Chinle, everything was happening to put her to work and scare her to death. A non-Indian teacher at the elementary school was accused of child molesting, and Kendall Hansen, the county attorney, appropriately filed the felony complaint in my court. I knew that any decision I made could be appealed *de novo* to the Superior Court in St. Johns, and there was comfort in that. My only duty in a preliminary hearing was to find probable cause, or not. But I also knew that finding probable cause would be very damning, especially in a child molestation case, and that even if the accused were found innocent later, that accusation would be impossible to erase. I was terrified by what hung in the balance. I hadn't thought I was going to have to deal with serious matters like this. Couldn't I just be the marrying and fining kind of J.P.? My predecessor in six years had had no excitement whatsoever, no preliminary hearing, nothing beyond his abilities. I got out the Justice of the Peace Manual and looked up preliminary hearings. I needed to get to work and master some of the legal terms. Bob was sitting at the kitchen table eating lunch.

"So, what's this 'rules of evidence' about?" I asked him, thinking how lucky I was to have an attorney for a husband.

He took a deep breath, but didn't say anything.

"You know . . . rules of evidence . . . like there's just a paragraph in this J.P. Manual about it, and I know there's a lot more I probably should know." Silence. "Don't you think?" I was beginning to wonder whether Bob was really a lawyer or not.

Finally, "I think it's better if you just read the paragraph, and use your instincts after that. They spend a lot of time on rules of evidence in law school, a whole lot of time, and . . ." he was visibly shaken by now, "and I just think you're better off not trying to learn it now."

I was disappointed, but, always happy for a shortcut to homework, I nodded. "Okay. I'll just wing it."

"Yeah, it'll be okay." He looked a little green.

I prepared myself as best I could, and lost sleep the night before the hearing, only to have it cancelled by agreement of the attorneys. The case was sent directly to the Superior Court at the request of the defendant's lawyer. I was relieved and disappointed at the same time. The teacher moved away at the end of the school year.

School politics was brutal on the reservation. It was one of the few accesses to power, and people fought over school board seats and constantly tried to recall each other. The school board election in early March was chaos, and now that there was a J.P. in town, everyone made a beeline to my door. The two sides hated each other. People wanted to file criminal complaints against each other for campaigning within the fifty-foot limit, or for not letting a poll watcher within the polling place, or they wanted to arrest someone for harassing them. I spent the day explaining how to file a complaint, how to get someone arrested, and what the voting statutes said. The radical, power-to-the-Navajos candidate, Mary Ina Ray, defeated the trader Gerald LaFont.

In May the opposition forced a recall election of School Board member Florence Paisano, one of Bob's paralegals and an outspoken activist for Navajo rights. They succeeded by a slim margin, and we were devastated. But in the process I made an interesting discovery. Over 1,000 people voted in the Chinle School District. That was more than double the number that voted in the whole Teec Nos Pos Precinct in November 1970. I had been traveling to chapter meetings throughout the precinct registering voters, a lot of whom were illiterate and signed their registration cards with thumb prints. I had also sworn in nineteen assistant voter registration officers—legal, but not encouraged by the County—in Chinle, Round Rock, Rough Rock, Salina, Cottonwood, Piñon, Many Farms, Rock Point, Mexican Water (Grace Reeves, wife of my predecessor!), Totso, and Lukachukai. I was seeing results, and it was exciting, even if this exercise of the ballot was personally disappointing.

Traffic citations were, of course, the bulk of my work. Every person cited, just like me six months earlier, had to appear in person or send in the money to the justice of the peace, now in Chinle. If they did neither, I sent a letter requesting the money and threatening consequences. I was amazed to look at my records after the first year, and find that only 2 out of 190 violators failed to pay up. Some entered into negotiations with me by mail, and I had several who paid on the installment plan. Others wrote complimentary notes along with their checks, about how lovely the buttes and plateaus were, or how pleased they were to see the traditional hogan they had heard so much about. Judging from this group of people, I would say that humanity was honest, dutiful, and gracious. Quite amazing.

My first traffic ticket contestant, however, was a surprise. It seemed that all the "firsts" in my J.P. term of office were unlike anything to follow. His name was Labib Barhoumi, and he appeared for his hearing to protest a speeding ticket. I invited him in, noting that he was no taller than I was, and probably weighed less, and that he was Middle Eastern and dressed in an expensive dark tailored suit. There was not a wrinkle or a spot on him, and from his ticket I knew he lived in Albuquerque. How did he get all the way here looking like a fashion plate, and smelling like one, too? It crossed my mind that he might have changed at Fleming's Shell station before coming over.

He smiled and strode inside. I could see him adjusting his strategies, seeing I was so young. With a thick accent and many apologetic flamboyant gestures he explained that he had just flown in from Albuquerque in his new plane for this hearing. He hoped that I would understand about his speeding ticket. He spoke rapidly as if I might not be able to scrutinize what he was really saying if he just kept the words flowing. He was in the Jordanian Air Force and was being trained in Albuquerque, and, he added with another flourish in the direction of his breast pocket, "I will show you my pilot's license."

No, I said, that was really not relevant to the ticket, and how did he plead to going 100 miles per hour in a 65-mile-per-hour zone?

Ah, yes, he begged me to understand, as he lit up a potent foreign cigarette that clashed with his aftershave lotion. He had just bought this new sports car in Albuquerque and was driving it out to Chinle to visit a friend. The dealer had told him not to go over 50 miles per hour for the first 200 miles, and he had just passed that mark at Ganado. So, he stepped on it, just to see how fast it would go, and it went well over 100, he was proud to report.

I took this as a guilty plea and said I would have to fine him $55. His face froze. He was enraged. He had clearly expected to snow me with the unbeatable combination of suit, smells, accent, sports car, and pilot's license. "Isn't there anything else I can do?" he stammered, trying to maintain an ingratiating smile.

"You could spend a few days in jail," I replied, wondering just what he meant by "anything else."

He wrote out the check and handed it to me coldly, "I will never come to Chinle again."

"If you do," I smiled, "maybe you'd better stick to your plane."

This being a Justice of the Peace was a kick, I thought to myself as I closed the door. What fun to have so much power! How clever I was to run for office! I had been reveling lately in my job—so entertaining, so ego-building, so satisfying to pass judgment with the sanction of the law, to do right while doing good. It was fun to surprise defendants when they saw how young I was, that I was female, that the so-called office was in the living room, that babies—mine and others—and dogs were everywhere. Yes, I congratulated myself, quite the perfect job. And at that moment, Coyote Trickster, the Navajo messenger of humility, tapped me on the shoulder.

It was April 15, 1971, and the wind was howling and flinging dust and sand everywhere. You could feel it between your teeth. How it got there I could never figure out. The phone rang. It was the dispatcher at the Navajo Police Department. "There's been a death up at Rough Rock School," he said bluntly. I felt sick, knowing why he called, but praying that somehow I could be excused. This was one of my duties I had not yet been asked to perform and had hoped that somehow I could avoid.

"You want me to be coroner?" I managed weakly.

"Yes. We've got three officers there guarding the house but they can't touch the body or do any investigations until the coroner pronounces the body dead, and says the cause of death."

My mind was racing. "How did the person die?" I asked stupidly, knowing that was up to me to determine, but hoping for a clue so I could prepare myself.

"It was a suicide . . . uh, I mean I guess it looks like a suicide . . . they don't know why he did it." That was all the clue I would get, so I said I would leave immediately for Rough Rock. I had been enjoying my role as J.P. Now I would have to pay the price.

Numb, I put Matt in the Bronco and headed for Linda Thelen's house in Low Rent. Linda had had a baby, Andrea, two months after Matt was born, and we were destined to be close friends. For now, she was a godsend, providing a warm and loving place to leave Matt while I went to do something unthinkable. I told Linda what lay ahead. We speculated on how he did it. I was thinking of pills or gas. I headed north to Many Farms and turned left off the highway for the last twenty miles of dirt to Rough Rock. I had to remind myself to keep breathing. I told myself over and over, "It's going to be okay. It's going to be over. Pretty soon, you'll be driving back down the road. Pretty soon you'll pick up your precious Matt and go home." Just before the school came into view, I tried to prepare myself. "Lucy, you'd better be ready. It might be awful. His eyes might be wide open, or there might be a horrible expression on his face."

The house was not hard to find. There was a crowd of people milling around the cordoned-off periphery. I went straight to the door. There were three Navajo policemen inside. They asked if I was ready to see the body, and the way they said it implied that I should be ready physically and emotionally, not just ready in the sense of time. I asked how he had done it, and Officer Benally said "shotgun to the head." I said I was ready. I didn't want to have to anticipate the sight one more second than necessary. I saw the other two policemen in profile, standing in the hall and looking into the bedroom. Their faces were unmoved, businesslike. "That's how I will be," I told myself. One of them stepped aside for me to pass. The other asked if I was sure I wanted to look. "You don't really have to if you don't want to," he added gently. Of course, I didn't want to, but it was my job. I would do it.

I entered the bedroom, and looked at Mr. Hoffman on the floor. My eyes registered what Mr. Hoffman had done to himself. My whole body, my whole being, took it in. And then I saw black, a second or two of blindness for which I was very grateful. And by the time my vision returned I was turned toward the door. I walked to the living room and sat on the floor. The police asked if I had seen him, although it was obvious from my collapse that I had. But I knew what they meant. They meant, now you're a member of the club. Now you know what we look at, what we deal with, now you know what it's like. I certainly did. I also knew that my role was tiny. I handled paperwork that declared there was no foul play involved. Their roles—cleaning up, transporting the body, dealing with relatives—were enormous.

I looked around the living room. It was such a lived-in room, with posters, books, letters, what looked like a half-drunk martini on the arm of a chair. I was stunned by Martin Hoffman's act. Did he really mean it? Was he drunk? Does he want to take it back? And I was haunted by the fact that the people he did it "for" wouldn't see what he wanted them to see. I silently raged at him. "You did this for *someone* to see, your ex-wife, your mother, your employer, you did it for someone, but not for *ME. I* saw it instead, and I didn't want to see it!" Later, the police called his ex-wife in California and got her address so they could send her the note he left. She said she wasn't surprised. His brother came to claim the coffin from the funeral parlor in Winslow. Judy Collins wrote a beautiful song in memory of her friend Martin. None of them saw what Mr. Hoffman left behind. The police saw it and I saw it. It would go no further. I knew that was as it should be.

I signed the death certificate, and waived the coroner's inquest, thereby sparing a few more people. As I drove home, I shook and mumbled to myself as the tears streamed down my face. How naive I had been to dread looking at the body for fear the eyes might be open, or the face in anguish. There were no eyes. There was no face.

Bob and Lucy, wedding day photo, Cambridge, Massachusetts, June 1968.

Lucy poses in midday heat, Mojave Desert, July 1968.

John Rockbridge, medicine man and community leader from Forest Lake, Arizona, and member of the first DNA Legal Services board of directors. Mr. Rockbridge carried a briefcase to board meetings that contained only two things: an ink pad and stamp with his name on it for signing documents, 1969 (Gallup Independent).

Bob in his DNA Legal Services office, above Fleming Begaye's Trading Post, 1969.

Our house in the cottonwoods. A Jim Walters home, it was brought from Albuquerque in numbered pieces, and featured a ceiling of sparkly foam insulation, 1969.

Bob and Lucy, holding puppies, Louise and Harold Mutt, on edge of Canyon de Chelly, Tsegi Overlook, Christmas card photo, 1969.

Chinle Headstart Preschoolers laugh at a good joke, probably having to do with their teacher, 1969.

Valentino Hadley, Headstart student, dressed as an Indian for Thanksgiving, eats lunch in the Chinle Chapter House, 1968.

Horse-drawn wagon passes Garcia's Trading Post, now the site of the Holiday Inn, 1969.

Harold Mutt and wife Louise share an intimate moment,1970.

*Lucy finishes the endless rug, which took nine months to weave,
every bit as hard as having a baby, 1970.*

(top) Lucy holds Matt in cradleboard, 1971— note arms sticking out.

(bottom) Verna Harvey Salabye holds Vaughn in cradleboard 1974— note proper wrap.

*Lucy with baby goat,
near Rough Rock, 1971.*

Matt and Harry B. Charley mugging for the camera, 1972.

Irene Teller starts a fire for lunch at the Tellers' land in Canyon del Muerto, 1972.

Ben Teller and Bob shove cement into the cracks between the logs of the cabin on the Tellers' land in Canyon del Muerto, 1972.

Lucy, Matt, and Bob in front of the nearly complete cabin in Canyon del Muerto, 1972

Lucy in front of Justice of the Peace sign marking the turnoff to her home office. The choice of pose, on the rarely ridden bicycle, was that of the newspaper photographer. (Arizona Republic photograph, August 1973).

Matt on his pony, Canyon del Muerto, 1974.

Matt in back of Bronco with harvest from the canyon, fall 1974.

Peterson Zah (later Navajo Nation President) and Nathan get acquainted. Peterson named Nathan "Little J.P." 1974.

Matt and Nathan enjoy the mud in front of the house, 1975.

Barbara Leigh and Joe Lewis, Hollywood starlet and Karate World Champion, after their marriage ceremony by Lucy on the rim of Canyon de Chelly, 1975.

Irene and Ben Teller, 1979.

Tanya, Aleta, and Adam Teller, 1979.

Eighteen members of the Amos Yazzie family visit Bob and Lucy in Santa Fe, 1979.

Irene Teller and daughter Tanya selling food and more at their concession near Antelope House, Canyon del Muerto, 2001.

Tanya Teller and son, Javis, 2001.

Adam Teller at First Ruin, Canyon de Chelly, 2001.

A reunion at the Holiday Inn in Chinle, 2001 (left to right), Verna Salabye, Ivan Salabye, Robert Salabye, Nathan Hilgendorf, Lucy Moore.

NINE

The Grassroots Wake Up

$\blacktriangle$

When we first arrived in Chinle, before DNA Legal Services had made its mark, most Navajos assumed we were VISTA volunteers, and it was not a bad guess. We had much in common and many became good friends. Volunteers in Service to America (VISTA) were mostly young, mostly white, and mostly eager to help disadvantaged people in some unknown part of the country, either urban or rural. Some had education or training in legal or health fields, and could help in law offices or clinics; some were simply ready to do whatever seemed useful. It was a domestic Peace Corps, and attracted the same spirit of adventure and good works. Some VISTA volunteers came and went relatively quickly. Like the DNA couple from New York who had fled the red dust of Tuba City, there were those who couldn't handle the foreign landscape and alien ways. Their own roles were often confusing to them and to those they were supposed to be helping.

We heard stories of a volunteer who had been assigned to the Forest Lake Chapter House, eighteen miles past Piñon on a dirt road. He lived in an abandoned hogan and learned to haul water, build fires, and generally survive Navajo-style. But he had ambitions for the community. He wanted to bring economic development to the area. He wanted to help start sheep marketing cooperatives, rug weavers' guilds, land conservation initiatives. He wanted to bring electricity and running water to Forest Lake and introduce them to the modern world. It was not that community leaders weren't interested in the same things. They probably had the same dreams. But it was inappropriate for this outsider to arrive with these big ideas and ignore the local pace and more immediate needs.

The volunteer went to his first chapter meeting, introduced himself, laid out several ambitious economic development options, and asked how he could help the community. His remarks were translated into Navajo and he, like many of us, probably wondered why it seemed the translation took three times as long as the remarks themselves, and why the "translation" included a lively back and forth discussion in Navajo among attendees. Finally, the chapter president turned to the eager volunteer. He said that they needed someone to sweep the chapter house floor before and after meetings and to set up and put away the folding chairs. That would be a big help. The volunteer was crushed. He performed these duties for a couple of months, and seeing that community members were not ready to let him advance any of his ideas, he left. He was insulted and disappointed. Had he stayed on a few more months...who knows? Maybe he would have persuaded the chapter to dig a community well. Maybe he would have fallen in love, married into a clan, and still be herding sheep. Or maybe Forest Lake would have become known for its perfectly swept chapter house floor.

Another VISTA Volunteer had set herself up in Many Farms, offering knitting classes for Navajo women. They could knit their beautiful hand-spun, vegetal-dyed wool into sweaters, and make much more money per hour than weaving it into rugs. She had done all the calculating. And furthermore she had connections with a department store in Dallas that would be interested in carrying the sweaters. All the women had to do was learn to knit! She sat in the room at the elementary school that she had reserved for three nights a week and waited for customers.

Two Anglo girls came who needed to earn Girl Scout badges for "homemaking" and thought that knitting skills might qualify. A Navajo woman came with a picture from a magazine showing an afghan for a new baby. She wondered if the volunteer knew where she could get that kind of yarn, with many colors in one strand, pink, blue, light green. Finally, a kind soul told the young woman why her classes were a flop. "Oh, you know how it is. Hopi men knit socks, so we Navajos don't knit." Her informant suggested that she might want to give cooking classes. "I always wondered how to make that macaroni and cheese, like we used to have in boarding school. I really liked that." The volunteer left on the heels of her colleague from Forest Lake.

Some volunteers welcomed these tests and stuck around, curious about this culture that would lust for macaroni and cheese on the one hand, and be in no hurry for electricity and indoor plumbing on the other. In Chinle four VISTAs—Jon Colvin, Bob Faxon, Richard Jones, and David Lundberg—moved into "Club 49" in Low Rent, set up housekeeping (sort of), and listened and learned. They volunteered in all kinds of places, at the school, the DNA office, the fire station, the chapter house. They were open and good natured, and although some locals wondered whether they were actually the dreaded hippies with a government stipend, many in the community welcomed them.

❖

In 1970, the tribe created its own VISTA-type program, DAI, which stood for Diné Ahilndáálnish, Inc., or The People Working Together. Funded with the same federal dollars, DAI was an effort to shift the direction and priorities of the volunteer projects to suit Navajo needs. The Anglo VISTA volunteers became staff in a sense to the grassroots community organizing effort, led by Navajo DAI volunteers like Leroy Mitchell in Chinle. The DAI focus was economic justice and consumer rights. Here they were in concert with DNA, and in Chinle DAI initiatives and DNA legal actions were often mutually supportive. The grass roots were sprouting.

In the Gallup area, heart of economic activity for so many Navajos from the central and eastern parts of the reservation, activists were also raising issues that attracted the attention of the power structure and support from DNA. Michael Benson, a Navajo who grew up near Two Grey Hills, half way between Gallup and Shiprock, had gone east to Wesleyan University. Just as my eyes were opened by leaving the eastern college environment and moving west, Michael was hit hard by moving in the reverse direction. He experienced the civil rights movement and was impressed by the passion and commitment of Anglos, who were determined to make life better for minorities in this country. And, for the first time, he met strangers—teachers and students—who were interested in him and his background. They were respectful and supportive of his ethnic identity, and he was shocked.

His first summer back from the east, in 1968, he attended a workshop organized by Southwest Indian Development Corporation (SID). SID was a nonprofit created by Navajos to build the capacity for economic development and social justice within Navajo communities. Their first board of directors included Peterson Zah of DNA Legal Services, educator Gloria Emerson, and community organizers Louis Tracy and Lorene Bennett (now Lorene Ferguson and a justice on the Navajo Nation Supreme Court). It was a powerful group and they were determined to fire up young Navajos to take responsibility for the betterment of their people in a variety of ways. Speakers at that first workshop included Acoma Pueblo poet and activist Simon Ortiz, Navajo activist Herb Blatchford, and Shirley Hill Witt, an Akwesasne Mohawk who at the time was earning her Ph.D. in biological anthropology from UNM. Blatchford and Witt had been among the original members of the National Indian Youth Council, created in 1961. For those like Michael who were ready to speak out and force change, SID activities provided inspiration and resources both within Navajo country, and outside.

The next summer, in 1969, Michael, along with fellow students June Tracey, Linda Hubbard, and Eddie Brown, took action. Outraged over its discriminatory treatment of Indians, they attacked the Inter-tribal Indian Ceremonial. Billed as "Today's Greatest Living Tribute to the American Indian," the Ceremonial was seen by Benson and many others as a blatant exploitation of Native Americans by the City of Gallup and a group of Anglo businessmen. The students appeared at the Ceremonial Grounds and distributed leaflets (which they had printed through the DNA Legal Services office in Shiprock) entitled "When Our Grandfathers Carried Guns" on the Ceremonial Grounds. Local police seized the leaflets, which were critical of the Ceremonial, and escorted the students off the grounds. They in turn brought suit, through DNA, against the City of Gallup for violation of civil rights and free speech. Ted Mitchell represented the four in Federal District Court in Santa Fe, demanding a public apology for the violation, return of the leaflets, and monetary damages. The students lost the suit, but they were not deterred.

The next August, in 1970, we went to Gallup to meet some friends and were drawn unwittingly into the Ceremonial parade route. My impression was not good. I remarked that the Ceremonial was supposed to honor the American Indian, but that the parade was full of row after row of glum-faced Indians from all over the country, trooping past squash blossom-bedecked Anglo women and bolo-wearing Anglo men who were shouting and gyrating to get the best photos. What kind of honor was that? The last straw for me was a group of Plains Indians, following a "buffalo," which was in reality a donkey with a hump-shaped wooden structure tied to its back and covered with a moth-eaten buffalo robe. I was very depressed.

Benson and associates, now organized as Indians Against Exploitation (IAE) and joined by Indian activists who had been occupying Alcatraz, demonstrated throughout the Ceremonial, demanding that the event either be put out of its misery or given over to Indian control. They had a broadcast system on a flatbed truck inside the grounds, and at one point the operators were arrested for "excess noise." They were also arrested for a staged sit-in at the office of Ceremonial Director Edward "Ike" Merry. Merry blamed DNA for instigating the demonstrations and criticized the Navajo Tribe for not setting guidelines to keep the legal services program in line.

By August 1971, the climate in the country was increasingly hostile to, and fearful of, protests, as civil rights riots and anti-war demonstrations intensified. In Gallup local leaders were worried about the young but seasoned Navajo college students who were the core of IAE. These activists used their mainstream education to defend their grandparents' culture, values, and traditional way of life. They were incensed that the

Ceremonial had gone on for fifty years and that many middle-aged, middle-class Indians tolerated and even supported it. They saw the event as a way for Gallup businesses to make money, sell liquor, and exploit Indian traditions, in particular those of the Navajo. Much of what happened at the Ceremonial was sacrilegious, they said. A snippet of the Yeibichei dance, for instance, was regularly performed in the grandstand, wedged between snippets of Kiowa war dances, Aztec sacrifice rituals, and Pueblo corn dances. The thousands of chattering and cheering tourists had no idea of the sacred and seasonal nature of the Yeibichei healing ritual. If the Ceremonial was to truly honor the Native American, they said, the board should be in Indian control so that these offenses would not happen.

IAE negotiated with the City prior to the 1971 Ceremonial, and agreed to a silent march before the official parade, peaceful leaflet distributing, and two loudspeaker locations on the grounds. About sixty people took part in the silent march, led by three traditionally dressed young Navajo women carrying a banner that read: "The Long Walk Must End," referring, of course, to the forced march in 1864 to Fort Sumner. The mayor had the National Guard on alert just in case.

One of the ongoing complaints from Benson and IAE leadership centered on Gallup Mayor Emmett "Frankie" Garcia, who owned one of the most dangerous and profitable liquor stores along the border of the dry reservation. The Navajo Inn, on Highway 264 just over the line from Window Rock, was famous for its remarkable and disgusting litter, its traffic fatality rate (thirty-six in three years), and its human dramas of sex and public urination played out for highway travelers to see. Recently a Navajo man had drowned face down in a mud puddle 400 feet from the Navajo Inn. DNA had brought suit against Garcia on behalf of six of the Inn's Navajo neighbors who regularly suffered property damage.

The drinking scene in Gallup was renowned. The UPI newspaper account of the 1970 Ceremonial featured a city report that "434 drunks, mostly from the nearby Navajo Reservation, had been arrested during the four day event" (*Diné Baa-Hani*, October 1970). Calvin Trillin wrote an article in the *New Yorker* (September 1971) that was highly embarrassing for the city and probably very accurate. Minors were routinely served; anyone who could crawl to the bar was served; and the jails (10,000 arrests for drunkenness per year) were disgusting beyond description. Those not incarcerated were likely to die of cold in the winter or be executed by a train if they passed out on the tracks.

By 1973, Gallup had thirty-nine liquor licenses, thirty-two more than allowed by law. A state formula permitted one license per 2,000 population, and with under 15,000 people, Gallup was entitled to seven. Albuquerque and Santa Fe also were over the limit, a phenomenon resulting from licenses grandfathered in after the passage of the law. Mayor Garcia declared that Gallup would not issue any new licenses until the population justified the current number, a date many decades in the future. To address its severe alcohol-related problems, the city formed the Gallup Inter-agency Alcoholism Committee, which planned to raise federal funds for a treatment center. In a particularly ironic move, the mayor became an active member of the committee, giving rise to conflict of interest charges because of his ownership of the Navajo Inn.

On March 1, 1973, the tension between the city and Navajo activists exploded, and the mayor was at the center of the explosion. Larry Wayne Casuse was a nineteen-year-old sophomore at the University of New Mexico, where he was president of the Kiva Club and active in IAE. With a Navajo friend, Robert Nakaidine, also from UNM, Casuse abducted Mayor Garcia and held him hostage in a Gallup sporting goods store. The act was to protest the city's treatment of Indian people, and to draw attention to the inappropriate actions of the mayor in dealing with Navajos. Besides his role in intoxicating Indians, Garcia promoted and hosted the degrading Ceremonial, and recently had been appointed to the University of New Mexico Board of Regents. Not even a college graduate, and symbol of so much pain for the Navajo people, in the eyes of the activists the mayor did not deserve that respected seat.

A member of the IAE Central Committee, Casuse had been a strong critic of the Ceremonial, and had always advocated peaceful protests, but for a variety of reasons he took this violent, fatal step. Friends speculated that Larry was in a difficult position, particularly as an advocate for the rights and values of the traditional Indian (*Gallup Independent*, March 22, 1973). He was considered an urban Indian, not raised traditionally, and unable to speak Navajo. His father was Navajo and his mother was German. Casuse in the end was Gallup's latest victim, shot in a confusing barrage of bullets that followed the mayor's flinging himself through the plate glass window onto the sidewalk in front of the store. It was never clear whether or not Casuse killed himself or was shot by a police gun, but in any case, he died in Gallup violently, and he brought the Gallup-Indian conflict into sharp focus.

In response to the tragedy, the *Albuquerque Journal* (March 25, 1973) ran a feature on "Gallup: City of Growing Indian Discontent." Middle-aged Indians, members of the mainstream establishment, spoke of the repressed anger they dealt with daily. These voices meant a lot to the IAE leadership, who had suffered from criticism from older Indians who accused them of being "un-Indian" and acting like white people, making trouble and a lot of noise.

"We older people," said Joe Savillas, a Pueblo Indian and BIA employee, "have always suppressed our feelings. Now they have started to come out in the open. Indian people get treated like dogs. In Gallup, they take all your money until they can't take anymore.... The bars for Indians here are overcrowded, the bathrooms are like filth. This is what we have against Gallup. The state should be inspecting these bars but the liquor interests are so powerful that nothing is done. And any time an Indian is killed, it's a forgotten matter. An Indian is just run down like a dog in this town and the police never do anything about it. This is partly due to the fact that we never spoke up.... We agree with everything the younger Indians in Gallup want, but we disagree with their methods... it is the Indian way to go slow and talk.... Looking over the whole Indian picture, sometimes I think the young ones are right, though."

One of the most painful parts of the Casuse death for Navajos was the publication in the *Gallup Independent* of a photo of his body sprawled on the sidewalk in a pool of blood. "You wouldn't do that to a dog; you'd cover up a dog," said an outraged middle-aged Navajo woman. The publisher, John Zollinger, defended the publication, "It was news, that's all. It was a news item." IAE leader Michael Benson said that attendance at meetings and demonstrations after the shooting increased dramatically, and the militant American Indian Movement (AIM) was rumored to be sending reinforcements to Gallup from their stronghold at Wounded Knee. Some Gallup citizens responded by buying new guns, or cleaning old ones, in preparation for a showdown.

But the crisis also provided an opportunity for Indians and non-Indians to negotiate and create some kind of workable future together. Gallup knew that its economic viability was facing new threats from Navajo activism and the ensuing publicity, competition from businesses sprouting up on the reservation, and DNA lawsuits against traders, merchants, car dealers, and police departments. Navajo activists knew that, although negotiations were risky, violence was only going to beget more violence. They planned a march that would end at Rollie Mortuary with a viewing of Casuse's body. The city had refused the permit to march, and the activists were poised to defy the police. In this setting, IAE prepared to negotiate.

The negotiations were not easy. IAE was pressured by AIM leadership to respond with force to the Casuse killing. AIM's Carter Camp hustled down from South Dakota and argued with Benson and others "not to be sissies," not to let themselves be pushed around. AIM would help local Indians create a situation to be reckoned with, as at Alcatraz or Wounded Knee. The federal Department of Justice was also present, with mediators from the Community Relations division, trying to promote a peaceful resolution. According to Michael Benson, who at that time was working at the Gallup Indian Community Center, they helped him have the courage to take a leadership role in the face of some stiff pressure from AIM. They encouraged local Indians to maintain control of the situation and make their own decisions about what course to take. In the end, AIM was rejected and local leadership prevailed. Negotiations with the City resumed. The march permit was issued, there was police protection for those who marched, and the result was a peaceful and powerful demonstration with more than 600 participants.

I was stunned by the Casuse shooting. Depressed and frustrated that Navajos weren't more outspoken and outraged by their colonization, past and present, I had been yearning for a little grassroots uppityness, and here it was. In a gesture of suicidal defiance a young Navajo did the unthinkable, and died as a result. Suddenly an uprising like those I had seen on TV in cities and at Wounded Knee was right in front of me. I was drawn to the march. I wanted to be there, to show support for the Navajo people who were discriminated against in subtle and not-so-subtle ways, and to mourn with the others the sad loss of Mr. and Mrs.

Casuse's son Larry. I left Matt with my friend Linda, who had agreed to support the cause by babysitting for me.

I parked north of town and joined the gathering crowd. It was somber and a little tense. No one knew what to expect from the Gallup citizenry or from law enforcement. There were very few Anglos, and I was glad I was there. Some Navajo events should be all Navajo, and Anglos should stay away. Others, like this one, needed other faces as well, to show that this was not just a Navajo problem. It was bigger than that. It was a justice problem. We walked silently. A few people had signs, but most just walked. Some, including me, cried. It was very moving, and I was glad that I had come.

Following the shooting, the city created a Gallup Indian Commission to ease tensions and address some of the problems that were now in sharp focus. Ben Hanley, a Navajo and remarkably an Arizona state representative, sat on the commission, along with young activists John Redhouse, Phil Loretto, Mitch Fowler, and Victor Cutnose. Hanley announced at a rally after the march that all bars in Gallup would be closed on Saturday in honor of Casuse's funeral. The last closing of the Gallup bars had been in November 1963 for Kennedy's funeral. Mayor Garcia closed the Navajo Inn for one month following the Casuse shooting. Some suspected that this move was more in the interest of the upcoming mayoral election in April than in the interest of respecting Navajo wellbeing or feelings.

Hanley also announced a new agreement among the state police, the city, and the Gallup Indian Community Center, whereby the center would be notified of any major trouble involving an Indian and would act as a clearinghouse for complaints against the city and law enforcement officers. The new commissioners were ready with a list of ten demands for the city, which they presented at the press conference that day. They asked for an immediate investigation by the U.S. Attorney General into the death of Casuse. They also demanded other investigations of civil rights abuses, health care services, education, and economic development in Indian country, and the release of promised but never delivered funds for a variety of programs. Finally, they targeted Mayor Garcia, demanding his removal from the Board of Regents and the Gallup Inter-Agency Alcoholism Committee, and demanding that he step down as mayor (*Gallup Independent*, March 5, 1973).

Bob and I participated in the official memorial march in Gallup on March 31. It was estimated that between 3,000 and 5,000 people participated, including spectators who spontaneously joined in. The event was remarkably peaceful, and very moving, and represented all kinds of people, Navajo and non-Navajo. It stretched more than a mile and filled both lanes of traffic. Greatly relieved city officials issued statements of congratulation to the organizers, the UNM Kiva Club and the Gallup Indian Community Center, for the law-abiding way in which the protest was planned and executed. The march was preceded by speeches at the Ceremonial grounds by Indian leaders, including Peterson Zah, now director of DNA Legal Services, and Chester Yazzie from the tribal chairman's office. Organizers urged non-violence in the parade, and provided Indian parade marshals to help keep the peace. Four organizations joined to present seventeen demands to the city relating to Mayor Garcia and the treatment of Indians. Sam Ray, appointed mayor for the day because Garcia was out of town, accepted the demands from the Kiva Club, the Gallup Indian Community Center, the new Gallup Indian Commission, and IAE.

The demands duplicated some of those submitted earlier by the Indian Commissioners relating to the mayor, but there were additional ones as well. They asked for the dismissal of Police Chief Gonzales "because he is responsible for racist police attitudes and actions as evidenced by numerous complaints concerning police brutality and general harassment." They asked for a citizens review committee to monitor and investigate police actions against Indians, and for the establishment of a liquor tax to fund treatment programs. They urged rescinding the thirty-two illegal liquor licenses, and putting a majority of Indians on the city's Inter-Agency Alcoholism Committee. Some of the demands from both the March 3 and March 31 protests were eventually addressed. The mayor, of course, held onto his positions and was re-elected in April. But the activists kept those issues in the public eye, where they belonged. Changes did come to Gallup eventually.

The marches, the negotiations, the press conferences and speeches of those years demonstrated that Navajo activism did not need to follow in the more radical footsteps of those who had occupied the BIA offices in Washington, taken over Alcatraz, or resisted at Wounded Knee. But the activists did have to walk a very fine line. By rejecting the advances of AIM and others who tried to capitalize on their struggle, the young leaders ran the risk of being labeled weak and passive by other activists. Yet when they stood up to the powers in Gallup and rocked the boat, they risked criticism from older Navajos who labeled them "un-Indian" because of their aggressive style.

Above all, this particular Navajo brand of activism was committed to the local grassroots and to their elders. Their protests included local leaders, and their speeches were translated into Navajo, or simply given in Navajo without translation. The target audience for their activism was fellow Navajos, particularly traditional Navajos, not the press or the outside Anglo world. DNA had helped those activists in a variety of ways. They had defended their right to free speech, had sued Mayor Garcia's Navajo Inn, and had represented several of the demonstrators in police brutality and discrimination cases.

❖

DAI, the Navajo VISTA volunteer program, was also playing an increasingly important role in nurturing the grass roots. In 1970 they began publishing an alternative newspaper, *Dine Baa-Hani*, which was an instant hit. The paper's masthead included a quote from John F. Kennedy: "Those who make peaceful revolution impossible make violent revolution inevitable." Staff and writers included Leroy Mitchell, Susie Wauneka, Leroy Keams, Robert Salabye, Verna Harvey, and cartoonist Richard Mike, all feisty young native activists. Some articles were reprints from elsewhere; some were written locally. And some were serious calls to action, with angry invectives against the white man, the government, corporations, missionaries, and mainstream poisons like alcohol, preservatives, and pollutants. The paper covered the Gallup Ceremonial issues and the latest lawsuits filed by DNA, and uncovered abuses by tribal government as well as outsiders. I was excited by the eloquent outrage in the pages of *Dine Baa-Hani*, and there was great Navajo humor in the comic strips *Super Navajo* (aka Richard Mike) and later *Lone Navajo*. The paper was in English, but for the first time I saw Navajo words in print, scattered here and there, not just to translate the

Bible, or to name a new laundromat, but to make jokes, make points, arouse passion.

One of the most effective joint projects of DNA and its grassroots cousin DAI involved attacking the illegal and immoral practices of many trading post owners on or near the reservation. Anglo traders had played a critical role in the life of Navajo communities for over a hundred years. They brought the latest in goods to the isolated areas, including canned food, flour, sugar, coffee, pots and pans, cloth, and tools. Usually fluent in Navajo, they also provided many services, reading and writing letters, handling mail, cashing checks, preparing and burying bodies, buying livestock, rugs and jewelry, and generally serving as a link between the outside Anglo world and that of the traditional Navajo. Their power was easy to abuse, and in a growing number of places traders took advantage of vulnerable clients.

By 1971, DNA was ready to mount a major challenge to the weak and rarely enforced Bureau of Indian Affairs trading post regulations. Some reservation traders were nervous that their practices would be scrutinized and their livelihood seriously curtailed. DNA and DAI realized that there would be repercussions for trading post customers as the traders felt the squeeze. Their strategy involved two fronts, reforming trader practices (which would probably put some out of business) and developing an alternative source of goods and services for Navajo customers who were dependent on the trader for so much.

On October 1, 1971, the Chinle DNA office led the charge against the traders, filing two class action lawsuits in Federal District Court against William and C. F. McGee and their associates. The McGees were owners of Piñon Mercantile at Piñon, as well as trading posts at Keams Canyon and Pollaca (both on Hopi land), and "Indian Curio" stores off reservation in Holbrook and Scottsdale, Arizona. The suits charged that the McGees violated the Code of Federal Regulations, the Navajo Tribal Code, and the 1969 Truth in Lending Act, which required merchants and traders to disclose to customers any finance charges, late fees, and the rate of interest, and to issue periodic statements showing the balance remaining on accounts, description of merchandise charged, and amounts paid.

DNA clients from Piñon complained that they paid on accounts, never knowing what interest was charged, and when they believed an account was paid, they were told that there was still—and always—more owing. It was also common for traders, and the McGees were no exception, to refuse to let a customer redeem pawned items until the credit account was paid in full. This enabled traders to keep pawn until it had expired, and move it to other outlets, off the reservation, for resale to wealthy Anglos looking for a good deal on a unique piece of handmade Indian jewelry. It was no coincidence that the McGees had a shop in Scottsdale, Arizona. Traders were also known to open credit customers' mail, sequester checks until the credit amount was equal or greater than the check, and then have the customer sign it over. Some traders used scrip, and gave change in gas coupons to be used at the trading post only.

At Piñon Mercantile, the reaction to the suit was swift. McGee threatened to cut off credit for those who didn't withdraw from the lawsuit. He circulated a letter for people to sign that stated "what a good man the trader is" and "how good he treats Navajo people" (*Diné Baa-Hani*, 12/22/1971). Senator Edward Kennedy flew to Farmington, New Mexico, for informal hearings on the problems facing Navajos in the areas of health, education, economy, and natural resource protection. Hundreds greeted the senator at the airport, eager to see a living member of the legendary Kennedy family. He met with a small group of DNA staff and attorneys, including Bob, who explained what they saw as abuses of the Navajo people. The McGees and other traders must have fumed with anger when they read the report of the visit in the *Gallup Independent* (January 3, 1972). Fuming or not, they settled the lawsuit out of court, agreeing to pay $32,500 in cash to their Piñon area credit and pawn customers and to stop all illegal practices. Bob, and John Silko, who brought the case, were pleased that their clients would see money sooner rather than later, and that the practices would end immediately, at least in that location.

Following the settlement, the Federal Trade Commission and the Bureau of Indian Affairs held hearings throughout Navajo country on trading post practices. Those critical of the system described an economic bondage that was as real, demoralizing, and degrading as the physical subjugation of the past. They painted a picture of a very powerful trader who served as banker, post office, finance company, hiring agent, retail merchant, adviser, pawn broker, and purchaser of wool, livestock, and arts and crafts. *Akwesasne Notes* (Early Autumn 1972), repeated some of the stories.

Carmie Toulouse, a social worker, said a trader in Two Grey Hills regularly underpays the Navajos in the area for their sought-after woven rugs. "They sell it to him for $25 and then the trader sells it for ten times that much," she said.

Mr. and Mrs. Tsosie said they received an extra $150 in their welfare check last month in order to buy their 11 children clothes for school. The trader refused to give the couple any cash, and applied all the money to what he said they owed him. As a result, the children have not been able to return to school yet.

According to Mrs. Carl Grace, the markup on most goods at a trading post near Leupp, Arizona, was 100%, and Anglos were given a 10% discount "to keep objections down."

Mrs. Velma Lewis complained about the unsanitary conditions of the trading post. She had seen a snake in the meat counter, and when she asked the trader about it, he said the snake helped keep the rats away.

Michael Benson also testified at these hearings, pointing out that the trader class had developed a dangerously broad base of power in Navajo communities, often being elected to school boards, county commissions, and other positions of influence over Navajo life.

A Shiprock trader justified his 25–45 percent markup on food and hardware, saying that carrying a large amount of credit was risky. He had grossed $450,000 the previous year, and cleared a profit of $30,000. This trader and others admitted that their financial records had never been audited by the BIA or the tribe. Traders leased tribal land and buildings for twenty-five years for a 1.5 percent tax paid to the tribe. They were reluctant, they explained, to make any investment in the property for fear the lease would not be renewed. The commissioners were particularly critical of Graham Holmes, former BIA Navajo Area Director, who failed to respond appropriately to the hundreds of complaints received against traders during his tenure (*Gallup Independent,* August 29, 1972).

Peterson Zah, speaking for DNA, told the commissioners he didn't expect any changes as a result of the hearings, since hearings in the past had produced no enforcement and no changes in regulations. Ernie Stevens, BIA Director of Economic Development, told Zah that within sixty days the BIA would produce a new set of regulations. At the hearings in Chinle and Piñon, the FTC announced that traders who had violated the law would be prosecuted and that some could lose their licenses. Some had thought that once new regulations were promulgated all past sins would be forgiven, but those hopes were dashed.

Near the end of that sixty-day period, DNA offered the BIA a set of regulations to govern trading post practices. The intent was not to eliminate credit, which they admitted was a necessity in many cases, but to provide for recording information by the trader and disclosure of that information to the customer. They also recommended that traders be required to notify those pawning items of the deadline for redemption of the piece and of the method of calculating late charges and finance charges. Before a piece is lost, the owner should be notified in writing, they said, and payment for the pawn should be made in cash not credit. The DNA regulations also urged tribal courts to take jurisdiction over traders on the reservation in order to insure more direct accountability and efficient enforcement. There were many other provisions, including an end to the postmaster role of the trader.

Not until June 1973 was the report from the FTC released. According to *Newsweek* (June 25, 1973) the report was "held up for months to spare the Administration embarrassment." Highly critical of trading practices and the lack of enforcement by the BIA, the commissioners recommended that supervision of the traders be taken away from the BIA and given to the Navajo Tribe. Finally, in September 1975, the BIA released new regulations governing traders. Although three years later than promised by the BIA, the regulations had been carefully developed, and the process had included not only the responsible bureaucracies but also DNA attorneys, tribal officials, and traders themselves. Peterson Zah was very pleased with the result and the process used to get there. The new regulations, he said, stood as a landmark not only in terms of legal reform, but also in terms of the best kind of cooperation among the people in this area (*Gallup Independent,* September 6, 1975.). The reforms addressed almost all the complaints that had been raised during the hearings. They also increased the traders' accountability to the community and customers. A trader was forbidden to take any kind of revenge, like cutting off credit, on a customer who complained to tribal authorities or to DNA. Traders were also required by regulation to attend tribal council, chapter, or other community meetings if requested by tribal leaders.

Happy with their victory, DNA staff realized that it was critical not to destroy a system that was serving a vital function without offering an alternative. A casualty of the war with the trader would be the Navajo weaver who brought a rug to the local trading post and received credit— often an amount unknown to the weaver—to be spent in the store. Although perhaps taken advantage of, the weaver was reluctant to lose this relationship. Without the trader, where could she take the rug? DAI had the answer. They worked with local chapter houses to create rug auctions, where the weaver could set her own minimum and receive 90 percent of the sale price. These auctions became very popular, both on the reservation and off. There were regular auctions in Crownpoint, Chinle, Tuba City, Kayenta, and occasionally in San Francisco, Phoenix, and Denver. Buyers, both locals and tourists, were happy to support the weavers and take home rugs at reasonable prices. The Navajo rug auction is now an institution in the Southwest.

As John Silko and Bob were readying to file the first suit against the Piñon Mercantile and the McGees, Robert Salabye, a paralegal at DNA, and Lynn Cianci, an IHS doctor's wife in Chinle, worked to help the Piñon community start a food cooperative. The Coop was an alternative for people who wanted to leave the traders' clutches but were forty-five miles from Chinle and much farther from a major shopping center. Diné Bi-Naa-Yei opened in April 1971 with a membership of 136. The opening was memorable. The food was late in arriving, but a medicine man blessed the empty shelves, and, of course, there was mutton stew and fry bread for all.

In its first nine months of operation, the Coop grossed $80,964 and realized a profit of almost $14,000. Part of the profit—$5,749—was allocated in dividends to the 470 members. There was a one-dollar fee to join the Coop, and for those who needed credit there was a federally chartered credit union, also with a one-dollar membership fee. A member had to have at least $5 in shares before he or she could borrow from the credit union. By September 1972, Robert Salabye had left DNA and was employed by Food Advocates of California on behalf of the Piñon Coop. That year the store grossed $245,322, and returned $17,910 in dividends to the members. By 1974, the Coop membership reached almost 900.

From this beginning was born Dineh Cooperatives, Inc., which today is a Chinle-based incubator for a huge variety of Navajo-owned businesses that provides technical assistance to communities needing economic development opportunities. One of those original VISTA volunteers, Jon Colvin, is still spearheading the work of DCI over thirty years later. Those who know and love Jon accuse him of staying in Chinle just so that he could accrue enough seniority to be the fire marshal and drive the fire truck in the Chinle parade, a dream that he fulfilled several years ago.

❖

Grassroots activity suddenly seemed alive everywhere. Activists moved to protect Navajo natural resources and formed the Committee to Save Black Mesa. The committee met every Thursday evening at 7:30 P.M. in the Chinle DNA office and advertised its meetings in the paper. DNA was not hiding from activism; in fact it was in full support. I was excited and pleased by what was happening, but I also had a slightly queasy feeling about the relationship between my roles as Justice of the Peace and as wife of a DNA lawyer. Being J.P. was not something I took lightly. Sure, it was amusing at times, and fun to be in a position that surprised myself and others. But the job was a very serious thing to me. I performed life-and-death duties; I was responsible for justice and for equal treatment of all under the law. I wanted to be sure that my DNA connections did not influence in any way my attitude or my actions with respect to anyone who might come before me. I felt sure that I could maintain integrity in office, but wanted to avoid any perception that I might be a tainted judge. I found myself consciously staying away from meetings of the committee. I helped *Diné Baa-Hani* to save Black Mesa by typing mailing labels and other tasks I could do at home. I hoped that my low-profile support was understood.

There were legal, environmental, and cultural reasons why the development of Black Mesa was a very serious concern for many. Navajo Tribal Chairman Raymond Nakai, in the belief that the salvation of the Navajo people was in the development of resources on the reservation, had entered into two leases with Peabody Coal Company in 1964 and 1966 for the mining of coal on 45,000 acres of Navajoland, 20,000 of which were in the Navajo-Hopi Joint Use Area. The lease period was thirty-five years, and the return to the tribe was twenty-five cents per ton for coal used off the reservation and twenty cents per ton for coal used on the reservation. The lease also gave the company the right to pump 2,000 gallons of water per minute from under Black Mesa for the purpose of slurrying coal to the Mohave Power Plant 273 miles away. The Tribe would receive between five and six dollars for every 325,000 gallons (one acre foot) of water.

The Committee to Save Black Mesa spoke for Navajos living in the area that was to be mined or that would be impacted by the mining. These residents had not been consulted by the tribe before the leases were signed. They were promised benefits from the mining, which were not coming to pass, and they were not told of hazards and damages, which were happening daily. Grazing land and watering holes were being destroyed. Runoff from the strip mining operations was creating sulfuric acid and contaminating watercourses and killing livestock. Construction of facilities and roads had interrupted irrigation systems. The air was foul with dust and fumes. The noise level for those living nearby was intolerable. We visited a client of Bob's, a family on Black Mesa whose hogan was dwarfed by the giant shovel that had chewed up the mesa in the background. As a final insult, Peabody reneged on its promise to hire local people.

The destruction of Black Mesa brought Navajos and Hopis together just at the moment that the government was driving them apart by means of the Navajo Hopi Land Dispute. Black Mesa was a shrine with great religious and cultural importance to both peoples. Anglos joined in support, and took part in a demonstration on the Mesa April 17, 1971. Kee Shelton's mother spoke and *Diné Baa-Hani* quoted her: "The noise and the ripping of land, trees, everything is taking the life out of us. This is not legal and you people who came from across the sea to slaughter our people, it is time to go back home. . . . When you destroy sacred land such as the female mountain, it is bleeding, it is helpless without us, and we are helpless without it. . . . We on Black Mesa never surrendered to Kit Carson, and we will not surrender to you." David Monyogye, a Hopi Traditionalist leader, offered a prayer and a corn pollen blessing to help the earth defend herself. He was jeered by Peabody workers in hard hats who stood nearby. Leroy Keams posed for the picture of the day, which became a symbol of resistance. He stood, defiant, rifle raised in one hand, in front of the huge Peabody earth mover.

In May 1971 the Senate Committee on Interior and Insular Affairs held hearings on pollution and electrical power plants in the Southwest, in Page, Arizona, near Black Mesa, and in Albuquerque, New Mexico. *Diné Baa-Hani* (May 11, 1971) ran an article urging testimony against the coal mining and proposed power plant construction, and offering van rides to the hearings. The non-Indian environmentalist movement had joined the effort, and both the Black Mesa Defense from Santa Fe and the Sierra Club in Tucson were organizing testimony as well. We went to the hearing in Page, and it was a powerful event, covered in the June 3 issue of *Diné Baa-Hani*.

Peterson Zah asked the senators: "Why are millions spent by the power giants to saturate the media with propaganda which seeks to increase the demand for electricity? Why is this money not being used for developing new and clean sources of power? Do people really need electric shoe buffers, toothbrushes, garage door openers, can openers?" Those who are using this power, he said, should produce it in their own backyards and leave the Indians alone. He pointed to the Four Corners Power Plant, in the Navajo backyard, and accused the utility companies of broken promises. "They promised to install the most advanced air pollution control devices on the smoke stacks. This promise was broken. You have heard the power plant people make many promises about improving the power plant, and they haven't. Do you really think they will keep the promises they are making to the Senate Committee?"

Robert Salabye also spoke. "The contracts with Peabody took place while I was in Viet Nam. It was done by trickery and misrepresentation. My community near Piñon knew nothing. Black Mesa is as sacred and holy as St. Peters Square is to the Christians. Why should we sacrifice our precious water, our holy element, for the deep wells of Black Mesa, when we badly need that water on the Reservation?" Relocating Navajos is no solution, he added. Leaving the remains of loved ones, and knowing they will be disturbed is a terrible thought.

The Hopis testified as well. Thomas Banyacya, a traditionalist from New Oraibi, criticized the Hopi Council for not consulting with tradition-al Hopi leadership before signing the contract. The strip mining, he explained, is a serious violation of nature, a wound to the heart of our mother, and Hopi prophecies warn that disturbing nature may bring on severe drought and famine. He held up a drawing on fabric that showed the elements of the prophecy and the uncertain future.

Navajo Tribal Chairman Peter MacDonald was eloquent. "The Navajo Tribe has thousands of eyes and ears that have lived and commu-nicated with the earth since our beginning. We see smoke, hear noise and feel any basic alteration to our land and water, being at one with nature." He went on to criticize the Department of the Interior for allow-ing the power companies themselves to prepare studies for the environ-mental impact statements newly required under the National Environmental Policy Act. "I have no doubt," he concluded, "that this committee will be holding these same hearings in this same building on this same subject ten years from today—except that ten years of oppor-tunity will have been lost. I, for one, do not want to tell my children why the legendary Window Rock has been blackened with fly-ash, why the sheep are dying from sulphur-oxide poisoning, why part of the Reservation must be abandoned due to the loss of an adequate water table. . . . We must stop all present and future development of power plants in this area until we are guaranteed that such operations are safe for human and animal life."

For me the most impressive speaker was Kee Shelton's Mother. Aside from the confusion among the Senators about how to address her—Mrs. Shelton? Mrs. Mother? Mrs. Kee Shelton's Mother?—it was a very serious presentation, in Navajo. She submitted a sworn statement as well. She closed with the following:

> Our prayers and healing have been tampered with and they
> don't work as good anymore. How can we give something of

value to Mother Earth to repay the damages that the mining has done to her? We still ask for her blessings and healing, even when she is hurt. They are taking water and other Holy Elements from her veins.... I want to see them stop taking water from inside the Mesa. The water underground works with the water that falls to the surface of Mother Earth. I want to see the burial grounds left alone. All of my relatives' graves are being disturbed. I want to see the mining stopped.

But Navajo communities, and even families, were not unified in their opposition to Peabody. Some valued jobs with the company, or held out hope for a job in the future. Many of the leaders at the chapter level and higher had been influenced by the company or bought off, and area residents felt abandoned and as if they needed to take their own defense into their own hands. Families were divided. A son told his medicine man father, "Shut up about Peabody. I don't want to lose my job."

In an ironic twist, archaeology students from Prescott College in northern Arizona were hired by Peabody to dig up graves in locations prior to strip mining, in order to preserve the contents. *Diné Baa-Hani* interviewed one of the students. "In a year or so all these sites will be destroyed with the rest of the land. I don't enjoy anything being destroyed." Mr. Hat, a lifetime resident of Black Mesa, saw his own father's remains dug up by the students, laid out for photographing, and then left there to be destroyed once again by the strip mining machinery.

DNA supported the Committee to Save Black Mesa against the actions of former tribal administrations and utility and mining companies, and filed lawsuits as well. In April 1972, Bob brought suit against Peabody on behalf of four Navajos whose traditional grazing area had been destroyed by the mining operations. DNA also supported the establishment of cooperatives and off-reservation markets for Navajo arts and crafts to offer alternatives to the trader's stranglehold. They criticized the Bureau of Indian Affairs and other federal agencies for violating trust responsibilities and for conflict of interest. The Bureau of Reclamation had entered into contracts, for instance, with the Bureau of Indian Affairs that deprived the Navajo Reservation of valuable water rights for its own use.

Nor was the Navajo tribal government itself immune to DNA scrutiny. DNA revealed that the tribe had entered into very bad deals over Black Mesa that netted the tribe less than half the income that would go to the State of Arizona, and that sent precious Navajo water in a coal slurry line to Bull Head City to run power plants and casinos. And there were the same civil rights violations at the hands of the tribal government that seemed rampant off the reservation. The new administration, with Peter MacDonald as chairman, offered hope. We saw a potential ally in the struggle for Navajo rights and empowerment. And at DNA there was a new administration as well. Peterson Zah, later to become Navajo Nation president himself, became director of the legal services program.

Ted Mitchell's departure in early 1971 to found a similar program in Micronesia did not reflect on the strength or the future of DNA. He had been a brilliant creator and inspirer, and the program was full of energetic and passionate staff who would charge ahead with or without him. Over 300 people had applied for the Micronesia position, and Ted was pleased with the recognition and excited by the move. He repeated his performance in Micronesia, perhaps a little wiser for the experience, or perhaps not. There were occasional sensational stories from the South Pacific about both his personal and professional life, some from former DNA staff who followed him and spent time with the Micronesian program. Ted died there in 2001. He left an important legacy, as well as dozens of legendary stories, and empowered populations an ocean apart.

TEN

Having Faith

The winter of 1971 had been a record-breaking cold one. On January 5, in sub-zero temperature, we attended the inaugural ceremony at the Window Rock Fairgrounds for the new tribal chairman, Peter MacDonald. It was so cold that the Marine Corps Band horns froze to the players' lips. It was so cold that Matt, who was already weeks overdue, decided to stay inside where it was warm for a few more days. The bitter wind whipped up under my pitiful polyester maternity dress, the only thing left in the closet that I could fit into. Navy blue with fake nautical buttons, it had once been a conservative (for the times) length, but now was raised well above the knee by the huge beach ball sticking out in front of me. Neither my high boots nor my parka helped address the problem; they both left the crucial region unprotected. I stood on the bleachers, witnessing one auspicious event, the birth of a new administration for the Navajo people, and believing that the other event, the birth of my baby, was never going to happen. I would be pregnant forever.

But one year and four days later, on January 9, 1972, Matt celebrated his first birthday. It was another cold—but not record-breaking—winter, and we were inside, gathered around Matt's high chair watching him plunge both hands into a round, white Sara Lee layer cake from Imperial Mart. Harry and Louise wagged happily, waiting for chunks to fall from the high chair tray, as they certainly did. We were all—two-legged and four-legged—a very contented family. Things were stabilizing for us. DNA was on firmer ground in this administration. Bob was able to concentrate on some of the systemic problems, and his victories benefitted multiple clients. By now I hoped I had seen what the Justice of the Peace role had to offer, and looked forward to smooth sailing in the future. We were working on good causes, like Black Mesa, and were beginning to see the grassroots sprouting in an exciting way. We had made friends, Navajo and Anglo, and even had a social life that included poker games, a movie rental club, cook outs and occasional golfing at the sand dunes—one big sand trap, said Bob. Perhaps, I speculated, these are the early signs of colonial behavior. One becomes comfortable and then does what comes naturally.

Matt was a wonderful companion, both indoors and out. He walked early, and loved to help feed the horses, goats, and chickens. Teetering and weaving, he was determined to conquer the harsh ruts and ridges of frozen mud that lay between the house and the corral. It was sometimes a long trip, but he helped me see wonders in that landscape that I would have missed from my higher elevation. He had friends as well, most notably Harry B. Charley, the son of Lilly Charley from Cottonwood, who babysat for us from time to time. He and Harry interacted under the watchful eye of Lilly or her daughter Lillian, who was about ten at the time. Lilly and her family became very important to us, and we missed them terribly when we left Chinle.

Ben and Irene Teller remained close friends. Their third child, Tanya, was one year older than Matt, and even though I no longer worked in Del Muerto, Irene and I saw a lot of each other. Ben and Bob were more businesslike in their relationship and cooked up a joint venture, which involved building a cabin in the canyon. We went into the canyon frequently with the Tellers, and Ben's hints—"Sure would be good to have a cabin around here"—were not lost on us. Bob agreed to buy the logs, and Ben and Irene would provide the land. Together the two families would build a cabin. In January, just after Matt's first birthday, Ben bought a home site lease just up the canyon from Antelope House Ruin. He was eager for us all to look at the site together and see if it would be appropriate for a cabin.

I was always ready for a trip to the canyon, but I was also beginning to think a little like a Navajo. I thought to myself, "Navajos don't drive into the canyon in the winter. There must be a reason for that. I need to understand this better, and respect the knowledge and actions of those who go before me." When Kee Yazzie taught me to drive the Headstart van on muddy roads, slick with a layer of chocolate pudding, he made sure that I understood the importance of stopping before driving into a mud puddle. Some of the puddles were huge, water covering low spots in the road that might have turned into a foot of ooze. "Look at that puddle. If you see fresh tire tracks going in and you see them coming out the other side, it's probably ok to go through. If there are no tracks going in and none coming out, look for other tracks that have gone around the puddle, through a field maybe. If you don't see how anyone got through or around that spot, then turn around. You won't make it." He was a very wise man. That advice covers more situations than driving in the mud.

And so I asked, "How come no one drives in the canyon in the winter? Are you sure it's OK for us to drive in there?"

"It's OK," Ben answered. "I don't know why they don't. They just don't. Maybe they're scared." And he laughed, watching Bob's reaction carefully.

"Well, I don't see why we shouldn't," said Bob, who was eager to get to work on the project, and who, for all his hours spent with Navajos, was more used to teaching than to learning.

Irene offered a voice of reason. "You can get stuck in there."

"Well, you can *always* get stuck in there," Bob replied quickly. "But Ben's the best driver around, right?" It was Bob's turn to laugh and watch for a reaction.

And, so it was that Ben, Adam, now eight, Bob, Matt, and I took the Bronco into the canyon, with no tracks ahead of us, on a very cold January day. We went early to take advantage of the frozen layer of water and mud on the surface. It was a beautiful, but eerie, trip. The cottonwoods were bare, with black trunks and branches against the sandstone walls, and the grasses were dried yellow. The canyon bottom was streaked with frozen rivulets, wet sand, and some patches of snow in the shade of the walls. The sun arced low behind a gray sky and shone briefly on certain sections of walls and floor. It was almost a black-and-white scene save for the red walls, which were on that day more cold than warm. Ben drove fast, cutting through the frozen strips with an uncharacteristic crunching sound. The sounds in other seasons were of splashing water, or of churning sand, or of tires on hard-packed dirt.

I was nervous, and as we rounded the last turn and Antelope House was in sight, I sighed with relief. "We're almost there, Mattie, almost there." He was on my lap in the front seat and I held him perhaps a little too tight. He hadn't made a sound the whole trip. I loosened my grip, and at that moment the Bronco dropped, crashing through a layer of ice, and sinking into the half-frozen sand. It was like ice cream, I thought later as hunger overcame me, exactly like coffee ice cream. Ben got out methodically and pulled the shovel out of the back. Silently, he began to dig in front of the tires, while Bob fussed with a broken jack, trying to imagine how it might help. Bob got into the driver's seat and randomly tried to drive forward or backward, depending, it seemed, on how he could best cover Ben with frozen slush. After a few minutes, Ben announced that it was not possible to dig it out and that he was leaving for help. He headed up the canyon, past the ruin, planning to climb up Baby Trail and get help in Del Muerto. The sight of him disappearing around the bend gave me an extra chill.

I already knew that this could be very serious, or at least very unpleasant. We had stupidly assumed that we would be back out of the canyon in plenty of time for lunch, so we had brought no food or water. I had stopped nursing Matt two weeks earlier, and had nothing to offer him except a half-size bottle of milk that I had planned for his mid-morning snack. I was sick with worry about how to deal with a hungry one-year-old once that bottle was drained. Bob kept struggling with the Bronco, digging, stuffing sticks and stones under the tires, grinding and whirring the engine, all to no purpose. He and I knew it was hopeless, but he needed an activity. Adam was a big help, gathering firewood, playing with Matt, and generally distracting us with cheerful chatter. We built a fire and huddled in what was a brief window of sunlight. I looked at the narrow opening between the Canyon walls, and knew that the sun would be making a very short visit.

I held off as long as I could giving Matt the bottle, and at noon I gave in. He drank it lustily, and fortunately fell asleep on my parka on a dry patch of sand. I dreaded the end of his nap, and when he woke up at 2:00 my heart sank. He was obviously hungry but was able to be distracted, and seemed somehow to understand that this was a time to be brave. Brave for a one-year-old meant not crying for food. He didn't. Another hour went by. We had been stuck since 9:30. What was going to become of us? Had Ben made it up that treacherous trail, now coated in ice in some spots? Wasn't it time for something to be happening?

And then I looked in the direction we had last seen him, and I saw what I thought at first was a mirage. Two people, not very big, were walking toward us. It was two boys from Del Muerto with a big pillowcase bulging with goods. Ben had made it home. Irene had sent the boys down Baby Trail, loaded with supplies for us—baloney and cheese sandwiches, pop, a thermos of coffee, a full milk bottle for Matt, dry socks for Adam, and two disposable diapers. That was another of my worries, no diapers, and I had already hung out a soggy one to dry in front of the fire for re-use if need be. I was never so happy to see a pillowcase, and to this day I have a special attachment to them. We were so enthusiastic in thanking the two boys that we almost frightened them back up the canyon. But we convinced them to stay, eat with us, and wait for the next stage of the rescue, which we were not sure was in our future.

Around 4:00 P.M., as the temperature began to drop, we decided that we should abandon ship and walk back down the canyon about three miles where we could hike up a relatively easy trail to the rim. We hoped to make it to the top before dark. Just as we were ready to set out, we heard the rumbling echoes of a vehicle. It was a Park Service truck, with towing rig. Ben was in the passenger seat. How could we have doubted him? They worked a long time and finally got us unstuck. Full of apologies and gratitude, we started the Bronco and with great delicacy drove out, with the Park Service truck behind us just in case. We later found out that we moved a little too fast on our way out, losing sight of our rescue truck, which itself got stuck and had to be rescued.

Later that spring we drove in again, to examine the home site lease and choose the location for the cabin. The trip was pure pleasure, and by that time we were almost able to laugh about the winter disaster. I never did understand why we had gone into the canyon in the winter, with no tire tracks ahead of us. But perhaps, looking back, there were clues.

When we stood on the land near Antelope House and exclaimed on its beauty, Ben asked us where we wanted the cabin. Bob looked around and asked how it would work to put it under a big cottonwood, away from the rim and near the road. Ben thought that would be fine, and it was settled. Years later, on a visit back to Chinle, Ben told us that he had moved the cabin. "That wasn't a good place to put it," he declared. "Too close to the rim. People could drop things on you." There was a deference to us about decisions that we were not capable of making. Perhaps that's how we ended up in the canyon in the winter. Perhaps that sheds light on the following cabin-building adventure.

The next trip into the canyon was for the purpose of delivering the logs and beginning construction. That day as we four stood staring at the stack of logs, deposited earlier by a lumber truck from Gallup, Ben asked, "How do you want to start?"

"Start?" asked Bob. "What do you mean?"

"Well, what should we do? What do you want to do . . . to make the cabin?"

"I don't know. You tell me. How do we make a cabin?"

"Well, you can make it however you want." Ben stared at the logs as if they might speak for themselves. He had built a beautiful, many-roomed log house for his family at Del Muerto, as well as numerous hogans. He could obviously build a foundation, put up walls, install windows and a door, affix a roof, and everything else required to build a simple cabin.

Irene broke a long silence, with a rather final "It's up to you" in our direction.

I was very uncomfortable. I didn't understand what was going on. We were city people, Anglos with no such knowledge or experience. We never pretended to know how to build a cabin. They needed to tell us what to do and we would do it. What were they thinking? I tried to explain, "We don't know anything about building a cabin or anything else. You guys are the experts, not us. You've built great houses and hogans. You tell us what to do."

More silence, more staring. Bob couldn't bear the standoff any longer. "Well, I had Lincoln Logs when I was a kid. You know, you stacked them at the corners, one on top of another. They stayed put cuz they had little chopped out places . . . flat places on each end . . . that's all I know. . . ." he trailed off, knowing he was just filling the silence with words, any old words.

I couldn't help myself. I laughed weakly. "This is crazy. You know about this and we don't. Please tell us."

Finally, Ben spoke, with a touch of stinginess, as if he was only going to reveal the minimal information. "Well, there are two ways."

We leapt at him, "Yes? Two ways? Ok, what are they?" The eager Anglos wanted what Ben and Irene had, and they wanted it bad.

"You can do it like that, like you said, with the corners on top of each other, or . . ." We were so relieved that the ice was broken we could hardly keep from grabbing him by the collar and shaking him to make him get on with it. He was deliberately and painfully slow. Waiting was a Navajo specialty. They waited for bureaucracies to move, they waited for the clinic doctor to see their child, they waited for wool to grow on sheep, they waited for the trader to calculate the debt, they waited for their pawn to go dead, they waited for the ceremony chant to end, they waited for a son to come home from Viet Nam. They were very, very patient, or perhaps they were simply good at waiting. Rushing was an Anglo specialty. We rushed through silences, through jobs, through meals, through conversations, through stories, through fights, through lovemaking.

". . . or, you can put four posts in the ground for the corners and then fit the logs in between," he finished the alternative. More silence. "If you do it that way, you have to dig really deep holes for the posts."

"Oh, right." We were so happy to finally be discussing building techniques. "So is it easier to do it the other way?"

"The other way, you have to make all those cuts in each end of each log. It's kind of hard that way, too."

"We'll do it however you think is better. You decide," I said.

"Well, I guess we'll do it with the posts," said Ben with more hesitation than authority.

"OK, great. We'll do it with the posts!" Bob and I were almost crying with relief. "What's first?" The Anglos rush forward.

"First, we better build a fire for lunch," said Irene. She smiled, a gift at that moment of understanding and intimacy.

It had been a strange and unsettling experience for us. These were our best friends. There were things that we were good at: the law, reading and writing difficult material, winning debates, dealing with the mainstream power structure. There were things that they were good at: surviving in Navajoland, building houses, growing food, fixing trucks, speaking Navajo. Wasn't that clear? Why did they defer to us so inappropriately, insisting that we knew how to build a cabin? Or, did they want to put us in an uncomfortable position, one which might be very familiar to them, where we would be asked to do something very foreign and strange, while the experts stand and watch? We never talked about it with Ben and Irene. But I have hung onto that image of us, squirming, feeling inadequate, our so-called superior skills getting us nowhere, knowing that there is a lesson there, a lesson about how it can feel to be Navajo.

Building the cabin was a wonderful experience that took many weekends that summer. The working days were always broken up with other chores, which were not chores at all—delivering a tractor part to Irene's grandfather farther up the canyon, near Massacre Cave, or watching someone's baby for a few hours while they tilled a field. Each Sunday we came home tired, satisfied, full of mutton ribs, fry bread, peaches and melon. The hardest part was pounding thousands of nails, tens of thousands of nails in at an angle, nails every few inches along the top and bottom curve, inside and outside, of each log after it was in place. That was women's and children's work, and Irene and I worked with Adam and Eva hour after hour, hammering this lattice work in place to hold the cement calking. Matt had a little hammer (and no nails) and he banged away on the lower row of logs, feeling, I hope, very much a part of the project. The cabin had windows and a door, and I made curtains. Before we put the wooden floor in place, Ben scattered broken glass on the dirt that would be below the floorboards.

"What's that for, Ben?" Lucy walks into his trap.

"Keep the snakes away," Ben lays the bait.

"SNAKES?! There won't be snakes in the cabin, will there?" Lucy takes the bait.

"Not if we put this broken glass in here. It'll keep 'em away... I'm pretty sure."

"PRETTY SURE?! Be-e-en, don't scare me like that!" Much laughter all around.

To this day, Ben teases me about snakes in the cabin, and I have to admit that thirty years later, I have yet to spend a night in the cabin.

❖

The next summer, when Matt was two and a half, we decided to go to the Hopi snake dance. On a scorchingly hot day in August we climbed into the Bronco and took off for Second Mesa. I told Matt this was going to be a special, special trip. After two hours, we unstuck ourselves from the vinyl seats, lifted Matt out of his car seat, and walked toward the pueblo. Every step created a cloud of dust. We could hear the dancers, the shells rattling, the chanting, and we hurried. When we reached the pueblo, and slid in between the buildings, we saw the small plaza still open in the center, but ringed with people perhaps fifteen deep. We were slightly above the crowd, not yet in the plaza, and could see that everyone was Hopi. The dances were still open to the public, but on this day, we seemed to be the only representatives from the outside world.

I was irritated that we were apparently too late to get a good view of the dance. I could barely see the tops of the heads of the dancers, and Matt, in Bob's arms, was no better off. I had hoped this would be an important event for Matt, an opportunity for him to absorb some culture, to be imprinted with the colors, the rhythms, the spirituality of a long and meaningful tradition. And here we were, pinned against the adobe wall with a sea of bodies between us and the action.

And then somehow the sea parted. People turned around and saw us, one row after another, and motioned us forward, smiling and stepping aside so we could pass. I was thrilled. How warm and inviting these people are, I thought. They understand how much I value their culture and traditions, how important it is for us to be able to see, how respectful and appreciative we will be. Silently we were passed from one row to the next, until we were in front, the very front, where people were sitting on the ground. I smiled gratefully at those around us, who scooted over to make room. We sat down, as inconspicuously as possible, ready for a powerful experience.

Six Hopi men were in the center of the plaza dancing around a large basket, which I imagined held the snakes. The sounds were mesmerizing. Matt was in my lap, still and staring. I was quite content, and probably a little too pleased with myself for initiating this significant trip. At my most self-congratulatory moment, the lid of the basket was raised, and the dancers pulled out the rattlesnakes. They held them in their mouths, right behind the head, and moved slowly around the plaza. I could see the snakes' eyes and tongues darting in every direction, and their rattle-ringed tails slowly grasped the air, as one dancer passed another.

What a remarkable sight! What an unforgettable experience! What wonderful, generous people! How lucky we were to be there! My mind and heart were filled with excitement and wonder. I patted Matt's tanned and chubby thigh. We are giving our son a remarkable experience, I thought to myself.

And then it happened. One dancer carefully released the snake from his mouth, and with a kind of pirouette, he turned and set the snake on the ground. It hesitated for a second, then took off, like lightning, straight for me—me, the one who so cleverly brought her family here, who was so fortunate as to find a front row seat, who was going to give her son an experience that would last a lifetime. But how long a lifetime would any of us have with a rattlesnake—no, now it was *two* rattlesnakes—on the ground, streaking toward us? This innocent little Anglo family only a moment earlier was so flattered to be ushered up front, and now the plaza was full of snakes, all rushing toward the audience, and two were headed straight for us.

No one around us moved or even flinched. No one cried out or even gasped. The scene was frozen, except for the snakes that were racing in slow motion, if there is such a thing, toward us. Bob was leaning toward me, whispering, also in slow motion, "Lucy, do something!" Foremost in our minds was Matt, who was sitting serenely, patiently on my lap, unaware that his tranquility was about to be shattered by a snake bite.

I was frozen. I pictured myself leaping to my feet, and, with Matt clutched tight, bolting back into the safety of the crowd. I pictured the commotion and disruption I would cause, the embarrassment I would feel. I pictured remaining motionless as the snakes neared us, and eventually bit us. I felt the bites. I would hold Matt up above the ground, so the snakes could satisfy themselves on my succulent thighs. And, finally, at the end of the split second in which I rehearsed these scenarios, I knew what I would do. I would simply sit there, as the Hopis were, waiting and trusting.

We had struggled for a front row seat, on the very edge of the action, and now we had a role to play. We had not understood that role, the part that we were auditioning for, but now it was clear. We were going to be the stoic, patient Anglos. We were going to be respectful, we were going to dig down deep for some kind of faith, faith that these people would not allow us to be hurt. It was a test, a very great test, and I didn't want to fail.

The first snake was inches from my hiking boot when it vanished into the air. A dancer had plucked it from the ground with a forked stick, and with the same pirouetting motion returned it to the basket. One after the other, they were all retrieved. We stayed at the dance until it was over. The snakes came out two more times, were released two more times, and retrieved two more times. And each time I reached a deeper level of trust, and with it came a serenity I am not sure I have felt since.

As the dancers left the plaza, and the basket of snakes was carried away, Matt turned around in my lap. "No more snakes?" he asked. "No, Mattie, not for now. No more snakes." We stood up, and dusted off our jeans. I smiled cautiously at an old woman who had been sitting behind us in a lawn chair.

She touched Matt's blond head. "He's a pretty boy," she said.

"Thank you," I replied. "And thank you for letting us sit here."

She laughed. "Oh, I like to have someone in front of my feet! Just in case!"

"But, they don't ever bite anyone, do they?" I asked, unwilling to give up my newfound faith.

"Oh, maybe sometimes they do." Her answer made me wonder whether sometimes they did, or sometime they might. But, I looked at her face, and decided not to pursue it. Her eyes were big, and her mouth was pursed, and for a second I could see her as a small child watching the snake dance, wondering and waiting. Maybe sometimes they did bite, maybe sometime they might bite. Each time was different. Each time she wondered and waited, and now I knew what that was like, to wonder and wait, to have faith and be rewarded.

ELEVEN

Bucking
the System

Having the Navajo Community College
so close, in Many Farms, was a great blessing. The courses were tempting, and what I learned was often more than was advertised. I took weaving, and learned that carding can be fun and spinning can be impossible.
My warp was thread-thin in some places, which was good, and thick and
lumpy in others, which was bad. When I was ready to weave the rug,
described earlier, I bought a warp from the weaving teacher. I figured
that given the weaver, my rug would be odd enough without using a
bulging warp.

Leslie, Linda, and I spotted a Beginning Ballet Class in the mimeographed catalog the second year, and wanting to regain our pre-baby
figures, we enrolled. It was one of the cultural surprises that awaited us
newcomers to Chinle, to find ourselves in the Many Farms High School
gym, moving through the first five classical ballet positions, arms frozen
in what was supposed to be a graceful pose, thighs screaming, chin held

high, and suppressing giggles. We loved our teacher, Ben Barney, a Navajo who went on to dance in New York, and eventually returned to teach at Rock Point.

And then there was silversmithing. Peterson Zah's father-in-law, Kenneth Begay,* was an outstanding and revered silversmith, and we were very lucky to have him as instructor at the Community College. I was determined to learn how to make my own jewelry, and invested in tools and a torch under his direction. Bob joined me for awhile, and we went weekly down to Many Farms to learn from the master. Mr. Begay's style was harsh. He apparently had not read my early childhood philosophy books about the importance of positive reinforcement and developing self-esteem and independence in the child. Nor had he read about fostering creativity in the student. He gave orders and we obeyed. He scrutinized our work, giving us criticism and orders to do something over, or if we passed, giving a faint grunt of approval. We lived for those grunts.

Once we had learned the basics of stamping, cutting, overlay, and soldering, we were allowed to make a bracelet. Mr. Begay told us to draw our design on paper first, and then bring it to him for approval before beginning the project. One young Anglo woman from California, who was teaching at the boarding school, wanted to learn the craft in order to express her creativity. She drew a very elaborate picture. She planned on making a two-inch-wide silver bracelet with a landscape in overlay, with grazing goats, a hogan, bushes, mesas in the background. She showed it to Mr. Begay. His jaw tightened, his eyes narrowed. He hated it.

"You can't make this," he said. It would be difficult, she admitted, but she was determined and this was what she wanted to make. He repeated that she could not make it. It wasn't a matter of being able to, it was a matter of having permission to.

"But it's my bracelet," she protested, her young, female, Californian feistiness on the rise. "This is what I want to make. It's my design. I want to make it."

"It's not a good design. It's bad. You can't make it."

They were both flustered and red. Mr. Begay and the young woman both realized that they were dealing with someone who offered no

---

*Begay's daughters, Sylvia, Kay, and Roz (Peterson's wife), all followed in his footsteps.

respect. They were equally headstrong and sure of themselves. He knew good design for Navajo jewelry and he was the master. She knew what she wanted to make and she had learned the skills and was ready to go her own way. He valued tradition and authority. She valued creativity and self-expression.

"I'm going to make it," and turning, she headed for her work space.

"I'm not going to help. I don't want to see it," Mr. Begay raised his voice ever so slightly.

She did make the bracelet. It was really difficult, especially with no help from the instructor. The goat's legs were too thin and the solder ran in between them; the bushes looked more like little explosions than vegetation; the hogan could have been an anthill. She had a hard time, but by the end of the term, she was wearing her bracelet and we were pretty impressed. We all told her it looked good, and added that it sure must have been a lot of work. Mr. Begay averted his eyes and never said a word.

My bracelet experience was a variation on the same theme. I had seen a bracelet in the pawn section of the trading post at Round Rock. It struck me as extremely beautiful in its simplicity. It was overlay, and the cut-out layer was simply a strip down the center of the band, with each edge scalloped. The result was an elegant band of oxidized black, defined by the silver scalloped edges facing each other. That was it. I was quite taken with it. I even dreamed about it.

I felt I was destined to make that bracelet. I drew the design and cautiously presented it to Mr. Begay. He looked at it awhile, and then said, "Put little balls right here," and he pointed to the negative spaces created as the two scalloped edges dipped toward each other.

"Well," I began, hoping to demonstrate enormous respect, "I was thinking it was nice just plain like this. I really didn't want to add anything." I added that I had seen one like it in Round Rock, hoping that this might give it a little authenticity that the Californian's design had lacked.

"You need to put little balls there," and he pointed to those spaces again. I could see what he meant, and it made some sense to fill in that black space with a string of silver dots. But I had my heart set on seeing it plain, like in my dream.

"Could I make it without the balls, first, and then see what it looks like, and . . ." I knew from his scowl that this was not going to work. I acceded, "Can you show me how to make little balls?"

"Yes, after you do the overlay I'll show you," and he dismissed me.

I was grouchy and felt pushed around. I knew what I wanted, and he seemed to think he knew better. The irony was that he *did* know better. I made the bracelet with little balls, put it on, and haven't taken it off for decades. The balls, now flattened on top with wear, make the bracelet just what it should be. I can't imagine it without them. I often think about Mr. Begay and what it means to be a master, and what it means to be a student.

Bob and I were perennial beginning students of the Navajo language, always starting over with different teachers, determined to break through and become facile if not fluent. We had let our Jim Parrish tapes collect dust, and now worked with a new book, *Navajo Made Easier,* by Irvy Goossen. The title said it all—it would never be easy, but maybe it could be easier. The verbs were overwhelming, and the pronunciation very foreign to our Anglo tongues. We clicked and spat out *tł'izi* (goat) a thousand times, trying get the right sound without drenching the listener. We nasal-ed and hissed our way through the slash "l" sound in *łįį'* (horse). We had piles of mimeographed sheets from Paul Platero, our teacher at the college, and from Stan Weaver, another teacher who was Mennonite and ran a trading post, a legitimate and service-oriented one, at Blue Gap. We learned enough to amuse dozens who crossed our paths, but we never got close to facile.

Bob was better than I about spouting out Navajo phrases without a lot of forethought. I was more afraid of embarrassing myself. He seemed to accept that that was inevitable, and perhaps even one of his roles in Navajoland. One morning during our first year, I stopped by the DNA office to drop off his lunch. I knocked on the door, and found Bob with Sam Gorman, a client who was a coucilman from Cottonwood. Bob wanted to introduce me to Sam. Showing off, he blurted out, "*Sam, nich'ooní, Lucy wolyé.*" He had meant to say, "Sam, this is my wife, her name is Lucy," but he was sloppy with the pronoun, and mixed up "*ni,*" which means "your," and "*shi,*" which means "my," in the process giving Sam Gorman a new wife. Sam's eyes got big, and he smiled a big smile, and reached out to claim his new prize. More proficient with pronouns than Bob, I knew immediately what had happened, and Sam and I pretended to play out the mistake at Bob's expense. By the time he left, the whole office was laughing about how Bob had given away his wife to Sam Gorman. Soon it was the whole town, I'm sure.

But this was a trivial mistake compared to what Bob was capable of. His finest moment took place downstairs in Fleming's café one hot afternoon. He had gone to the trading post to buy a carton of juice to help him get through the afternoon, and had walked through the café next door on his way back to his office. There he saw a client sitting in a booth, and stopped to say hello. Again, Navajo flowed easily from his lips. He thought he said to the man, "It's hot out today, isn't it?" But the word for "hot" wasn't quite right, and there were probably more subtle errors as well, and the result was that Bob asked his client, a tough middle-aged Navajo cowboy, if he was still nursing his baby. The restaurant collapsed in hysteria, while Bob patiently waited to find out what he had said this time. Apparently, the fact that he was holding a paper sack with what might have been a carton of milk peeking out the top added to the joke. I am sure that story is alive and well in the greater Chinle area today.

We socialized with some of the DNA staff and others working on social justice issues. Although the work was serious, the partying was anything but. There were cookouts and parties in remote areas where we could laugh as loud as we wanted and not disturb any spirits of a spiritual kind while we partook of spirits of the other kind. A group of us met a few memorable times near a canyon rim, and whooped and hollered around a fire. It was a miracle someone didn't fall into either the canyon or the fire. The dancing was wild, particularly when certain young native women took up the Apache Devil Dance, satirizing with razor sharp accuracy the moves of their cousins the Apaches. It was a real treat to be there, and we all laughed until we rolled on the ground. I envied my Navajo friends their ability to let loose completely and outrageously, at the expense of traditions of their own tribe and others. I held onto a little dose of guilt, perhaps appropriate for an Anglo, and hesitated to follow in those outrageous footsteps—hesitated, but eventually succumbed! The songs, made up on the spot, in traditional style but with contemporary content, often featured political figures or agencies in compromising positions. The BIA—"Bossing Indians Around"—received much abuse.

If we had some laughs in Chinle, I was not so amused when I looked at national politics. After almost four years of the Nixon administration it was election time again. Now that I was an elected official, and a Democrat, I was becoming a political animal. I participated in precinct meetings, and in January 1972, I was part of a slate of committed delegates to the state convention for John Lindsay. It seems like a strange choice, but he was making a point of paying attention to the disadvantaged of the country, and he even gave a special nod to Indians. He made a trip to Window Rock, and spent an hour with a few of us, including Peterson Zah, talking about his platform. I found him appealing, and surprisingly accessible and easy to talk with, considering he was an easterner in very foreign territory. He was clearly sincere in his concern for the problems facing Indian country, but his frame of reference was New York City, and that made for some incongruities.

The student body president from the Navajo Community College told Lindsay about the pollution of the reservation air, water, and land from strip mining and power plants. Lindsay was immediately sympathetic, but his first words were, "I certainly understand. We have terrible pollution problems in New York City, but we're working on them, with a lot of success." He went on about air pollution from cars, and said that he felt strongly that something had to be done about the proliferation of cars in this country. Attacking the motorized vehicle was not a winning platform in Navajoland, where the pickup was a member of the family. I was embarrassed for him. He meant well, but needed better advice before bringing the New York experience to Window Rock. Perhaps he had the same problem elsewhere.

After the nominating convention, we desperately wanted McGovern to win but knew he had no chance. We hoped for a good showing at least, and helped with the campaign, which emphasized decreased military spending and an increase in spending for health, education, and welfare programs. In Indian country, McGovern spoke of supporting Indian-owned businesses and economic development, and of expanded school lunch and food stamp programs.

Chairman MacDonald was supporting Nixon in spite of drastic cuts in next year's BIA funding for Navajoland. Teachers had already been fired, and classroom size was up to thirty-five or forty children. Welfare benefits were being cut, and there would be no new roads in the near future. I was disappointed that the Navajo leadership was spending time and money campaigning on behalf of Republicans. Nixon's passage of the Indian Self-Determination Act had made him a hero for many in Indian Country, and it was one of those quirks of history that he remains a hero for many Indians. The bugging of the Democratic headquarters seemed in the fall of 1972 to be no more than a cute prank to most people in the country. Watergate had not yet flowered.

But not all the Navajo interest in non-Indian politics centered on the re-election of Nixon. In June 1972, the newly formed Navajo Party announced a slate of candidates for the primary election in September. It was exciting to read in the *Gallup Independent* (June 12) that Peterson Zah and Arthur Hubbard were considering running for Congress and the State Senate, respectively, and that Ben Hanley and Milton Bluehouse had decided to try for the House of Representatives. There were other candidates looking at positions in Apache and Navajo counties. The response from Apache County was quick. "Navajos Reported Out for Apache County Control," read the headline in the weekly *Apache County Independent News*. This was in response to the Navajo Party's request for county nominating petitions, and for 10,000 voter registration forms. It was a wake-up call for the county, and it was music to my ears. I was more determined than ever to register voters who could vote Navajo in these state and national elections.

I was worried that the polling places would not be able to handle the swelling numbers of voters expected in November 1972. I had been busy, and Chester Yazzie, the Navajo Tribe's director of voter registration, was mounting a major push. A tally before the general election showed almost 3,000 registered in Chinle Precinct, and 9,994 in Apache County, a sharp increase from the 6,378 registered for the election two years earlier.

My worries were justified. On November 7, 1972, the Community Center, the one polling place in the Chinle Precinct, was overwhelmed. It was a cold and muddy day. People came in wagons from fifty miles and more to vote, most for the first time. Of the 3,000 registered voters in the Precinct over 1,300 had the patience and stamina to wait in line to vote. For most of the day, the wait was two and a half hours. The last ones in line at 7:00 P.M. when the polls closed finally voted at 9:15. I spent most of the day there, fussing over the lines, bringing people coffee, trying to speed things up at the point where people were checked on the one list of registered voters. I was also documenting the situation for the Department of Justice in D.C.

The day after the election, I wrote a letter to the Apache County Manager, Mr. Haws, describing the scene and asking for more polling places at the next election in 1974. The note back was apologetic. He said that the county "could see what was going to happen," but explained that state law required that polling places be assigned based on the registration numbers in November of the year prior to the election. At that point, the Chinle numbers had been much lower. Next time, in 1974, things would be different, he assured me. In a footnote, he also assured me the county would take seriously any suggestions I had for additional polling places.

I took him up on that invitation, and mounted a campaign that alerted all the communities in the Chinle Precinct about the opportunity to become a site for voting in the next election in 1974. I spoke at chapter meetings, contacted the councilman in each district, and just for good measure helped form a League of Women Voters chapter in Chinle–Window Rock to push for a variety of voting rights issues. I collected petitions from several chapters with hundreds of names asking for designation as a polling place. Councilmen pointed out the problem to county officials in letters from all parts of the precinct. In the fall of 1973, the November prior to the next election, the Board of Supervisors approved eight additional polling places for the Chinle Precinct at Nazlini, Tsaile-Wheatfields, Mexican Water, Red Rock, Rock Point, Many Farms, Rough Rock, and

Cottonwood. I was very pleased. I was also grateful to the assistant U.S. attorney general in the Civil Rights Division who responded to my report with carefully placed pressures on county officials.

The League of Women Voters invited County Manager Haws and County Attorney Hansen to come to Chinle to discuss county issues with the community. I said in the invitation letter that I hoped they would be able to come early enough to have dinner with us. They declined the dinner, but the meeting was cordial and informative, clarifying many misconceptions about the drain of money going in one direction or another across the reservation boundary. The county spent $600,000 a year on the reservation and received $690,000 from the reservation. They admitted that gasoline taxes collected on the reservation were spent almost entirely off the reservation, and that Chinle High School was categorized as an elementary school because its district included an elementary school, reducing the per student annual funding from $500 to $350.

In the meantime, DNA was suing Apache County for violations of the Fourteenth Amendment, the one-man, one-vote law invoked to remedy unequal districting. The three Apache County Supervisor Districts, each entitled to elect one supervisor, had the following populations:

District 1, St. Johns	1,598
District 2, south of St. Johns	3,905
District 3, all Navajo Reservation within County	26,984

This case seemed a sure thing, and it was. But before it happened, the County announced that they would rather split the county than risk having two, or even three, supervisors from the reservation. Bills to that effect had been introduced in the last two legislative sessions, but had failed due to opposition from the Navajo and Hopi tribes and officials from other counties. Tom Shirley, on the Navajo Party ticket in 1972, had won election to the Board of Supervisors. But he had been unable to take his seat because of a lawsuit claiming that he was ineligible because he did not pay county taxes, and because he could not be served papers by state or county officials. After a year of legal battles, he was now sitting on the Board.

The county split movement was under way. A St. Johns attorney, Harvey Platt, fueled the fire in February 1974 by declaring that Indians were not U.S. citizens. In a hearing before a state legislative committee considering yet another bill to split the County, he claimed that the Fourteenth Amendment did not apply to reservation Indians. Fortunately, this made inch-high headlines in the *Gallup Independent* on February 28. Navajo, and other, leadership decried the attempt to divide the county on racial lines, or to "put the Navajos off on an island." With 81 percent of the population of the existing county, an all-Navajo county would have only 57 percent of its property valuation. The bill failed, and its sponsor from St. Johns was ousted in the next election by Daniel Peaches, a Navajo.

That election, in 1974, was remarkable in many ways. Observers called the turnout "fantastic" and "unbelievable" (*Gallup Independent*, November 6). Over 5,000, or 51 percent of registered Navajo voters, went to the polls in Apache County. In Navajo County the Navajo Tribe's voter registration drive was particularly impressive. In 1970 one person had voted at the remote Hard Rocks Chapterhouse; in 1974, 336 voted there. In Dilkon, 2 people had voted in 1970; in 1974, 322. These numbers were typical in many of the most rural parts of the reservation. It was exciting to see those numbers and to know the Navajo voter was going to be a force.

An easy winner in the rest of the state, Barry Goldwater lost heavily in Navajo country, perhaps because of his seeming favoritism toward the Hopis in the land dispute. Raul Castro won the race for Governor by less than 5,000 votes. Navajos gave him about 9,000 votes reservation-wide. Ben Hanley joined Daniel Peaches as a new representative to the legislature from District 3. Navajo voters were becoming a force in state and local politics. Phoenix attorney Jack E. Brown, a loyal and generous supporter of Navajo causes and a DNA Board member, narrowly lost his bid for Congress.

In Chinle, I had my eye on the election process that day, although, because I was on the ballot myself, I needed to exercise restraint and not get too close to the action. I had been worried about the numbers of people who would need interpreters in order to vote. Although we now had an adequate number of polling places and voting booths, would there be enough interpreters to help people vote intelligently? I had planted this question in the ear of my contacts in the Justice Department and the Commission on Civil Rights, and had sent them copies of my correspondence with the County Clerk of Elections, Virgie Heap. I was hoping that the illiterate voter would be able to bring a relative into the voting booth to help out. This turned out to be possible. I wrote to the Commission on Civil Rights to report good news on the election process in northern Apache County. No polling place seemed to be overloaded. Bob was a poll watcher in Chinle. He reported that the longest wait was half an hour, and that interpretation by family members was allowed.

And so, I entered my second term as Justice of the Peace, pleased to be part of an electoral uprising on the reservation. My one reluctance, as always, was the prospect of more calls for the coroner. I had had a few more of those dreaded calls, following the suicide at Rough Rock. They were always difficult, but I was trying to convince myself that I was getting used to it. In one case, I was positively uppity. The Canyon de Chelly Motel called to say that the maid had found an elderly man dead in one of the rooms, and I was needed to determine if there had been foul play. I drove over, went in, and looked at the body. He was slumped, half on and half off the bed, partly dressed. I didn't see any signs of attack or struggle. The room had been locked and it seemed to be a death of natural causes. But there were dark blotches on his neck and upper chest. I didn't know what that meant. Might he have been struck, or choked, or poisoned? How did I know? I called the Public Health Clinic, and asked to talk to the doctor on call. I told him my predicament and asked him to come over and tell me what he saw. He refused. "What do you care? He's dead. I've got things to do over here."

I was not happy with that response. He sounded more uncooperative than busy to me. "I'm sorry, but I really need you to give me some advice. I need to be sure."

"No, I'm not coming," and he hung up.

I was furious, but not powerless. I turned to the Navajo Policeman standing outside the room. "I need help. Do you have an arrest warrant?"

He brightened up. "Sure," and dug around in his police car, emerging with one.

I filled it out, ordering the arrest of the doctor and that he be brought immediately to me at the motel. The officer hopped into the car and took off, as if it were a matter of life and death, instead of just death.

He returned in a few minutes with the doctor, who was very angry, but who did what I asked. He looked at the body and explained to me about pooling blood, and that those blotches meant that the man had been dead a certain period of time, and the blood had settled. He saw nothing out of the ordinary. I thanked him for his help, and the officer took him back to the clinic.

This may have been good for my power-hungry ego, but in general being coroner was not worth it. I joined other J.P.'s in pressing for relief from that duty. At the annual Justice of the Peace and Constables Convention in 1973 held in Williams, we voted unanimously to support the introduction of legislation to place that duty in the hands of a state medical examiner. The bill eventually passed, but not in time to spare me.

The annual conventions were always entertaining. I hobnobbed with my colleagues, exchanging stories and gossip, and getting tips on dealing with certain troublesome aspects of the job. That year we all wanted to hear from the J.P. in Flagstaff. He had just held a high-profile preliminary hearing involving the son of a prominent Phoenix attorney. The young man had been caught with drug paraphernalia outside Flagstaff, probably on his way to Tuba City, and had been brought before our colleague in Flagstaff. The J.P. was full of outrage over the whole case. The kid was a hippie, the father was a rich snob, and all the lawyers in his courtroom were pains in the butt.

"They all had lawyers there, the kid, the father, the police, the 'legalize marijuana people,' there were lawyers everywhere. Like to drove me crazy. They was jumpin' up and down, up and down, all the time, objectin' to this, objectin' to that. I couldn't hear myself think. I finally had enough, and I just banged my gavel, and shouted at one of 'em, 'You sit down and shut up, and don't you dare jump outta that chair again! And that goes for the rest of ya', too!' Well, that did it. They was all quiet as mice, and we could get on with our business." His story brought many sympathetic groans from the others. They all felt their lives would be a lot easier without those lawyers getting in the way. I told Bob that story, and his response was "Oh, boy, that's an automatic appeal right there."

Lawyer talk. I scoffed at him, and told him to sit down and shut up.

By that time Bob had lured me into yet another career, just as unexpected as the first. Border town car dealers generated hundreds of clients for DNA over the years. All the attorneys saw countless vehicle contracts thumb-printed by a buyer who was sweet-talked by an unscrupulous salesman. Typically, a Navajo family went to Gallup—or Farmington or Flagstaff or Winslow—to buy a truck. With little or no knowledge of English, they were very vulnerable to dishonest dealers who often charged outrageous prices for substandard products. A truck might have been seriously damaged, or repossessed, fixed up cosmetically, and sold for new. And, of course, the illegal repossessions continued.

There was another opportunity for unfair profit, and that was in the financing of the vehicle. Interest rates were as high as 20 percent and there was no chance that the buyer would have any access to any other payment plan. Finally, if the dealer wanted to squeeze a drop more out of the transaction, he could do so on the "insurance" line of the contract. A Navajo customer almost never came in with liability and collision insurance in hand, and of course he was not allowed to drive the desperately needed pickup out of the dealership without insurance. Hence, the dealer added insurance, through the financing company arm of the auto company, to the contract, and the customer, eager to get behind the wheel, thumb printed on the appropriate line.

The insurance rates were horrendous. If we, Bob and Lucy, paid $100 a year, these contracts were for $800 a year. Reminiscent of "Why is there no Justice of the Peace in Chinle?" I asked innocently "Isn't there an insurance company on the reservation somewhere?" The answer was no. In an area the size of West Virginia, there was not one insurance salesman—a blessing, some might say, but in this case, it was a tragedy. I did a little research. I contacted the Farmers Insurance Group, and inquired of their regional manager in Flagstaff if he thought the company might be interested in an agent in Chinle. His little insurance agent heart must have skipped a beat. Yes, indeed, he was sure they were interested. He came for a visit the next week, and left me with a pile of completely mystifying material to study so that I could take the Arizona State Insurance Exam at the next possible opportunity, which I did, in Phoenix late in 1971. By early 1972 I had a sign in the window of the livingroom/J.P. office, "Farmers Insurance Group—Home-Auto-Life."

Lloyd Siebert, the agent and regional manager in Flagstaff, was ecstatic. This was virgin territory, and someone was going to till it for him. I would get a commission for each sale, and he got a piece as well. And I did well for him, selling hundreds of policies in our remaining time in Chinle. People began to understand that if they came to visit me before they went to buy the truck, they could say "no" to the insurance offered by the dealer, and end up with a much lower monthly payment.

Besides, I found that with careful reading of the underwriting manual, I could qualify many Navajos for the "Preferred Farmers Rate." A non-smoking driver, of a certain age, with an unblemished driving record, who drove fewer than 30,000 miles a year could apply for the Preferred status, and save an additional 25 percent on the standard rate. I had an unusually high percentage of Preferred Rate customers, most of whom signed the application with a thumb print. I don't think the company had in mind Preferred customers who spoke no English, lived in a hogan, and were twenty miles from pavement—but then the application never asked about those things. And, after all, I *never* sold a policy to anyone in the two lowest, least desirable categories of customers according to the underwriting guidelines—divorced waitresses and itinerant musicians. Never.

Mr. Siebert was so pleased with my performance, and so impressed with the potential in Navajoland, that he urged me to push life insurance. Home insurance he was not so excited about. With no fire hydrants and an antique fire engine every hundred miles, insuring homes heated with wood stoves did not look like a smart move. "But, Lucy," his eyes lit up, "life insurance—that could be a gold mine!" He outfitted me with packets and rehearsed with me selling door-to-door. I was polite, and said that maybe I would try it, but I knew that there was no chance in the world that I would walk up to a Navajo door and offer the opener of the door life insurance. Many Navajos were superstitious about things like life insurance, believing that if you entertained such thoughts you might bring on the very thing you were trying to protect yourself against. No, I would have to disappoint my regional manager. I was not the company person he had hoped.

TWELVE

Identity
Crises

▲

Why would a grown woman eat an entire package of twelve chocolate-covered, dome-shaped, marshmallow-goo-on-top-of-round-graham-cracker cookies? I had walked to Imperial Mart, ostensibly for a carton of milk, and there they were, beckoning to me. I probably hadn't had one for fifteen years. I could give Matt a treat, and Bob, too. When I got home, I ate all twelve. They were so good, and I was so pregnant.

It was ironic. The day Matt was born, January 9, 1971, had been a record-breaking cold day. Now, in June 1974, I waddled around, pregnant, with puffy feet and sausage toes, knowing that my second baby would be born in record-breaking heat. Our good friends Alan and Sue Liebgott had a wading pool for their two little girls in the grass (!) of their PHS backyard. It was divine to sit there, laughing with Susie, in my maternity shorts, with my cotton sleeveless smock billowing out in front of me. Of course, there was no room for Matt and the girls in the pool, and when I got out, the water level dropped a foot.

And who was this mystery person I was carrying around with me? When I was pregnant with Matt three years earlier, Navajo women would ask me if the baby kicked a lot. I had no basis for comparison, but it seemed to me that I was taking an internal beating and usually answered "yes."

"It's a boy," was always the answer. "They're too rough!"

This pregnancy was a quieter one, and so my answer was, "No, it doesn't kick much, seems pretty quiet."

"It's a boy" again was the answer. "They're so lazy!"

Apparently boys couldn't win, and the prediction was right both times. Nathan was born on June 29 at the Project Hope Hospital in Ganado. He was a hefty 8½ pounds, apparently having enjoyed those marshmallow domes as much as I did. Bob and I were more relaxed about this birth, and the shoelaces traveled with us more as a totem than anything else. The trip to the hospital was little more than half an hour, and we arrived in plenty of time. Project Hope was a program for delivering health care to needy people around the world, and those who volunteered expected to be assigned to a Project Hope ship. If the ships were filled, then the leftovers ended up in Ganado, Arizona, a strange substitute. The doctor who delivered Nathan was less than enthusiastic. It was his last night on call, and then he was going to veterinarian school. I was probably the last human patient he had. But I didn't care. I had a new baby, another beautiful little boy, and all was right with the world.

The hospital was small and of the seven new mothers, I was the only Anglo and the only one nursing. It was the era of formula and many Navajo mothers were choosing the modern ways over the traditional ways. When we had arrived six years earlier, nursing was the rule. Now it seemed the exception. But I was committed—in truth addicted—and nursed Nathan until he insisted on weaning himself around fifteen months. He was a wonderful addition to the family, and responded to his surroundings, including a brother and many animals, with a cheerful outlook. He was Matt's understudy. He crawled after him, stood at his big round table and watched him build with blocks or drive toy trucks around. Matt had been given a name that included references to the cotton fluff from cottonwood trees and white hair. Nathan was dubbed "Little J.P." by Peterson Zah, who took a special liking to him.

That summer included more trips into the canyon, Nathan usually riding up front in my arms or Irene's. He enjoyed his time between the canyon walls, I'm sure, snoozing on a quilt in the dappled light under the huge cottonwood tree by the cabin, a soft, silent breeze fluttering the leaves and caressing the fuzz on his head. He nursed on demand, and was surrounded by adults and children ready to entertain, to brush away ants that threatened him, to take him for a walk in the carrier. Matt, at 3½, was finding his independence and spent hours playing in the sand, with Adam, Eva, and Tanya. The big event of the day for them was heralded by the rumbling sound, in the distance, echoing around the corners, of the Thunderbird Jeep Tour. The big open World War II convoy trucks brought tourists into the canyon twice a day, and we were usually there for at least one of the trips.

As soon as one of the kids heard the sound of the truck, he or she leapt up and shouted "Candy Jeep!" The others followed and they ran as fast as they could down to the open area where vehicles drove through that stretch of the canyon. They jumped up and down and called out "Here we are! Candy Jeep!" The driver, often an uncle or a cousin of one of the Teller clan, stopped beside them, giving the twenty passengers a chance to take pictures of little Navajo children, or in this case *mostly* Navajo children. Among the black-haired brown-skinned ones, scrambling for the candy the tourists tossed, was a little blond head, just as eager, just as worthy. It was not perhaps the photo op that was anticipated, and I am sure that, peering from behind the bushes on one occasion, I saw a photographer trying to figure out how to avoid that blond head in the lens.

Tourists provided a lot of educational opportunities for Navajo children in ways they never dreamed. I was driving a Navajo friend to Ganado to see the dentist there. Her two children, five and seven years old were with us, and before we even passed Fleming's, they needed a soda. I stopped the car in front of the trading post, and they ran inside. They came tearing back out the door, in too short a time, and empty-handed. Their eyes were popping and they were breathless.

"What happened?" asked their mother. "Where's your soda?"

"There's Indians in there!" gasped the older girl, and the two of them clutched each other in the safety of the car.

"What are you talking about?"

"A lady, a white lady, we heard her, she said 'Look at the little Indians,' we heard her."

We saw what had happened and laughed. "Did you see the Indians?" I asked.

"No, we just ran as fast as we could."

What followed was a brief lesson in race and culture, in which they learned that Navajos are a kind of Indian, and that the tourist ladies had probably been pointing at them! It was no wonder they had been confused. The most vivid impression of an Indian came from the old, racist Western movies shown monthly at the Community Center. Soon after our arrival we had gone to see *War Arrow*, and had been astonished to hear the entire audience, old and young, cheering for the cavalry, and shrieking in fright at the Indians. I suppose it was understandable. The Indians were certain-ly cast in a demon role, with war paint, tomahawks, strings of scalps—nothing more in common with the residents of Chinle than with me.

The mixup about identity was not limited to Navajo children. Matt, Nathan, and I went to a special meal honoring graduating seniors from Rough Rock Demonstration School. I was teary-eyed at the event. It was touching to see the young graduates, ready for the world, being sent off by an older generation in a traditional way. There were long tables and benches set up under a summer shelter, and grandmas cooked huge vats of mutton stew and piles of fry bread. There was also plenty of macaroni salad, Jello-O and marshmallow salad, cake and fruit.

I maneuvered two bowls of stew, for me and Matt, and enough extra fry bread to feed over my shoulder to Nathan, who was on my back. Now almost five, Matt was experienced in the ways of stew and fry bread, and also enjoyed dunking bits of bread in the stew and slurping up the chunks of meat. As he popped a piece of mutton into his mouth, he looked up from his bowl and spotted half a lamb, skinned, and hanging upside down from the corner post of the shelter. It was pretty graphic for a city slicker accustomed to securing meat shrink-wrapped in a styrofoam tray. I had adjusted over the years, and hardly gave the carcass a second glance. Matt, however, spotted it, pointed, and spoke from some place deep in his cultural identity.

In a loud and rather alarmed voice, he asked "What's that?"

Surrounding tables quieted and turned in our direction. I leaned in toward Matt, trying to keep the cultural commentary relatively private. "That's a sheep, sweetie. Half a sheep. That's what Navajos use to make the mutton stew. It's just hanging there . . . that's where they keep it."

He took in my explanation, staring all the while at the carcass that used to be a sheep. And then even louder, as if he had just reached an important conclusion, "*I'm* not going to be Navajo when I grow up!"

"No, sweetie, you're not," I said, amid much laughter. Anglos could always be counted on to be entertaining.

We attended a variety of traditional events during our years in Chinle, including a puberty ceremony, healing ceremonies of different kinds, and a squaw dance or two. I was even asked to officiate on behalf of the State of Arizona at the traditional Navajo wedding of our friends Ella Natonabah and Richard Jones. I was included in all the preparations, both the serious and the joking parts, and sat under the summer shelter with the family, witnessing the traditional ceremony and signing the marriage certificate afterward. The wedding of Robert Salabye and Verna Harvey was another thrill, a ceremony at Verna's mother's house near the Canyon Rim.

It was always an honor to be invited and we felt grateful to be included. But we were always aware that, although we were welcome, we did not really belong. There was a slight sadness to it, a feeling of isolation, but I never doubted that it was worth it, and that we were very lucky to see some of things we saw, and hear some of the things we heard. I had come to grips with being an Anglo on the Reservation, and had given up that quest for some special non-Anglo, almost-Navajo status. It wasn't going to happen, except in my fantasies, and Navajos didn't want it to happen. For them, our being Anglo was less significant than it was for me. They saw that we had chosen Chinle as home, and that we didn't seem to be on the two-year rotation schedule of the PHS professionals. Near the date of our second anniversary in Chinle, we began to receive visits from community members.

"It's been nice having you here, and we hope you'll come back for a visit sometime," we heard more than once. When we explained that we weren't going anywhere, that we were staying, that this was our home for now and we liked it in Chinle, the well-wishers were surprised. They assumed that all Anglo professionals would only stay as long as they had to and then would go back where they came from. In some cases, I imagine that was a day for rejoicing; in our case, I was glad that it wasn't. It mattered to people that we wanted to stay. They knew that we could be helpful to the community and to individuals, and that we seemed to have our hearts in the right place. That was all anyone asked, and I eventually understood that was enough.

Being helpful could look a lot of different ways. We had our formal roles, as lawyer, teacher, judge, and insurance agent. But as the years went by we learned that it was important to remain open to whatever other opportunities came along. Although picture taking could be a delicate issue, the Tellers asked us to take pictures of them and their children, to document those years for them. I made countless cakes for cake walks, wrote dozens of newsletters and flyers, and edited letters for people. I even taught someone to knit. Bob judged a Miss Chinle Contest (a strange and painful event), helped groups write by-laws, and guided students toward college. He responded to every request that he could. One, however, was too much.

John Rockbridge, always called Mr. Rockbridge, had been on the DNA board of directors from the very beginning, and always spoke up with great conviction and eloquence in defense of the work of the attorneys. He was a community leader, an elder, and medicine man from the Piñon area, and had widespread respect from Navajos at the grassroots and the governmental levels. He was a wonderful ally for the program, giving both spiritual and political support in generous amounts.

The first time we met Mr. Rockbridge was at a board meeting in Window Rock shortly after we arrived. He spoke no English, and did not read or write, but carried a briefcase to all important occasions where he might need to perform an Anglo duty. I puzzled over that briefcase and what might be inside. When the board members were required to sign a document, Mr. Rockbridge placed the case on the table in front of him, and opened it with all the self-possession and ease of a Wall Street lawyer. Inside were two things, a rubber stamp with his name on it, and an ink pad. That was all. He took them out and proceeded to sign the document.

We gave Mr. Rockbridge a ride to Chinle that day, and he spent the night with us in our little apartment. He talked non-stop in Navajo and we listened. It was quite remarkable all that we learned, or perhaps absorbed is the better word. There were some prayers and there were some jokes, and in between there were stories and commentaries on a wide variety of subjects . . . I'm sure. He enjoyed whatever we served, and when the watermelon was set in front of him, I asked "*Haash wolyé?*" for the umpteenth time that evening, trying to increase my vocabulary. "Waddymelon!" and he beamed a toothless smile. "Waddymelon!" I repeated. OK, waddymelon it is! In the morning, a nephew picked him up at the DNA office and took him home to Forest Lake, many miles past Piñon.

When Mr. Rockbridge died in 1974, Bob was invited to the funeral at Forest Lake, as a representative of DNA and as a friend. I decided this was not an event for the children, and stayed home with them. When he returned, he was shaken. It had been a very emotional experience, and the most surprising and upsetting part was that he had been asked to shoot Mr. Rockbridge's horse, which according to tradition was to die with its owner. Bob was confused and reluctant, and in the end said he couldn't do it. The horse was led away, he said, behind a hill, and he heard the shot. Bob would have done anything to help, but not what he was incapable of.

I had challenges as well. There was so much help that was needed, in so many areas, and there were surprise requests I filled as best I could. In October 1972, there were two suicides that hit me hard. One was Ned Hatathli, who some believed had accidentally shot himself cleaning a gun. That never made sense to me, but whatever happened it was a very serious loss to Navajoland. He had been a fine silversmith as a young man, and there is a photo of him in Laura Gilpin's *Enduring Navajo*, looking so quietly pleased, holding a silver bridle in his hands. He had become Director of the Navajo Arts and Crafts Guild, and then had moved into politics, perhaps an arena too harsh for him. He had been on the Resources Committee when the Black Mesa coal lease had been signed, and later became president of the Navajo Community College. There was enormous pressure on the few Navajo leaders capable of operating in both the Navajo and Anglo worlds. Some of them were inevitably extruded upward beyond their desire, and perhaps their ability. It was a terrible loss, and it came just days after my favorite Navajo policeman, Sergeant Yazzie, shot himself. He was knowledgeable, kind, and professional. He was polite with defendants, a rarity among law enforcement officers with whom I dealt. I was shocked and crushed. These were personal losses, and they were losses to the future wellbeing of Navajoland. That week was a week of steady rain, very unusual for Navajo country, and it seemed as if the mood of the community was mirrored in the gray drizzle. The mud—often a source of wonder and amusement—was depressing.

One afternoon that week there was a knock on the back door of the house. I went through the pantry and opened it and found a Navajo in his twenties standing at the bottom of the steps in the mud, soaking wet, drunk and desperate. I expected to be asked for a couple of dollars, or a ride to the store. Instead, he said, "I saw your sign [Justice of the Peace] and I want some kind of identification card." I told him that I didn't have any kind of identification card to give him, that that wasn't what the Justice of the Peace did. I asked what he needed it for to see if there was a way I could help.

"I'm a prisoner of war and I have to go back to Albuquerque to the Veterans Hospital. I was in Viet Nam and now I don't have any identification papers." The way he said "identification papers" made me understand that they were very important to him. Having papers confirmed having an identity, and the poor guy seemed to have lost both. He went on, "I went to the Census Office but they don't have me on their lists there, so they told me to go to Window Rock, but I don't have any way to get there."

He needed to get to Albuquerque for an appointment next Friday, and he was desperate for some kind of card. "Don't you have a card, some kind of card, any kind of card that says who I am?"

I explained again that I didn't have any cards, or I would be glad to give him one. I told him that if he went to DNA, the lawyers there could write up a legal paper for him, with witnesses and everything, that would say who he was. He was cheered up.

"Can you write me a letter for them at DNA, tell them who I am? Tell them about the identification papers?" he pressed me. I repeated that they could do it for him, if he just told them what he had told me. He began to cry. "Please write it down for me, so I can have a paper."

This was much bigger than I had thought. I invited him inside. I got a sheet of Justice of the Peace stationery and an envelope, and began to write.

"What's your name?"

He brightened. "Bobby H. Begay. Bobby *H.* Begay."

"OK, that's good. I've got it here." I continued to write. "I'm telling them at DNA that you want some kind of identification paper, right?"

He was pointing to the palm of his hand. "And here's a scar for identification. They use this for identification." He was talking excitedly, "And there are three more scars back here," and he pointed to his thigh. I made a note of the scars, and read him the letter, and then pressed my Notary Public seal at the bottom, just for good measure. He took it, felt the raised seal, and maybe he smiled faintly. He put the letter in the envelope, shook my hand in thanks, and went back out the back door. I watched as he walked through the mud toward the highway, holding the envelope carefully in both hands. Sometimes Chinle was a sad place to be.

But the clouds always lifted, and there were other knocks at the door. Although the tourist boom slowed down in October, and with it the traffic ticket business, the police continued to call with occasional problems. One of these problems was Arthur Williams. Officer Benally called one evening, almost hysterical, to say there was a "colored" man in the middle of the street by Fleming's Trading Post. A picture of his corpse in the middle of the street sprang to mind, but fortunately he was very much alive and apparently "jumping at cars" as they went by. I told the police to find an appropriate statute and arrest him, and I would see them in the morning, when hopefully Mr. Williams would have calmed down.

Next morning, very early, so they wouldn't have to feed him breakfast, Officer Benally brought the defendant over on charges of hitchhiking and clinging to cars. He was huge, at least 6'8", very thin, and moved in a kind of crazy, erratic way. There was a moment of fear, as the tiny officer brought him into my tiny courtroom, with tiny me behind my flimsy door-on-legs desk. Mr. Williams soon proved me wrong, as he began "ma'am-ing" and "I'm sorry-ing" so continually that I couldn't proceed with the arraignment. I used my gavel, which quieted him enough for me to advise him of his rights. I told him that I was going to read out loud the laws that he was accused of breaking, and that he should think carefully about whether or not he was guilty. Then I would ask for his plea.

"Yes, ma'am, oh yes, ma'am, thank you, ma'am."

I read the hitch-hiking statute, and as soon as I had uttered the last word, he shouted "Guilty! Guilty! Guilty!" I asked him if he really thought he had broken that law, and he "yes ma'am-ed" me into submission.

The second charge against him was entitled "Clinging to a Vehicle." I read the statute that prohibited hanging onto a moving vehicle while riding roller skates, a skate board, a bicycle, a wagon, and things like that. I couldn't help smiling at Officer Benally as I read it, because it obviously did not apply in this case, but was the closest thing he could find to "jumping at" cars. No sooner had I read the statute than Mr. Williams again shouted, "Guilty! Guilty! Guilty! I am guilty, guilty, guilty!"

I used the gavel again. "Now listen, Mr. Williams, I explained to you that I wanted you to listen carefully while I read these laws, and then think about whether or not you did anything wrong, and *then* plead guilty or not guilty." He listened and looked concerned. Hadn't he said "guilty?" like he was supposed to? What was I talking about? I went on.

"Let's take each part of the law separately, and you see if you did anything wrong, OK?" He nodded. "Did you ride on a skate board last night?"

"Oh, no ma'am, no skate board!"

"Were you on roller skates at any time last night?"

"Oh, no, no roller skates. No, ma'am."

"How about a wagon, or bike?"

"Oh, no, I was just on my feet, ma'am, just my two feet."

"OK then, how do you plead?" I looked at him very seriously.

He hesitated and said, "Not guilty?"

"Charge dismissed," I said.

After a moment of disbelief, Mr. Williams exploded in one long "Thaaaank youuuuu, ma'am" accompanied by much arm waving and head wagging.

I suspended the sentence for illegal hitchhiking and made sure that he knew the Arizona law on the subject.

He responded with, "You won't never see Arthur Williams in this town again, I promise you that, ma'am. Thank you, ma'am."

I tried to explain to him that that wasn't the point, but I gave up.

On his way out the door he picked up a comb on my desk. "Can I use this comb a minute?"

"Sure," I said, watching in amazement as he spruced up his Afro. "Thank you, ma'am. Sure appreciate it. Here's something for you. Goodbye." He returned the comb, with a handful of coupons for free slot machines in Las Vegas, and bounced out the door with little Officer Benally mystified in his wake.

My life was busy, serving as J.P., selling insurance, and being a wife and a mother. I tried to insure that I had some time for friends, too. I was surprised to find that language was not a prerequisite to friendship. Mr. Rockbridge had shown us that, but in his case he was such a personage that it was easy just to be in his presence and receive whatever emanated from him. It was a little one-sided, although totally enjoyable. With Eunice Lee it was different.

John Billie Lee had been a client of Bob's, in another illegal repossession, and his wife Eunice had woven a rug for us in appreciation of his help. We went out to visit them several times in their house just northwest of the junction to Piñon. They lived traditionally, with no utilities, in a compound of three dwellings—an abandoned hogan, a newer hogan, and a small rectangular one-room house, with a kitchen in the corner. *Kitchen* in this case meant a sink, filled with water from big Igloo coolers, which drained to the outside, and some shelves with dishes and pots. The wood stove was in the middle of the room, to maximize its heating capacity. John Billie and Eunice had several children; the oldest was fourteen when we first met them. Roger was born after Matt and before Nathan. Eunice was Verna Harvey's (later Salabye) older sister, and they shared a special beauty, a beauty that is still there in both of them. Eunice's face was smooth and peaceful, her teeth straight and strong, her eyes deep with experience and thought. She dressed traditionally, in velveteen skirts and blouses, and jewelry. Her rugs were the finest.

Eunice and I became close friends, although we had no common language, unless my very primitive Navajo counted. I have often marveled how that came to pass, that one of my closest friends is someone with whom I have had no real conversations, intimate or otherwise. We used her children, when they were around, as interpreters, and they allowed us to exchange important factual information, about a broken vehicle, a sick lamb, a trip to Gallup, a graduation from elementary school, the price of the new rug. But there were times when I went to visit, especially after Nathan was born, and simply sat with her, drinking coffee. We watched Matt and Roger play, we cooed over Nathan, or sometimes we just sat in silence. I absorbed the hogan sights and smells, as an antidote to a busy, materialistic life. I found it immensely comforting to be with her. I think that there was some mutual feeling of peacefulness, safety, and warmth that we generated for each other.

THIRTEEN

Tracks
Out

When we arrived in 1968, we promised to stay at least two years, to satisfy our obligation to legal services. Although we always assumed that we probably would leave some day, as the years went by, I, especially, began to entertain the idea of staying. Chinle was our home, we knew no other. We had begun our married life here. We had had babies here. We had grown here in so many ways, thanks to the generosity and/or perseverance of good friends and colleagues. Each day had been touched with some kind of experience that was valuable, perhaps frightening, enlightening, entertaining, or moving, but always valuable. How could we leave all that? And what could the outside world, the mainstream America, possibly have to offer us?

There were three answers. First, Matt would soon be ready for the first grade. Did we really want to subject him to the strange life of an Anglo student in the Chinle school system? One of Bob's first clients,

Frank, had shown us how tough and isolating it could be to grow up that way. We were also aware that any Anglo child in a classroom probably would be treated like royalty by the Anglo teacher. The teacher and the Anglo students tended to bond in a colonial rite, and the result could be a graduate of the system who had a hard time getting a grip on reality. Perhaps Matt should go to a school off the reservation. On the other hand, some of our closest friends, Winton and Tavita Dorow, who were non-Indian, had enrolled their children in Chinle Elementary School, and they seemed to be doing fine. But, the Dorows were a remarkably calm family, able to assume the best about everyone and make the most of every situation. Could we expect to live up to that standard?

Second, Bob was beginning to wonder about himself as a lawyer. To stay seven years with a legal services program was unusual. Most attorneys spent one or two years doing good, and then returned to a more normal career path. Bob wondered if he had dallied too long. He considered going into private practice, and talked with Louis Denetsosie,* the first Navajo to graduate from law school and pass the bar exam, about a potential partnership with offices in Chinle and Window Rock. Bob talked to Fleming about remodeling a space downstairs from DNA for a private law office. Fleming, of course, was accommodating and ready to expand his "professional plaza." But that left the problem of schools unsolved.

Third, tribal laws prohibited non-Indians from owning land and building houses on the reservation. We loved our house, although it did seem to be shrinking now that there were four of us, but it was not ours and never would be. Some (cultural) instinct to own property, to have security, to invest and get old, began to creep into our consciousness.

In late summer 1975 we decided to leave Chinle. Bob began to look for jobs elsewhere. He found a good one with Bruce Babbitt, then the attorney general of Arizona, in Phoenix. He was pleased with himself, and encouraged that he still was a marketable commodity. I nixed it. "I hate Phoenix. I'll die in that heat. I don't want to live there."

---

*Ironically, Louis had made DNA history with a remark years earlier. When asked what he was going to do after graduating from college, he had quipped, "I think I'll go to law school. If Hilgendorf did it, I sure as hell can!" Although he and Bob missed the chance to practice together, Louis went on to become the Attorney General of the Navajo Nation, confirmed in 2003.

A little exasperated, he asked, "OK, where *do* you want to live?"

"I want to live here! I don't want to go anywhere," and I burst into tears. I knew better, that we were leaving, that it was the right decision, but I didn't have to go graciously. After a while I reckoned that maybe Santa Fe or Albuquerque would be OK. They were at higher elevations so that my brain wouldn't fry, and they were close enough to Chinle to permit trips back. Bob dutifully pursued jobs with the State of New Mexico, and in October was offered the director of consumer affairs position at the Attorney General's Office. We would move in November.

There was a sadness and a frenzy that grew out of our decision to leave Chinle. The sadness played itself out in a variety of ways, weepiness seeing babies born that we would not be around to watch grow up, awareness that this would be the last fall in the cottonwoods, nostalgia in advance over every bowl of stew, every wild horse, every multi-skirted grandma. The frenzy drove us to try to do everything we could, to somehow stock up on experiences, as if we were setting out again, in reverse, for a long drive back across the Mojave in our Bronco. I imagined that Santa Fe would be a wasteland for me and that I would need to delve into as many memories as I could to keep myself going.

This was one reason that we embarked once again for Hopi land, to take in one last event of an unpredictable kind. We didn't know the exact nature of the dance at Second Mesa, but by now we understood that any trip to Hopi land was going to be exciting and worth it. We had seen dances where clowns pulled unsuspecting tourists out of the audience and made merciless fun of them, prancing around them, speaking a nonsense language that mocked English, dancing lewdly with them, all to the complete merriment of everyone, except perhaps the victim. We had seen dancers put young Hopi boys in chairs and force them to smoke giant cigars, to discourage them from ever even thinking about smoking. The boys were terrified and soon they were green as well. We had heard that a tourist at a dance at Walpi lunging for her purse, which a clown was dangling in front of her, had fallen off the cliff to her death. Another version of the story (or perhaps it was another purse-lunging woman) had her fall stopped by an outhouse perched several yards below. And of course, we had our own memorable experience from the snake dance the year before.

We plunged ahead, greedy for another Hopi adventure. We were more cautious this time about the location we chose for watching the events unfold. We stood in the back of the crowd. Matt was on Bob's shoulders so he could see. When we arrived, a "throw" was going on. The clowns were hurling every imaginable kind of food up to the roof tops and dozens of outstretched arms. It was a sophisticated welfare system, masked in a chaotic and raucous ritual of throwing food at people. I made sure that we were out of range of flying cans of peaches and boxes of cereal. Matt was enchanted. Nathan, in the carrier on my back, was enchanted that Matt was enchanted. Again, I was sure that this was going to be such an important and culturally rich experience for both my children, and again, I was veering dangerously close to self-congratulation.

The throw came to an end, the clowns disappeared, and the plaza was empty. Would something else happen? Surely this would not be the end. We took our cue from others, who stood and waited. After a few minutes a clown dressed like a woman, a rather slut-like woman, rode into the plaza on a donkey. Everyone laughed in a way that made us realize that we were a long way from understanding this one. Another clown dressed like a woman, this one fat and in traditional skirts, approached the slut-bedecked donkey. The two clowns began shouting at each other, in falsetto voices, and waving their arms and pointing in one direction and then another. The traditionally dressed clown pulled a large, rolled-up map out of a satchel and showed it to the other, with much gesticulating and cursing. The slut-clown dismounted—an act of great revelation greeted with much hilarity—to look at the map and make her own pronouncements. All this was in Hopi, and we couldn't understand what the story was about. But Matt and Nathan were very excited to see clowns playing with a donkey, and we all laughed along with the crowd.

A Hopi woman standing next to us explained that the donkey represented the disputed Navajo-Hopi land, and that the slut-woman was Wanda MacDonald, Chairman Peter's wife, and that the other woman was the wife of the Hopi Chairman. The two were fighting over the land, and that's what the shouting and the map were about. We were delighted to know the inside joke and thought it was all very funny. Matt was pointing, "Look, donkey can't see!" and when we looked back at the plaza to see the latest antics, a third clown was tying a scarf around the donkey's head, covering its eyes. Oh, how interesting, I thought, pondering the significance of the blind donkey, "the disputed land" unable to see. Hmmm, what could that mean? Bob and I got the picture at exactly the same moment. A fourth clown had arrived on the scene with a huge sledge hammer. The female clowns continued to fight, now in actual combat, wrestling on the ground, purses flying, high heels flailing, wigs askew. As Matt squealed with delight, Bob lowered him to the ground and we turned on our heels and headed as fast as we could for the car.

"I want to see," he pleaded. "I want to see the donkey." Nathan echoed, "wan-key?"

"It's OK, Mattie, I know you do, but we have to go now. It's time to go," I prayed we were moving fast enough. Just as we rounded the corner out of sight of the plaza, I heard a dull thud, followed by a burst of laughter, and the squealing of the two leaders' wives, dismayed to have lost their prize.

We had not understood. The food giveaway did not end with the throw. The next course was fresh meat. An event like that gave us food for thought, and a good story, for a long time. We were grateful—with that tinge of sadness—to return to our beloved Chinle, where the customs and culture were more comfortable.

❖

My last wedding as Justice of the Peace was truly a grande finale. It brought with it a culture clash, and again made me miss Navajoland in advance. In July I received a phone call from Barbara Leigh of Hollywood, California. She identified herself as an actress,* and said that she was engaged to Joe Lewis, the current heavyweight karate champion of the world. Being part Cherokee, she wanted to be married on Indian land, and she thought that the Canyon de Chelly would be just perfect. Could I oblige and perform the marriage ceremony? I was wondering if this was all fantasy—mine or hers—but as the weeks went by, we continued to talk, and nailed down certain details. They would have to bring the cake and champagne, and I would make reservations at the Thunderbird Lodge for

---

*In fact, her roles included starring opposite Steve McQueen in "Junior Bonner," and later she became Vampirella, the hostess of horror films.

their party of eight. They were bringing their own photographer, and Barbara would bring me something to wear, appropriate for the camera. I would pick them up at the airstrip when they arrived in their private jet.

The plane was scheduled to arrive at noon. Irene was going to help drive them to the motel, and she and I, quietly hysterical, sat in lawn chairs out in front of our house, with all the kids, eyes glued to the sky waiting for sight of the plane. Irene had Ben's truck and had told him that she didn't know when she would be home, that maybe she would send him a postcard from Hollywood. We were full of excitement, but no one more than Adam, now eleven, who had brought his two paperback books on karate—one a biography of Bruce Lee—and was boning up as if he were studying for an exam. He was a true karate nut, and could not believe that Joe Lewis was coming to Chinle. He was so excited, in fact, that he forgot to put on a clean shirt before they came down to Chinle, and he made Irene wash the one he had on by hand at our house and hang it out to dry on the line. Shirtless, he checked the line every few minutes to see if it was dry yet.

A plane landed at the airstrip at 1:30 and since Nathan was asleep, I told Irene to run over and see if they had arrived. We were all in a flurry, Adam putting on his damp shirt, Irene brushing Eva's hair, me scream-ing "hurry, hurry!" as if they might all get away if she weren't there when they landed. Of course, it was an ear-nose-throat doctor arriving for an ear clinic, and they all came back. But they had stopped at the post office, and fortune smiling on him, Adam had received his Bruce Lee karate t-shirt in the mail. He had been waiting for it for weeks, and it arrived just in time for this day of days. He put it on and beamed. We had several other false alarms before the right plane landed. And then we were off, Irene in the truck, I in the Bronco, and Bob, too, who jumped in the car after I called him at the office.

It was a big plane by Chinle standards—twelve seats. The door opened, and the passengers started to emerge—slowly. The ride had been rough, full of air pockets, and many of them, including the bride, had been sick. In order of appearance down the steps of the plane, were the trainer Joe Armijo, a jovial Chicano with a little soft-visored cap; Kathleen Quinlan, an actress, in a Levi culotte skirt and sleeveless Levi vest, and sporting a studied air of naturalness; psychologist Nathaniel

Brandon, older, a little heavy, who stepped off announcing, "Smell that air, Patreeecia, just smell that air! Isn't it wonderful? Let's go to the hotel and get some sun," with which he pulled up his polo shirt to his armpits, patted his stomach, and took a deep breath. Patreeecia was tall and lean, in jeans, but Hollywood jeans, no jeans I had ever seen, a little Levi jacket, and a lot of hair, tucked up under another one of these little Oliver Twist–type caps. A stage actress, she took long exaggerated steps and made sweeping gestures. Rounding out the cast were the photographer, small, blond-ringleted in cut-offs and a sleeveless undershirt; and the manager, talking non-stop in a thick New York accent, with a lot of "right, Joe, baby? huh?"s thrown in.

The Joe of Joe-baby, of course, was the karate champ himself, complete with shaggy blond hair, square Tarzan-like features, and very good teeth. He wore flared denims and a tight baby-blue knit shirt, muscles rippling underneath. I introduced myself to him, expressed condolences about the trip, and asked after Barbara. "Hell," he snapped, "this plane ride was *her* idea, serves her right." He adjusted his pants and threw out his chest. I shot a quick glance at Irene, whose face betrayed nothing.

Last to appear, head down, hair covering her whole face, was Barbara Leigh, the bride. She stood a long time with her head resting on the airplane wing. She really must have felt terrible to make an entrance like that, even at the Chinle airstrip. Bob eased her into the car since it was the most comfortable vehicle and took her straight to the motel. Irene and I divided the rest of them and the luggage, which was formidable, and followed. Adam was beside himself, and stuck to Joe Lewis's side like a barnacle. The Champ never looked directly at Adam. In fact, it seemed to me that most of them spent as little time as possible making eye contact with the outside world. Maybe that was what Hollywood did to you.

We left them in their motel rooms to get over the air sickness. The manager gave Adam a Joe Lewis medallion to wear around his neck, with Joe in a kicking position on one side and a blurb about him on the back.

The photographer and the pilot—both of whom seemed to be eager to start drinking—came home with us for gin and beer respectively. The pilot was conservative looking, with a tie (required by the charter company, he explained), and he didn't say much. He clearly wasn't part of this set. The photographer, too, was just there to do his job, which, he explained would not be easy, given the lack of organization and the tightness with money. Bob asked how he got the job, and he said that he had done Barbara's centerfold for *Playboy* a couple of years ago. He wanted to get out and see the canyon rim so that he could pick the spot for the wedding, based on the best light at dawn. He confessed that he would really love to do a nude wedding here, but he guessed that wasn't possible. "Well, filmy white gossamer blowing in the wind will work," he concluded.

We drove him to the Thunderbird where Irene joined us and we filled our vehicles for a trip up the rim. I was praying that they would not want to go *into* the canyon for the wedding, although I had been willing to do that when I talked to Barbara over the phone. She had sounded so sensitive to Indians, and so appreciative of everything Indian, and after all one some-teenth Cherokee herself. But I already realized that I would be very uncomfortable hosting this group from such a foreign culture in the mythical birthplace of the Navajo people. The rim would be close enough. I had no need to worry, because the photographer quickly announced that the canyon would be much too dark at dawn, wouldn't give any feeling of space, couldn't catch the rising sun behind the bride's head, etc. Good. We took them to Antelope House overlook. Nice, they said, but too far from the motel.

Back into the car. Bob and I are in front, the manager in back of Bob and the champ in back of me. The air conditioning is on, giving them the illusion of privacy, or perhaps they didn't care about us overhearing.

"Don't worry about the big fight in two days in Hawaii, Joe baby. You can kill him. Sure he's only 23, but you can kill him . . . this is good you're getting married, then to Hawaii to fight . . . real nice, real nice. . . ." He seemed to narrate Joe's life for him. "Barbara's quite a catch, you know, quite a catch."

Joe interrupts, "Quite a catch? You mean *she's* a catch for *me*?"

The manager had blown it. "Uh, Joe baby, I mean the two of you are really good for each other. She's good for you and you're good for her, you know what I mean, Joe baby?"

"Oh. Yeah." Silence for a while. "You know she's got manicurists and hairdressers coming to the house everyday? I can't keep supporting her *that* way."

"That's ok, Joe, don't worry about it, she can do those things herself, she's a good kid."

"Yeah, well, at least she's cultured, you know what I mean. She's got culture."

Joe was a North Carolina farm boy, who had learned karate in the service. He seemed to have picked up other habits either on the farm or in the service, like terrible jokes, sexual innuendoes, and a penchant for repeating himself. If it was funny the first time, it would surely be funnier the second time. Barbara, on the other hand, seemed to have an appreciation for where she was. She was capable of saying things like, "You know, the Indians used to live in those cave houses hundreds of years ago, isn't that beautiful? Look at the little farm down there . . . I love that green color with those red rocks."

We reached the White House overlook, and it proved to be a winner. Good light, good vistas, and close to the motel. On the drive back, there was an uncharacteristic silence in the back seat. I took a peek in the rear view mirror. The manager was tapping something out of a very fancy little cylindrical case onto the joint of his thumb and forefinger. I looked away, and heard a quick sniff.

Suddenly everyone was starving, and we dropped them at the Thunderbird for cafeteria fare. I was in shock, and needed to go home, to the warm, patient arms of Lilly Charley, who was cooking mutton stew and fry bread, in case the wedding party had been so inclined. Bob and Matt stayed and ate with them at Thunderbird. Matt, age four and a half, engaged in conversation with Nathaniel the psychologist, who later observed to Bob, "I think Matt may suffer from not being king of the castle since his little brother arrived." We took these LA insights very seriously.

At home, I worked myself into a frenzy of love for everything about Chinle and my life there. Bob seemed the most wonderful person in the world, my children were sensitive, kind and witty. My friends Irene and Lilly were the most beautiful, dignified, insightful people I could imagine. I couldn't bear to think of those Hollywood-ites intruding on any of this. They weren't worthy of landing on the airstrip. I was afraid that they would come back with Bob, as had been suggested. I didn't want to give them any fry bread; I didn't want them to see our house; I certainly didn't want them to talk to my Navajo friends. Uncharacteristically

inhospitable, I was desperately clinging to my Chinle life, trying to protect it from the outside world. The problem was that I was terrified by
the knowledge that soon I would be confronting, and perhaps slipping
into, that outside world myself.

When the car drove up I peered frantically out the window. Bob
and Matt were alone. I flung myself at them, covered them with kisses as
if we had all escaped some terrible disaster. Bob said, "Well, it's not over
yet," and he carried into the house the sheet cake ("Love Always, Barbara
and Joe" with huge orange roses), the bouquet (seven purple orchids),
and four bottles of champagne—all of which survived the plane ride,
and all of which we were to keep cold overnight.

I set the alarm for 4:45 A.M. I was instructed by the photographer to
be at the motel by 5:15, well before sunrise at 6:30, so that he could set
things up, and take pictures in the pre-dawn light. I had terrible dreams
all night—dreams of missing the ceremony, interspersed with horrible
things happening to Nathan and Matt—and jumped up with relief when
the alarm went off. I put on the robe Barbara brought for me—a kind of
gray-blue monkish pullover dress, with white cord tie. "It was hard to
find something priestly," she had said laughing when she gave it to me
the day before. I grabbed the bouquet, jumped in the car, and drove to
the motel in the dark.

There they all were, dressed and ready to go. I was amazed. Barbara
looked gorgeous, in a muslin-ish white long dress with wide bands of
elastic at the off-the-shoulder neckline, at the sleeves, and at the waist.
She also had on a huge squash blossom necklace, and as I handed her the
orchid bouquet, she said, "There are seven of them, look. Seven is our
lucky number." Joe had on white pants and a body shirt with a pastel
painting on it of a teepee and an Indian boy and girl. "His shirt was done
by a sixteen-year-old girl," boasted Barbara. The rest of the wedding
party was dressed casual-Hollywood, except the photographer, who had
on the same cutoffs and sleeveless undershirt. He could wear anything,
because he would be invisible behind the camera, and also because he
was really the most important person there. The photographer could do
anything he wanted to.

Joe had to stop at the pop machine in the Thunderbird parking lot
for a 7UP, and then we drove to the site. The photographer gave orders as

to who should stand where. We took pictures for an hour, as the horizon lightened. Everyone in the wedding party had cameras, too, mostly Polaroids. They took dozens of shots, and exchanged them and exclaimed, especially Patreeecia, over how great they were. Barbara, who was focusing on the real photographer, put on a winning smile and posed over and over. Her arms around Joe, light sky in back of them. Kissing Joe, light on their faces. Staring into Joe's eyes, moon in the background. Over and over. There were intermissions for another hair brushing, another application of lipstick, a little Murine for Joe's eyes. Joe was full of remarks like "C'mon out here, fella [to the trainer] and stand next to us . . . about ten feet to the left," which would have put him 800 feet down in the canyon bottom. He said the equivalent of this, using different victims, every ten or fifteen minutes. There was a lot of taunting from the audience, like "You're not getting *shot*, Joe! Why don't you smile!" which gave him the opportunity to say "rub it and I will," punctuated with a big laugh.

The sun finally peeked from behind the mesa, and Barbara abruptly said, "OK, let's do it." She struck a getting-married pose, checked Joe's hair, and I began. "Will you, Barbara, take Joe to be your lawfully wedded husband?" She paused, looked coy, and said, "I . . . will," as if she were really thinking about saying no, which I thought she should have been. Then she dropped her pose, and said, "Wait a minute, let me brush my hair, and turn a little this way." She flopped her head down between her knees, hair falling forward and Patreeecia ran up with a brush. When Barbara was posed again, we started over. "Will you, Barbara . . ." The ceremony took all of one minute—the kiss took much longer. I quickly excused myself to the sidelines where Matt, Nathan, and Bob, who had just arrived, sat sleepy eyed.

After more picture taking, more clowning around, and everyone kissing everyone else, we piled into the two vehicles and headed back to the motel for cake and champagne. Kathleen asked if she could hold Nathan, who was still half asleep, for the ride. I said of course and deposited him in her arms. I could see her in the rearview mirror as we drove away from the canyon rim. She was wedged between the photographer and the manager, looking wistful, as if she were touching something real. Or maybe it was my imagination.

While the couple changed into the cake-cutting outfits, we all wait-ed on the lawn in front of the motel. The trainer played with Matt and Nathan, teaching Matt how to say, "Gimme five," and hand-slap Hollywood style. Good natured and friendly, he was an LA cop when not training Joe. Nathaniel was enchanted that Nathan was named after him, and kept talking about "the little Nathan." He also informed us that Matt's body language was the same as his own, whatever that meant, but since we weren't addressed that often, we listened.

The couple reappeared in matching white pants, bright orange fringed tops, and she with a stylish head-band. The photographer saw them coming. "Oh, the film is going to *love* that orange!" he mumbled. They cut the cake, popped the champagne, took many more pictures. Nobody except us felt like much cake and champagne since they were all going to jump on the plane immediately and fly back to LA. The cake was delicious, and Barbara addressed me, "Lucy, there's so much cake. Would you like another piece?" I said yes, please, and helped myself. She looked vaguely around, at the staring tourists in the distance. "Would *they* like some cake?" Bob, never at a loss for words concerning food, said quickly, "I could take it to my office, the secretaries would love it." Yes, that met with her approval. Bob whisked the cake into the car. We weren't so lucky with the champagne. The two undrunk bottles went back to Hollywood.

The couple changed again, this time into traveling clothes—long limp lavender skirt and skinny lavender top laced up the front for Barbara. We drove the crowd back to the air strip, with only one stop for Joe, who made a last visit to the pop machine, this time for a strawberry soda. "We sure do appreciate all you've done," recited Joe. "Oh yes," added Barbara, "we couldn't have done it without you. When we get to Hollywood, I'm going to send you two Joe Lewis key chains for your boys. You know, with the little medallions on them." The photographer promised some pictures, the trainer said "gimme five" to Matt once more, Nathaniel took one last breath of Arizona air, Kathleen turned her frozen face to the sun one last time for a few more seconds of tan. They all climbed into the plane, seated themselves and turned their minds to the next destination, Hawaii.

We watched the plane take off. We went home and were just sitting down to one more piece of wedding cake when Irene and her mother, and

Adam, Eva, and Tanya arrived. Adam had a glazed look on his face, as he showed me a picture in one of his karate books of Joe Lewis holding a huge trophy. He touched the medallion around his neck. It had been a miraculous two days for him, and I was glad. We all ate mutton stew and wedding cake and talked about the big event. I had the feeling a myth was being born, right there in the kitchen, concerning the time the foreign beings came to visit Canyon de Chelly. "Well, Irene," I said, "that was a good lesson for us. Maybe we don't want to live in Hollywood after all."

"Well," she said thoughtfully, "I don't think they were feeling very well. Maybe if they hadn't been sick on the plane . . ." Irene was so kind, so gracious. I was missing her already.

❖

In the early fall, I sent a resignation letter to the Apache County Board of Supervisors, expressing my regret at not being able to serve out my second term as J.P., and thanking all involved for helping me grow in the office. I actually had warm feelings for my former adversaries. We had been through a lot together. I received a nice letter of appreciation. They appointed Florence Paisano, Bob's former legal counselor and school board activist, to take my place. Things seemed to be moving in a good direction. I told Lloyd Siebert, my Farmers Insurance regional manager, that I would be leaving soon, and he was truly sorry. A little reservation cash cow was moving on. I suggested that he encourage and train a young Navajo I knew to take my place. I don't think he followed through. I extricated myself from the Navajo Nation Health Advisory Board, and from the Chinle Day Care Center, which, in a final burst of energy, I had helped organize. The animals were a big worry. Matt's pony went to Eunice Lee's family along with two dogs and a cat, and a small trust fund to care for all of them. We had an enormous yard sale, and ironically sold the last of Bob's sports jackets, just as we were moving to a place where he could use them. We were both in a strange state of mind, not fully competent.

As we drove out of Chinle on a gray November day in 1975, I was filled with sadness. There was little, if any, excitement about the move. I felt as if we were going through motions, perhaps pointless motions, and that in a few months we would see the error we had made and would come back. But for now, we were leaving. Bob drove a Ryder truck and towed the car behind. He had Matt with him. At least someone was excited about the trip. Matt got to ride in a big truck at last!

I followed in the Bronco, with Nathan in his car seat, and Wanda, the one cat we decided to bring with us, yowling under my feet. I thought about that trip into Chinle over seven years ago, in the same Bronco, then filled with goods from Cambridge, including the reel to reel tape recorder with the Navajo language tapes. There were just two of us then, and we were sweetly ignorant and filled with excitement. We had hoped to do some good, and we had been ready for some adventures along the way. We were still outsiders, but we had changed. The experiences, the people, the landscape had all given us memories to treasure . . . mostly. The memories that made us cringe . . . well, they offered priceless lessons.

I remembered thinking on that first trip down the hill into Chinle, "Someday this strange road, these foreign features will be familiar, will be signs of nearing home." And now we were leaving, moving on, as I had suspected would happen some day. We were four, not two. The Bronco was stuffed, as it had been on our arrival, but this time with gifts from friends, toys and baby blankets, two cradle boards, a few Navajo rugs, and boxes of memorabilia. As I curved left across Black Wash on that familiar road, and headed up the hill out of town, I began to sob. Nathan was silent, staring somberly at me from his car seat. Wanda emerged from under my feet, climbed onto my lap, and peed. No one wanted to leave Chinle.

FOURTEEN

Tracks
Back

In July 2001, Nathan, then twenty-seven, and
I went back to Chinle. We both wanted to return for a visit, to check out
our roots, to make sure that we hadn't strayed too far. Although born in a
very different part of the planet, the Pacific Northwest, I had emerged, or
at least re-emerged in Chinle. I knew that the choices that took me to
Navajoland had been significant, and that I was a different person because
of those years.

For Nathan, Chinle was his place of emergence, his birthplace. We
had moved to Santa Fe when he was not yet two, but he had always
known that Navajos and Navajo country were part of his past, and
assumed they would be part of his future. He had always looked forward
to those long car trips, usually in the heat of summer, and the rewards at
the other end. Canyon de Chelly, the sand dunes, the lambs and baby

goats, the mutton ribs and fry bread, the funny stories about his parents, the warm smiles of recognition from Navajo friends who reabsorbed us into their lives for however long we needed or wanted to be reabsorbed—all these were part of his growing up.

There were times when Navajo friends came to visit us in Santa Fe as well, and I hoped that we were as welcoming and easy when the tables were turned. When Nathan was five, we had a visit from the Amos Yazzie family of Chinle. There were eighteen of them, from babies to grandmas. It was summer, fortunately. Some of them slept in their camper, some in the back of a pickup, and nine of them slept in our living room in sleeping bags, lined up on the carpet like sardines. Bob and I clung to our bedroom like a raft of security. Matt's room was so tiny no one expected him to open the door for any sleeping Yazzies, and he was able to defend his turf and treasures as any eight-year-old would hope to. I had carefully protected Nathan's room, which was spacious by Navajo standards and could have accommodated at least three or four on the floor. I felt that the whole experience of having his home invaded by a family of eighteen for a long weekend, and the quiet routine of the four of us disturbed, might be difficult for him.

In the morning, after the first night, as I was making a million pancakes in the kitchen and Yazzies were streaming in and out of the house, Nathan came out of his room looking less than happy. "Oh dear," I thought, "this has been just too much for him." He came up to me and stood close. Spatula in hand I bent down so he could confide in me.

"How come I didn't get to sleep with any Yazzies?" he asked reproachfully.

"Oh, sweetie!" I tried to recover. "I thought you would want your room to yourself . . . and I . . ." There really wasn't anything else to say except: "Tonight you can sleep with Yazzies, ok?"

"Ok," and he turned away from me to join the tide of Yazzies ebbing and flowing around the coffee and pancakes. That night there was one more sardine on the floor in the living room, and Nathan's room was empty. It was a good lesson for me. I may have wanted to protect my privacy—that luxury of those who could afford it in Anglo America—but for Nathan, this was not necessarily a desirable thing. He had indeed emerged in Chinle, and that red dust had left its mark.

❖

And so, mother and son made reservations at the Holiday Inn in Chinle, packed up the cooler, and headed west. We bought sun block and Cheetos, and admired the Hogger t-shirts and the coconut cream pies at the Giant truck stop just east of Gallup. We made the mandatory ritual stop in Ganado to honor the exact spot of Nathan's emergence, the Sage Memorial Hospital. I had sensed in recent trips that this was mildly irritating to him, that he had seen it once and that was enough. But, for me, it had become what one does on the way to Chinle, like looking for the tree that looks like a rooster just north of Burnsides on the right side of the highway.

The Holiday Inn was the "new" motel in Chinle, glitzier than the deteriorating Thunderbird Lodge near the mouth of the canyon, and the more modern Canyon de Chelly Motel, near the highway junction. It had been built eight years ago in what many considered—and some hoped—was the floodplain below the mouth of Canyon de Chelly. It had the Holiday Inn look, inside and outside, and it had a real restaurant with a real menu. Alcohol was still illegal on the reservation, and the ice machines did a brisk business before dinner. Tourists who had checked in with a variety of stylish pouches and satchels for the smuggling of cocktails, mixers, wine bottles and openers, lined up with their ice buckets and scurried back to happy hour in their rooms. I know this scene, because I was among them.

The Tellers were expecting us, and I called when we were ready for dinner and suggested that we meet at the Thunderbird Lodge. Nathan and I were nostalgic. We wanted to see the place that had been the site of so many launchings, adventures, and reunions both before and after we left Chinle. Especially, we wanted to go through the cafeteria line again. The decor had been redone several years earlier, and there were now chairs that rolled on wheels, carpet, beautiful rugs on the walls, and even little niches for Kachina dolls. But the food line was unchanged, both in terms of structure and offerings. We salivated for the mutton stew, and knew that we would end up choosing a cream pie for dessert.

We pulled into the parking lot, and there waiting in and around an SUV were Irene and Tanya, Tanya's husband Jarvis, and their five children between eighteen months and thirteen years old. It was wonderful to see them. Irene and I hugged and cried. Tanya took over and chattered introductions of her children. The youngest, Javis, was a twin, she explained matter-of-factly but not hiding raw grief. His brother was stillborn. It had been a terrible experience. She had been in the hospital in Phoenix and then Flagstaff during much of the pregnancy. She begged the doctors toward the end to take the babies out; she knew that one of them was in trouble. She could feel it. They waited, saying that the longer they could wait the bigger they would be. They waited too long, and when they delivered the twins by Caesarean section, one was already dead. It was no surprise to her. She knew it. She felt it, she told me later as we were eating our chocolate cream pie.

By this time, we had been joined by Adam, his wife and two children, and Aleta—it was hard for me not to call her Eva, her name when she was in my Headstart class—and her husband and daughter. Ben arrived last, clearly a natural born grandpa. Little Arianna leapt into his arms, dropping her spoonful of Jell-O without a second thought.

I noticed a change in eating habits. Irene was eating salad and a piece of fish. Her children were making sure that their children were drinking milk and juice, not Cokes and Sprites. Everyone had a little dish of fruit or a slice of melon. Sure, there were puddings, pies, and cakes on the trays as well, but they were proportionally a less major part of the food intake than in the past. Irene explained that she had been diagnosed with diabetes. Not the kind that meant shots, she added, but the kind that meant she had to eat a better diet. She was trying, and she was making sure that her grandkids had better habits, too.

Nathan was content. I noticed how comfortable he was in this setting, where people let you be and accepted how you were. There were no questions fired at him about what he was doing, what his plans were, what he thought about Chinle, did he like it better than Santa Fe, did he have a girlfriend, was he going to get married. I had always admired and appreciated that patience and calm among Navajo friends, and there were times when it had been invaluable to me. There are also times when I emulate that way of being and treating others. It is a powerful thing.

But that July night at the Thunderbird Lodge I was my exuberant and excited Anglo self. Although I deliberately did not pry into the children, I did a healthy amount of oohing and aahing. I gasped and exclaimed over adventures and near-misses, I emoted abundantly over tragedies, I laughed heartily, especially at myself, as we told some of our favorite stories from years ago. It was a good feeling, to be so accepted and included, and be able to be myself, whatever strange mixture of Seattle-raised and Navajo-re-emerged that might have produced.

In the morning, Tanya and Jarvis arrived in their SUV and picked us up to go into the canyon. We were going to be part of their Saturday routine. This began with a dash to Bashas for a few things, and a quick gas stop, and then a stop at the Park Service to sign Nathan and me in, as guests of Tanya's for the day. There was that old feeling of specialness as I stood in the Visitors' Center and looked at the tourists. They were milling around, glancing at the exhibits, wondering where they were, and what to expect. I knew where I was, I had Navajo friends, close friends, and I knew what to expect. At least, I used to know what to expect.

Back in the SUV, we headed for the canyon. Aleta and her daughter were now following us, and some of Tanya's kids had jumped into the back of their auntie's pickup. We bumped through the cottonwoods that border the canyon mouth, and just before we left the hard ground and sank into the sand of the canyon bottom Tanya gunned the accelerator. It was such a familiar feeling, from dozens of trips with her father or mother at the wheel of the old Ford Pick-up, or even at the Bronco wheel myself more than a few times. It's a feeling of excitement, because the canyon is always an unknown. You may get stuck, you may help dig someone else out who got stuck, you may pick up a friend or relative, you may find your melons have ripened or have been stolen.

It's also a feeling of timelessness, especially if you are in the back of a pickup. You are entering a space that is ancient, and somehow the time is ancient, too. It moves differently here. Anticipating this environment always makes my heart skip a beat, my throat tighten, and my eyes tear up. Maybe it's the blast of dry wind as we shoot forward . . . but I don't think so. I leaned back, looked up, and watched the canyon walls, with their chocolate streaks, rise around me.

We arrived at Antelope House, bumped the vehicles up out of the sand onto the hard–packed dirt and parked near the cabin. It was still there, waiting for Lucy to spend the night, waiting for Ben to see the skin walker. I glanced at it, not sure if I wanted to reconnect or not. It was the site of such good and profound times, and the logs, the cement chinks, the curtains, everything had a powerful message. I wasn't sure I wanted to listen at that moment. And I needn't have worried. Nathan and I were immediately put to work. Tanya and her crew were running a little late this morning, and we had to hurry to be ready before the first jeep load of tourists arrived.

The last time I had been in the canyon with Irene and Tanya, about four years earlier, they were selling jewelry and a few snacks to the tourists. They had blankets laid out on the ground, with Tanya's work carefully arranged in different price categories. The pieces were mostly necklaces and bracelets, made from beads and factory-made components she bought in Gallup. She assembled the silver, turquoise, coral, and hematite parts into jewelry that was attractive and affordable. Irene watched the babies while Tanya interacted with the tourists who were delighted to find such a charming scene, and to be able to take away a souvenir. She was doing very well. Her style was gregarious and outgoing. She introduced herself, her mother, and her children. She answered all questions comfortably, and she even asked some—where people were from, how old a child was, were they enjoying the canyon. She was a great saleswoman.

The Park Service had suffered some anxiety over Tanya's activities, and some of her relatives and neighbors were suffering over her success. Irene understood my present line of work as a mediator, and thought that I might be able to smooth things over with the Park Service. She was kind enough and smart enough to leave me out of the disputes with relatives. I jumped at an excuse to visit Chinle and see Irene and Tanya, and soon found myself sitting in a folding lawn chair behind Tanya's blanket, chatting with Irene and holding baby Valerie on my lap.

My visit with a Park Service ranger had been strained. He had had trouble finding the right words to explain to me that Tanya's business was inappropriate in a national monument where visitors came to experience the past. He felt responsible for providing an environment that as closely as possible resembled Navajo life in the early 1900s. The beautiful petroglyphs, the abandoned caves and rock houses, the foot and hand holds in the sandstone cliffs, all these contributed to the illusion of living in earlier times. Local Navajo families, he understood, had a right to continue to live and work in the canyon. In fact, this was one of the unique features of this national monument. It was a partnership with the Navajo Nation, and there were provisions for Navajo residents to continue to use the canyon as they always had. This included grazing sheep and goats, growing corn, squash, and melons, tending fruit orchards, having ceremonies, and recreating. The ideal from the point of view of the visitor would be to see Navajos traveling in and out of the canyon on horseback or in horse-drawn wagons. That would heighten their educational experience. He knew that was asking too much; he understood that current lifestyles made it impossible to travel so slowly.

But, he said somewhat awkwardly, he really felt that Tanya had gone too far. The goods she was selling were not authentic Navajo hand-made. She had also begun to sell snacks and sodas, and it was beginning to look like a 7–11 or an Allsups. It was not in keeping with the tradition-al look. And, besides, he added, he was getting a lot of complaints from other Navajos that she shouldn't be doing what she was doing. I was interested in what their reasons were, but he could not be specific. I sus-pected that it was jealousy and/or old family feuds resurfacing.

We discussed the various laws and regulations governing activities in the Canyon, and he admitted that there was nothing specifically pro-hibiting Navajos from conducting business in the Canyon. In fact, Navajos acted as guides and took private parties on tours in their own vehicles. Women, especially in the past, had woven rugs on looms set up outside a hogan with a stunning petroglyph as a backdrop and sheep grazing nearby. And then they had sold the rugs to tourists who consid-ered themselves very lucky indeed to be able to buy a rug, hot off the loom, in such a classic spot. With luck, they would even have a photo of themselves with the weaver standing by the loom. So, there seemed to be nothing to prevent Tanya from carrying on her business activities as long as she confined it to the piece of land held by her family under a use per-mit. I was very relieved, and reported to Irene that the Park Service was not able to interfere in their business activities.

And now in 2001 Nathan and I were about to witness a small-busi-ness success story. The location at the edge of the wash where Tanya had been selling a few necklaces in 1997 was now the site of several structures. From left to right, as the tourists would gaze as they filed off the tourist trucks, were five display tables. They were empty now, but soon would be filled with a great variety of arts and crafts, some manufactured like Tanya's, some hand made and quite elegant. To the far right was an L-shaped open-air wooden stand, about eight feet by twelve feet, with a ramada roof of branches. Tanya told us to unload things from the back of the SUV, and shouted to Aleta to get the fire going under the stew pot. Irene needed no instructions but went to work immediately mixing a huge bowl of flour, water, and vegetable shortening (no more lard) for fry bread. Nathan and I hauled out boxes and boxes of candy, gum, and every imaginable representative from the salty snacks food group. We set them on the short side of the L, where Tanya's oldest son and daughter took over, propping open the boxes at an alluring angle, and maximizing every square inch of plywood for sales potential. The display was enticing, so enticing that they helped themselves to one jaw breaker each.

Tanya then sent us to the cabin to help Ben, who often slept there on the weekends, bring out the sodas, cups, bowls, plates, and plastic ware. The sodas went into three giant coolers of ice behind the stand. Irene wiped the flour off her hands and pulled one of each kind of soda out of the cooler and set them up behind her on a horizontal beam, part of the ramada structure. That way the customers would know what the choices were. Not that there wasn't a menu! I was amazed to see a painted sign above the propane stove offering mutton stew, fry bread, hot dogs, hamburgers, peanut butter and jelly sandwiches, sodas, juice, water, coffee, chips, and candy. By now the stand was looking very complete, the plywood surface was covered with offerings, and the posts that held up the ramada were festooned with sun visors, disposable cameras, film, chap-stick, sun block, packets of aspirin and Advil, plastic water bottles, and key chains.

We delivered the plates and bowls to Tanya, who was cutting up mutton for the stew. She had on short Levi shorts and a pink tank top embroidered with pink valentines, and she was wielding an ancient carving knife. It looked vaguely familiar. It may have been the same one that Irene had used to cut the ribs after she pulled them off the fire in the old days when she and Ben, Bob and I and all the kids used to spend a Saturday afternoon in that same spot. But I was yanked out of my reverie by Tanya. She was barking more orders, to Aleta's daughter to start peeling the potatoes, to her father to watch the baby, to her son to stop fooling around. It should be a big crowd today, and there was a lot to do to get ready. I marveled at her ability to organize and orchestrate this production every day, from late spring to early fall. She was clearly the one in charge, and she managed to exercise that authority over her older siblings, her parents, and a flock of children with good cheer and lots of laughing. No one seemed resentful. She had created something out of nothing, and this business was providing a living, or supplemental living, for her parents and all three of their children.

In a quiet moment later in the afternoon Tanya told me that Aleta had left home after high school and had moved to Phoenix. She got a job with Avis Rent A Car, and after several years she became manager of the airport Avis counter. I was impressed, but Tanya was scoffing. "She just had a rented apartment, and only one car, and a TV. She didn't even have a VCR! All those years! I told her to come up here, back home, and help me in the canyon. She's doing good now. They've got their own house, a car and an SUV, and a TV-VCR and everything. It's much better here. That's what I told her." And sure enough, there was Aleta, with her community college degree, cutting up onions, crying and laughing at the same time.

Adam, the oldest, had gone to Tucson for a couple of years of college, but he, too, had come back to Chinle. He had an entrepreneurial spirit of his own, and was now in loose partnership with his little sister. He became a silversmith and made beautiful watchbands with complex designs and stonework. He made decent money, but he had other ideas. He invented himself as a tour guide, for private tours of Canyon del Muerto, where both sides of his family had long histories. He knew the twists and turns of those canyon walls intimately, and could elaborate each one with stories from his own life and from the oral tradition of his ancestors. He had groups that returned every year for his special tours. One group came into the canyon in the most expensive four-wheel-drive vehicles made. They were packed with all the luxuries required by the ultra-wealthy camper hooked on native culture. They set up white tents, "like Lawrence of Arabia," Adam told me. They had tables and chairs, tablecloths, wine glasses and plenty to put in them. They had cots with mattresses, and most amazing of all, they had portable toilets, not outhouse-style, but real toilets in little bathroom-like structures.

And they were devoted to Adam. He was their guide, their storyteller, their link to the Navajo world. They paid him well for these services, and they paid Tanya, too, for the "Traditional Mutton Stew Dinner"she produced on their final night. In this way, Adam and Tanya supported each other's enterprises. The day we were there in the canyon a church group from Virginia, guided by Adam, was stopping by for lunch at Tanya's place. Adam even had his own website, where you could browse his jewelry or sign up for a tour of the canyon. Irene told me later that other families in the canyon were jealous of Adam's success. "They say that he isn't telling the stories right, that he doesn't really know the stories, he's just making it all up. They say he never herded sheep with his grandma down here, like he says he did. They say mean things about him. They're like that," and she shook her head and wrinkled up her nose.

It turned out to be a big day for Tanya, and for her artisans. She allowed anyone related to her, by blood or by marriage, to set up a table at no charge and sell what they made. It was good for her business to have a shopping opportunity for her customers. It was good for them to have customers who were well satisfied by a good meal, perked up by a little candy, relieved that they found that tube of sunscreen. That day the goods offered varied from Dream Catchers and beaded coin purses to a several-hundred-dollar silver-and-turquoise necklace and a stone sculpture of ravens in flight. The big open-bed trucks unloaded their tourists, twenty at a time, beginning about 11:00 A.M. By that time, the stew and fry bread were ready, and Tanya and Irene were poised to take orders. The first in line were the drivers. They were able to scuttle past their passengers who were stretching out stiff backs, focusing cameras at the Antelope House petroglyphs, or just enjoying being on solid ground again after the jolting "shake and bake" ride. They spoke Navajo and joked with Tanya and Irene, as they waited for their steaming styrofoam bowl of stew and the accompanying slab of fry bread. The rest of the customers straggled up to the stand, some a little hesitant, a little skeptical, others clearly with only one thing in mind—a cold drink and food.

During an afternoon lull Adam's church group arrived and enthusiastically plunged into eating and drinking, buying souvenirs and taking pictures. They retired with him to an area in front of the cave in the canyon wall behind the cabin. He had created a storytelling circle, with logs to sit on, and he sat with his back to the wall so that the listeners could admire the cave and the beautiful red and black markings that streaked down the sandstone.

Adam's son, clearly a tour guide in the making, walked with Nathan and me a short distance up the canyon. He was careful to keep us away from the cactus, and away from a pile of rocks known to be favored by rattlesnakes. We climbed up to a shallow cave and watched the sun disappear and the shade grow along the opposite wall. It was a nice bit of solitude, with a gentle guide who treated us like friends.

When we returned to the hub of activity, the business was being put to bed. The non-perishables went back into the cabin, where Ben would stay another night. The rest went in the SUV for the trip back to Chinle and replenishment in the morning. We helped load the vehicle, and climbed in the back seat. Undoubtedly exhausted, Tanya didn't think twice about jumping in the driver's seat. She hustled everyone in place and took off, punctuating the jolts and swerves of the trip with laughter, or taking a hand off the wheel to re-create a moment from the day involving a particular tourist or driver. At the Holiday Inn parking lot, we unfolded ourselves from the backseat, gave everyone hugs and thank you's, and watched them pull back onto the road, turning left to Del Muerto. I felt so fortunate to be able to be absorbed into their family, even for a day, especially for a day in the canyon.

Nathan and I hosted another dinner, this time at the Holiday Inn, with old friends Robert and Verna Salabye, a grown son, a teenage daughter who was off for a summer program in New York, and a handful of grandchildren, or, perhaps, grandchildren that were a handful. We filled two long tables, with much commotion between the two, and a constant stream of laughter. We reminisced and drank coffee until closing time. I took dozens of pictures, mostly of two-year-olds in motion, and remembered photos from decades earlier of Verna and me holding our babies in cradle boards. I realized again that my connection to Chinle was now over thirty years old. Robert, Verna, Bob and I, and so many others, including the Tellers, had known each other when we were in our twenties, the ages of our children now. Our children had grown up, and we had aged, which, I thought, must be what you do once you are already a grown up.

And, Chinle, too, had grown up and/or aged. Here we were in the

Indian-motif-carpeted restaurant of the Holiday Inn, which seemed to be trying very hard to look and act like every other Holiday Inn in the country. Tourists ebbed and flowed through the lobby, the restaurant, and the gift shop, apparently feeling quite at home. The ice and vending machines were in the right place, as were the remote controls and the miniature shampoos. The reception desk was computerized and there were clocks on the wall to show the time in different parts of the country. Brochures, many with website addresses, abounded, advertising arts and crafts outlets and tours all over Navajoland. And, of course, there was the small business explosion in the canyon.

But, I reminded myself, this Holiday Inn sat on the site of the old Garcia's Trading Post, in a vulnerable spot at the mouth of the canyon. There was history here, and unpredictability, and perhaps even quick-sand just beneath the surface. I also gratefully observed that, in spite of corporate training in guest services and voice projection, the reception desk attendants and restaurant wait staff were still very much products of Navajo country. Chinle was becoming modernized, it was true, but in its own way and in its own time.

It is always a joy to go back to Chinle. That last stretch of road north from Burnsides is still the same, although the gnarled piñon off to the right that looked like a rooster is long gone. I watch eagerly for Fish Point, the little jagged but graceful landmark jutting skyward off the south end of Black Mesa, as if it might not be there. When it comes into view, I smile as I would thinking about a close friend. I slow down at the Piñon junction, and my mind takes me west, remembering friends, now gone, at Cottonwood and way beyond at Forest Lake. The car drops down the hill into Chinle, turns right, and crosses Black Wash. At the last minute, I take a quick glance to the left at our house in the cottonwoods, not giving myself enough time to become teary-eyed. I drive to the canyon rim, and take comfort in the view and the quiet. There is more vegetation in the bottom, since the salt cedar took over, but otherwise it looks the same. The vehicles may be newer, their colors more exotic, but they gun the engine across those sandy stretches just the same.